The Emperor and the Actress

By the same author:

THE EMPEROR & THE ACTRESS

The love story of Emperor Franz Josef
& Katharina Schratt

Joan Haslip

Weidenfeld and Nicolson
London

To Lallie in memory of our mother

First published in Great Britain in 1982 by
George Weidenfeld & Nicolson Limited
91 Clapham High Street London SW4 7TA

ISBN 0 297 78102 2

Printed in Great Britain by Butler & Tanner Ltd,
Frome and London

Contents

Illustrations

Acknowledgements

In 1949, nine years after the death of the Vienna Burgtheater actress, Frau Katharina Schratt, there appeared a selection of letters written to her by the Emperor Franz Josef. These letters, which were edited under the supervision of her son Baron Anton Kiss, naturally omitted anything which might be in any sense derogatory to Frau Schratt's reputation and so it was only after her son's death that the complete correspondence came onto the market and was acquired by my American publishers. Included in this correspondence are rough drafts and excerpts of Katharina Schratt's own letters to the Emperor of which the originals are presumed to have been destroyed – in many cases these were so much corrected as to be almost illegible and so I am very grateful to her great-niece, Frau Johanna Nebehay for her help in deciphering them.

I also wish to thank the many others who helped me in the preparation of this book, in particular His Imperial Highness the late Archduke Karl Theodor Habsburg Salvator for inviting me to Schloss Wallsee and for allowing me to read extracts from his mother, the Archduchess Valerie's diary. I wish to thank his sister-in-law the Archduchess Rosemarie and their nephew Count Ferdinand Stolberg, the current Austrian Ambassador to Sweden.

My thanks are also due to Frau Brigitte Hamann for putting me in touch with the directors of the Burgtheater who then supplied me with some of Katharina's theatrical correspondence; to the late Mr Eidwitz of the Burgtheater and to the late Mr Mayer-Gunthof, both of whom had personal recollections of Frau Schratt; to the late Mrs Frank Wooster and her daughter the Baroness Elie de Rothschild; to Count Hans Wilczek and his sister Countess Emma Traun who kindly allowed me to reproduce a photograph of their grand-father Count Hans Wilczek; to Mr and

Mrs Rudolf Weissweiller for the week that I spent with them at Schloss Wymsbach from where I was able to explore Bad Ischl and the Salzkammergut; to Mr Rudolf Mount, a godson of Katharina Schratt; to Hans H. Coudenhove for his expert advice on the manuscript and, above all, my gratitude is due to the British Ambassador in Vienna, Hugh Morgan and to his wife Alexandra for their wonderful hospitality at the Embassy in Vienna and for the help and encouragement that they gave me in my researches.

Last of all I want to thank Maria Ellis for the typing of the manuscript and for succeeding in deciphering my almost illegible handwriting.

THE HOUSE OF HABSBURG

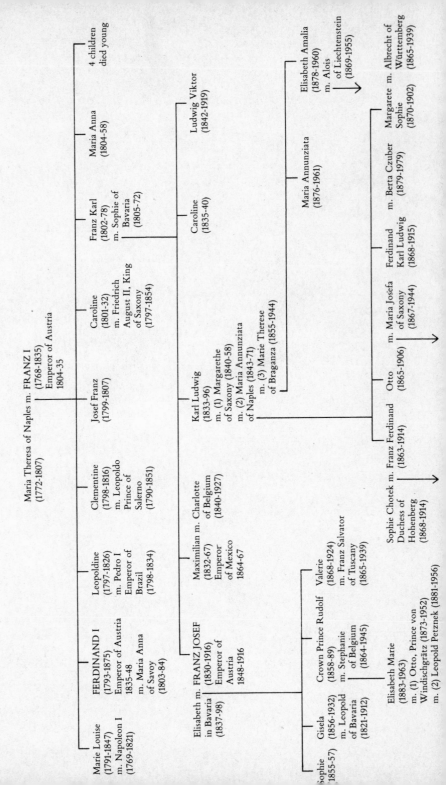

Prologue

The gardens of the Archbishop's palace were honeycombed with police, lest some Russian nihilist might attempt to assassinate the Tsar while he was on a state visit to Austria. It was the first time Alexander III had crossed the Russian frontier since his father's murder, the memory of which was to have a traumatic effect on his whole life. The palace of the Archbishop of Olmütz outside the little Moravian town of Kremsier had been chosen as a place where security would be easier to maintain than in the polyglot city of Vienna. Neither Franz Josef nor Alexander had wanted this meeting, which had been expressly arranged by Prince Bismarck in an attempt to hold together the tenuous bonds of the *Dreikaiserbund* – the Three Emperors' League.

It was 26 August 1885 and the baroque palace with its spectacular gardens and open-air theatre was a fitting background for the brilliant festivities which helped to hide the fact that the chief protagonists had very little to say to one another. The visit of the Tsar and Tsarina, accompanied by their eldest son and a bevy of grand dukes and duchesses, composing a suite of over a hundred people, was a strain on even the almost unlimited resources of one of the richest courts in Europe. Franz Josef was as always the perfect host, looking more elegant in his Russian uniform, worn out of courtesy to the Tsar, than any of his guests. At fifty-five he still had the figure and the carriage of a young man, but his blue eyes were tired, with wrinkles at the corners, and his face was that of a man who had learnt to accept the present rather than to have hope in the future.

It was here in this palace that his uncle Ferdinand had abdicated in his favour, when in 1848 he had succeeded as an eighteen-year-old boy to an Empire torn by revolution. He had grown up under the tutelage of Prince Metternich, who for thirty years had kept Austria and the confederated German states at peace, tied to a rigid, antiquated system imposed by the Vienna Congress. Worn out by the ravages of the Napoleonic Wars, the people had submitted to this system. Lulled into a soporific state of contentment, the middle classes had grown rich and prosperous and the last years of the reign of Franz Josef's grandfather, the old Emperor Franz, had been the golden age of the so-called *Biedermeierzeit*, when it was the bourgeoisie rather than the aristocracy who set the fashion in contemporary taste.

Franz Josef was only five years old when his grandfather died and Metternich allowed his uncle Ferdinand, a helpless epileptic, to succeed to the imperial throne, instead of passing him over in favour of Franz Josef's father, the Archduke Franz Karl, who, if not particularly brilliant, was at least *compos mentis*. It was a disastrous decision on the part of a statesman who wanted to keep all the power in his own hands. And when the flood gates of revolution opened in 1848, all the concentrated fury of the masses was directed against the ageing chancellor, who was among the first to take the road to exile. In this time of crisis when Vienna was given over to mob rule, Franz Josef's mother, the Archduchess Sophie, born a Bavarian princess, took matters into her own hands. Realizing that the country could only be saved by the strong, uncompromising leadership of youth, she persuaded both her brother-in-law and husband to renounce their hereditary rights in favour of her son. And with the help of generals like Windischgrätz and Radetzky, and statesmen such as Schwarzenberg, she brought the counter-revolution to a triumphant conclusion.

But the rebellion of 1848 left an indelible mark on Franz Josef's character. He never forgave what he regarded as the treachery of his Italian subjects for having enrolled under the banner of Charles Albert of Savoy. Nor did he ever forget the humiliation of having had to call in the help of the Russian Tsar in suppressing the Hungarian revolt. For their part, Italians and Hungarians never forgave the young Emperor for the floggings and the hangings committed in his name. Twenty years later, when the former Hungarian rebel, Count Julius Andrássy, became Foreign Minister of the dual monarchy, there were still men living in Hungary who refused to salute the Habsburg flag.

The year 1848 was the end of Franz Josef's youth. The cynical Schwarzenberg completed his education by teaching him that no autocrat could afford to be either grateful or humane: 'You can forgive the rebels but you must have some hangings first' – a doctrine which left behind a legacy of hate. Following in the steps of Schwarzenberg, Franz Josef astonished the world by his ingratitude in refusing to act as an ally of the Russian Tsar at the time of the Crimean War. Neither Nicholas I nor Alexander II ever forgave Franz Josef his policy of armed neutrality. The Austrians were left to fight alone when in 1859 the Piedmontese, together with the French, drove them out of Lombardy. Russia remained aloof when in 1866 Bismarck deliberately provoked a war to destroy the Habsburg hegemony in Germany, a loss more bitter for Franz Josef than that of Venice and Milan. In the aftermath of defeat he had come to terms with Hungary, terms put forward by the Hungarians themselves, giving them almost complete autonomy except for the army and foreign affairs. Franz Josef, descended from the Holy Roman Emperors, now ruled over a dual monarchy, as Emperor of Austria and King of Hungary. But at heart he still felt himself very much a German prince, who had little in common with the overbearing, chauvinistic Hungarians. The *Ausgleich* (Historic Compromise) dictated by expediency, the biggest and perhaps the most insoluble of all the problems of his multiracial Empire had brought him nothing but worry.

This meeting at Kremsier, to cement an uneasy alliance created by Bismarck who, having achieved all his own ambitions, was now the apostle of peace, was yet another sacrifice to expediency, one of the many irksome duties of Franz Josef's daily life. It had become a life of discipline and abnegation, for which he had renounced his own personal happiness in order to become what his wife described as 'the first bureaucrat of his Empire'.

His marriage to his fifteen-year-old Wittelsbach cousin had been the one romantic impulse of his youth, when he defied his mother by falling in love with the younger sister of the girl she had chosen for his bride. And however much Elisabeth had made him suffer, she still remained the object of his selfless and uncomplaining adoration. The word 'duty' had no meaning for a woman who worshipped at the shrine of her own beauty and who, bored by the restrictions of court life, regarded herself as a prisoner in her husband's palaces. In moments of crisis she was capable of rising to supreme heights. Her popularity in Hungary had prepared the way for the *Ausgleich*. But the compassionate Empress, who in times of war tended the dying in the hospitals and stood by her husband's side in defeat, could not bear the slightest tie which impinged upon her freedom. Vienna saw her less and less as the years went by, and she tried to escape from her unstable Wittelsbach inheritance on the hunting fields of England and Ireland. When she condescended to come home, it was to Budapest rather than to Vienna, for the Hungarians were the only people in her husband's Empire with whom she professed to have affinity.

This open preference for the Magyars cost her the affection of the Viennese. The Empress they had idolized was now criticized and resented, and not even the government's strict censorship could prevent her follies and extravagances from reaching the public's ear. In Parliament the opposition did not hesitate to question the enormous sums which were being spent on the new villa in the Lainzer Tiergarten, barely half an hour distant from the imperial summer residence of Schönbrunn. The Emperor was building this house in the hope of making his wife a home which would be more congenial to her than the fourteen-hundred-room Palace of Schönbrunn. At first she showed gratitude and took pleasure in what for her was a new toy, but Lainz was to satisfy her no more than Schönbrunn, and Franz Josef had to content himself with the few months or weeks she chose to spend in his company.

She had only consented to be present at the Russian visit on the promise of being allowed to go on a long cruise of the Greek Islands which, in view of the rising political tension in the Balkans, was the one place Franz Josef would have preferred her to avoid. But after over thirty years of marriage, Elisabeth's transcendent beauty and the magic of her smile still made it impossible for him to refuse her slightest whim. With the passing of time they had lost the few interests they ever had in common – a love of riding and hunting. Once the imperial couple had had their own pack of hounds at Gödöllo and acted as hosts to the best horsemen of Europe.

But suddenly Elisabeth lost all interest in hunting and sold her famous stud, turning her back on the hunting fields of Cheshire and Meath, and the normal happy life she had led as guest in the great English country houses. The first signs of age, the first wrinkles which affronted her beauty, moved her to tears and melancholia. The terror of losing her looks became obsessional, and every year the inherited Wittelsbach instability became more pronounced.

Like her cousin King Ludwig in his Bavarian castles, she was retreating more and more into a world of fantasy, making a cult of solitude, communing with the ghosts of dead poets, evoking the spirit of Heine and erecting the statue of a man whom the Emperor regarded as a subversive Jew in all the royal gardens. How could anyone as prosaic and unimaginative as Franz Josef follow his wife in all her poetical meanderings? But his loyalty was such that he never admitted either to himself or to his family that Elisabeth's obsessions bordered on the abnormal.

Having consented to attend the state banquet, the Empress sat in frozen silence, barely picking at the food to which her neighbour the Tsar, famed for his gargantuan appetite, did more than justice. Music, toasts, speeches, and the most famous wines of the imperial cellars failed to animate what the Crown Prince Rudolf described in a letter to his wife as 'a ghastly evening'. Everyone was glad when the dinner was over and it was time for the open-air performance to begin.

In his younger days the Tsar had been a devotee of both the theatre and the ballet, and the Burgtheater had produced their two greatest dramatic stars, Charlotte Wolther and Adolf Sonnenthal, to entertain the royal guests. But though both received their full measure of applause, the honours of the evening went to a young actress called Katharina Schratt who, in a one-act comedy, succeeded in enchanting her audience to such an extent that even the gloomy Tsar was seen to laugh, while Franz Josef's tired blue eyes lit up with pleasure. She was so natural and spontaneous in her manner that she appeared not so much to be acting as chatting with her audience, transmitting across the footlights the warmth of her own radiant personality, and revitalizing a tired and blasé court.

The Lord High Chamberlain, Prince Hohenlohe, congratulated himself on his choice, for there had been considerable discussion with the management as to whether Katharina Schratt, who was still a comparative newcomer to the Burg, should be chosen in preference to other worthier candidates. Prince Hohenlohe had admired the young actress from the time when, as a nineteen-year-old girl, she had made her Viennese début at the Stadttheater under the direction of the famous Laube, who had transformed her from a pretty, sturdy little ingénue into an accomplished comedienne, accentuating the essentially Viennese quality of her acting, the mixture of self-mockery and pathos, of homeliness and common sense, playing on the quicksilver changing of her moods which reflected the strains of the dozen races which converge in the Danube valley. The public had taken 'Kathi' Schratt to their heart long before she passed through the august portals of the Burgtheater, by which time she had over ten years of acting experience behind her, which included a season as a guest artist at the German court theatre in St Petersburg. In Russia she had played in front of the Tsar when he was still Crown Prince, which was probably the main reason for Prince Hohenlohe's choice. But no one could conceive that the Tsar's enthusiasm would go to the lengths of upsetting all the established rules of Hofburg etiquette by requesting that the charming ladies who had given them so much pleasure should be invited to have supper with Their Majesties.

There was consternation in the Austrian entourage, for though famous artists were sometimes received in private audience (and there was the famous occasion when the Emperor's mother, the formidable Archduchess Sophie, had invited Jenny Lind to tea), till this moment no Habsburg emperor had ever entertained a member of the Burgtheater to supper at court. Even Crown Prince Rudolf, who frequented circles where respectable ladies of the Burg would never have shown their faces, was sufficiently shocked to write home to his wife: 'Theatre at eight followed by supper with Misses Wolther, Schratt and Wessely in the same room with Their Majesties. It was very odd.'

Franz Josef looked stiff and embarrassed and Elisabeth, who welcomed any diversion which might relieve the tedium of the evening, noted with a certain amusement her husband's growing irritation at the way in which the Tsar was completely monopolizing Frau Schratt. The Emperor was not a great theatre-goer, but in the past year his visits to the Burgtheater had become more frequent, and he always seemed to choose the evening when Katharina Schratt was performing. This evening, however, he made no attempt to single her out from among her colleagues, and the young actress would have been the first to ridicule the idea that the great Emperor before whom everybody stood in awe should actually be jealous because the Tsar, who had had too much to drink, was pursuing her with heavy-handed compliments and insisting on taking her for a stroll in the illuminated gardens.

The following morning Franz Josef complained to his wife that Alexander's behaviour had been unpardonable. But Elisabeth only laughed. She was glad to see that her husband could still be human and take an interest in a pretty young actress, even to the extent of being jealous of the Tsar. There were times when she blamed herself for having, through her own neglect, allowed a warm and affectionate man, who wanted nothing more than a comfortable family life, to atrophy into a bureaucrat. And from that day she began to take an interest in Katharina Schratt.

I

The Grocer's Daughter

Baden bei Wien, which lies under the foothills of the Julian Alps at the edge of the Vienna woods, is a peaceful little town famed for its sulphurous, health-giving springs which have attracted visitors since Roman times. It reached the height of its prosperity at the beginning of the nineteenth century, when the old Emperor Franz made it his summer home, living not in a palace or a country villa but in a house in the public square which in its elegant simplicity reflects the Biedermeir style associated with his reign. Baden continued to flourish even after the imperial family had moved their summer residence ro Ischl, and from May to October the carriages and coaches crowded the highway from Vienna. Trade was good and Anton Schratt, who owned the biggest grocery store in town, could afford to buy the large house on Theresienstrasse which had formerly been a coaching inn, and where there was room for the handsome carriage and pair with which he vied with the local gentry. He was an ambitious, hard-working man and nothing was too good for his family, in particular for the little girl who was born in this house on 11 September 1853, at a time when loyal Baden was hung with black and yellow flags to celebrate the engagement of the twenty-three-year-old Emperor to his cousin Elisabeth of Wittelsbach. After four years of martial law the country was again at peace. There was an air of optimism and hope for the future, and the baby who was christened Maria Katharina Schratt was nursed to the sound of pealing church bells ringing out Te Deums.

The only girl among three brothers, Kathi, as she was called at home, was spoilt and cherished by her parents who were inordinately proud of their pretty little daughter with the golden curls and the large blue eyes, who could be so beguiling that it was almost impossible to resist her. From earliest childhood she displayed a precocious talent for memorizing and reciting verse, and at seven years old was already declaiming excerpts of Schiller and Grillparzer in front of admiring visitors. Drama and literature were the only subjects in which she excelled at school. Arithmetic was anathema, and whatever hopes her mother may have had of making her into a good and thrifty housewife were doomed to failure. She could never learn to keep her accounts and was bored by sewing and embroidery. Baden had many affiliations with the stage, and during the summer season the municipal theatre was visited by all the leading companies from Vienna. Kathi had no difficulty in persuading an indulgent father to take her to any play considered suitable for her age, and he would be amused at the way in which she mimicked every role from heroine to villain. But never for a moment did he consider the possibility of his daughter going on the stage, and it was only after taking part in an amateur performance, in which she won so much applause that it went completely to her head, that both father and mother realized it was time to put an end to their daughter's theatrical ambitions and send her to school in Germany. By now she was a lively, well-developed girl of fifteen, gay and headstrong by nature and very much in need of the discipline for which the establishment run by the sisters Haas at Cologne on the Rhine was famous.

It was the year 1868, only two years after Austria's disastrous defeat at Königgrätz, and the triumph of the Prussian needle-gun had turned the Habsburgs out of Germany and lost them the right to dictate to the confederated states. But what for the Emperor Franz Josef had been one of the cruellest blows of his unlucky destiny appears to have been of little consequence to the frivolous Viennese. There were a few days of panic when Baden was crowded with refugees, and horses and stabling rose to astronomical sums. But no sooner had peace negotiations begun, and the relative generosity of Bismarck's terms become known, than worthy burghers like Anton Schratt settled down to their jobs and ignored the humiliation inflicted on their army. Apart from the unlucky conscripts who were pressed into service, the war was largely a matter for the professionals and the upper classes, who, with an Emperor who was rarely seen out of uniform, could parade their ribbons and their decorations at court.

The wounded were still in the hospitals and the dead had barely been buried, but the carnival of 1867 had never been more brilliant, with Johann Strauss at the height of his fame and the Viennese dancing for the first time to the strains of the 'Blue Danube'. Saxons and Hanoverians who did not want to live under the hegemony of Prussia were flocking into Austria. Vienna was still the capital of a greater Germany in a sense Berlin could never aspire to be, and Cologne had too many links with the Empire to be considered a town in a foreign country. A man like Anton Schratt, proud of his German origins, had more in common with his cousins on the Rhine than on the Danube, but his daughter was not of a character to be turned into a genteel young Fräulein. From first to last she was a rebel, and school discipline only served to strengthen her resolve to go on the stage. By the end of the year the sisters Haas were longing to be rid of their refractory pupil before she had infected the other girls with her passion for the footlights. At the same time they were sufficiently intelligent to advise Herr Schratt to allow his daughter to follow her natural inclinations and send her to a good drama school, where they would soon find out if acting was for her a vocation or merely a passing fancy. Katharina had won only half the battle, for she had still to prove that she had sufficient talent to embark on a career which her parents considered to be fraught with hazards. The fact that she was accepted into Kirschner's Academy of Drama, to which no one was admitted unless they had serious intentions of going on the stage, shows that by now they had bowed to the inevitable, and Frau Schratt's principal concern was to find a suitable home for their sixteen-year-old daughter.

Katharina spent her first year in Vienna in the house of a middle-aged authoress of mediocre talent and impeccable morals who introduced her into a circle of writers, journalists and actors, many of whom became her friends for life. One of her salient qualities was her gift for making friends and for retaining them. Neighbours in Baden and colleagues in the Kirschner Academy still ranked among her guests at Hietzing and at Ischl, and in many of the Emperor Franz Josef's letters to Katharina he sends greetings to a Frau Dahn or a Fräulein Bauer.

The world of the Kirschner Academy centred round the Burgtheater, and in a town where the theatre was as important a part of the cultural life as in Vienna, the Burg represented the Mecca to which every aspiring actor hoped one day to be admitted and to earn the proud title of *Kaiserlicher und Königlicher Burgschauspieler* (Imperial and Royal Court Actor). Over a hundred years earlier Josef II, known as 'the people's Emperor', whose progressive views had often been in direct opposition to his mother the Empress Marie Therese, had opened his private theatre to the public. Now in the 1880s it was still entirely financed out of the Emperor's privy purse, and until 1888, when the new building opened on the Ring, it formed part of the imperial palace, with an entrance on the Michaelerplatz. Franz Josef had only to walk through the few rooms which led from his private apartments directly to his box in the theatre.

The rigid press censorship, in which political articles were cut down to the minimum, left a large amount of space for dramatic and literary reviews. The heroes of the educated bourgeoisie were the great actors, writers and musicians rather than the politicians. Though his plays were never performed at the Burg, the satirist Nestroy and similar writers had flourished in the age of Metternich, and were able to convey upon the stage thinly veiled criticism of the government which would never have been tolerated in the press.

When Katharina Schratt arrived in Vienna, the chief subject of controversy both in the Kirschner Academy and in the clubs and coffee houses was the bitter feud between the present and former directors of the Burg, dividing their supporters and detractors into Montagues and Capulets. Heinrich Laube was the fallen god, who for eighteen years had been the unchallenged dictator of the Burg. Under his inspired leadership an antiquated and lifeless institution, tied to old shibboleths and traditions, had evolved into one of the greatest of European theatres, the centre of the German-speaking world, in which every author's principal ambition was to have a play put on at the Burg. Laube had a passion for the spoken word and with the assistance of Alexander Strakosch, the most famous elocution master of the day, he did away with the mannered speeches and affected gestures of the old school of acting and taught his pupils to move and speak like ordinary human beings.

'Laube is God and Strakosch is his prophet' was a current phrase at the Burg. But gods will not stand for interference in their kingdom, and by the 1860s the court theatre, which was under the jurisdiction of the Lord High Chamberlain's office, was beset by rules and regulations made by petty court officials with whom Laube was in a state of constant warfare. A decision to place the opera house and the Burg under one administration led to his stormy resignation and the appointment of Franz von Dingelstedt in his place. Whereas Laube was a great director with a touch of genius, Dingelstedt was a brilliant impresario who, having been many years director of the court opera house, excelled in the theatrical effects, the trappings and décor which Laube tended to ignore. He was a superb scenographer, eminently suited to stage the magnificent spectacles and great classical dramas which were to be part of the approaching jubilee celebrations of the Emperor's twenty-five years of reign. Though many of the actors remained loyal to Laube, there were those who found Dingelstedt's charm and courtesy a welcome relief to his predecessor's biting and sarcastic tongue.

Strakosch had left the Burg at the same time as Laube to become principal instructor at the Kirschner Academy, where he found a promising pupil in Katharina Schratt. There were others who were prettier, more graceful and perhaps more talented, but behind that innocent little girl's face with the mischievous mouth and expressive eyes, which could change so easily from laughter into tears, was a strong personality and a driving ambition which would lead her to stardom. In the early months of 1872, the year in which Katharina Schratt graduated from the Kirschner Academy, Heinrich Laube, backed by a group of Jewish financiers, had become director of the new Stadttheater on the Seilerstätte, and ambitious young actresses in search of a job could now address themselves either to Dingelstedt or to Laube. The Burg had the greater prestige but Laube was the greater name, and Strakosch advised Katharina Schratt to try her luck in the Seilerstätte. In an article published many years later she wrote a description of her first interview with Heinrich Laube.

Strakosch brought me into a room where the great man sat writing at his desk. He looked me up and down without a smile and growled,

'So this is the young woman.' Then he ordered me to perform various excerpts from my repertoire while he leant back in an armchair looking at the ceiling. Trembling with fear I went through the various parts without him giving me a single word of encouragement. After an hour he stopped me, saying, 'That was no good. It has all got to be much more compact.' But the tone of his voice was kinder, and he added, 'We must see what can be done. Do not come to any decision before you hear from me.'

Strakosch, who was familiar with Laube's technique, assured her that the audition had been successful, but it was hardly calculated to reassure an intimidated young girl. A second audition on the same day, this time at the Burgtheater, was almost as terrifying.

I was called upon to step up to the footlights and perform my various roles in front of a pitch black house with an empty stage behind me; while invisible in the orchestra was director Dingelstedt together with the stage managers, who every now and then would call out of the dark the name of a part I was to perform. When the audition was over another invisible voice informed me that in a few days I would be hearing the management's decision with regard to an eventual engagement.

According to Katharina Schratt there was a third audition with director Ascher of the Karlstheater, a playhouse which specialized in light comedies which were called *Lustspiele*. This time the director appears to have been too enthusiastic for her taste. Overcome by her charms, he jumped out of his chair and asked her point blank to give him a kiss, whereupon she burst into a flood of tears and threatened to leave immediately. Ascher, who was not used to having his advances treated in this fashion, did his best to mollify her by assuring her that his behaviour was a purely innocent proof of his admiration. But she refused to listen, crying out that never under any circumstances could she be persuaded to work in such a place. When Ascher and Katharina Schratt later became friends they often laughed together over that first meeting, and he told her that he had never seen such bewildered and irresistibly comic facial expressions as those she had shown on that occasion. The results of the auditions of the Burg and at the Stadttheater were not of a nature to satisfy a young girl dreaming of stardom. Though both Dingelstedt and Laube recognized

Katharina Schratt's potential talents, and neither wanted to lose her to the other, they were not prepared to give a nineteen-year-old novice a contract for leading parts. Both offered to take her on the same terms, ones that would guarantee her no more than understudy and secondary roles. To their surprise little Miss Schratt kept them waiting on her decision.

Meanwhile the director of the court theatre at Berlin had arrived in Vienna in search of fresh talent. Hearing of a young actress in whom both Laube and Dingelstedt were interested, he immediately got in touch with her agent and, without even giving her an audition, made Katharina Schratt an offer which promised her leading parts. Katharina did not hesitate and the contract was signed after supper at Sacher's, before she had even received her parents' consent. Her father fumed, her mother wept, but both realized that by now they had lost their daughter to the stage. All poor Frau Schratt could do was to accompany her Kathi to Berlin and see her established in respectable lodgings. But even the most ambitious of girls must have felt very lost and tearful when she said goodbye to her mother at the station and came back to what was called a family *Pension*, but which lacked all the cosiness and warmth of her Vienna lodgings. Berlin itself was such a cold and friendless place. What had once been a charming old Prussian town was now swallowed up in the vast palaces and monuments of a new imperial capital given over to military display. It was a boom city, still celebrating its victory over France, a victory which the Prussians had not yet learnt to accept with grace. The proud young officers who were the heroes of the day had none of the nonchalance and easy laughter of those with whom she had flirted in Vienna. Here everything was heavy, humourless and grey. Even the surrounding countryside, the sad lakes, the sandy marshes and wind-blown pines contributed to her homesickness for Vienna.

But the lonely and unhappy year in Berlin developed her character, accentuating her natural independence, an unusual quality for a woman in those days, and which allied to her ultra-feminine appearance surprised and fascinated at the same time. No one could ever claim to have possessed Katharina Schratt, nor in her first ten years on the stage was she ever known to have had a rich protector like so many of her theatrical colleagues. Success came overnight when she appeared for the first time in the title role of *Gustl von Blasewitz*, an adaptation of a Schiller anecdote. And for the first time she saw her name billed in large letters as 'Fräulein Schratt, a guest artist from Vienna', acclaimed by the critics as a fresh and original talent. From now on she was overwhelmed with work, and received more and more parts to study and rehearse. Her popularity with the public was such that by the end of the spring season she had been chosen to act the part of Käthchen in Kleist's masterpiece *Das Käthchen von Heilbronn*, one of the most popular classics of the German stage. A new adaptation was to be put on in the autumn, done by none other than Heinrich Laube who was then almost as well known as a dramatist as a director.

Katharina Schratt's great ambition was to find favour in the eyes of Laube and to have the German critics acclaim her as the perfect Käthchen. She forfeited her holiday to stay on in the hot and airless city, studying her part, identifying herself so completely with Käthchen that her friends had difficulty in recognizing jolly, plump little Kathi in the wan, romantic-looking girl who, by the opening night in October, was in as great a state of nerves as her ill-starred heroine.

It was a tremendous challenge for someone so young and inexperienced, and the result was a triumph. There was not a critic, even including the demanding *Vossiche Zeitung*, who did not write that in spite of her youth and immaturity Fräulein Schratt gave the finest interpretation of Käthchen that had been seen on the German stage for many a decade. There was one exception. Sitting at the back of the stage box was Heinrich Laube, who had come from Vienna to see his adaptation performed for the first time. He agreed that Katharina Schratt was an excellent Käthchen and that it would be difficult to find a better one. But he still felt, as when he saw her for the first time, that the girl had too much personality for the part of a sentimental ingénue, and that given proper training what now appeared to be a little dove could develop into a bird of paradise. He wanted her for the Stadttheater and he wanted her to play Käthchen when he presented his own adaptation in the forthcoming jubilee season. But he gave her little encouragement beyond telling her to come and see him when she got back to Vienna.

These few words were sufficient for Katharina to terminate her engagement in Berlin at the end of the year. On her return to Vienna her fist visit was to the Stadttheater, where Laube received her in his gruff, undemonstrative fashion, offering her much the same contract as before she went to Berlin. But Katharina Schratt had grown up in the past year, and she knew that Laube was the one director who could make her into a star; she signed the contract placing herself entirely in his hands, and before many weeks had passed the cafés in the newly completed Ringstrasse hummed with the news that the nineteen-year-old Katharina Schratt was to play the lead in Laube's jubilee production of *Das Käthchen von Heilbronn*. All she had learnt and studied during that long hot summer in Berlin had to be forgotten and learnt again under the personal direction of Laube, who kept her rehearsing from morning until night, bullying her till she was on the verge of tears. But in that brilliant theatrical season of 1873 it was Laube's Stadttheater presenting Katharina Schratt as Käthchen von Heilbronn which drew the largest crowds. As one of the critics wrote, 'With her blonde hair and fresh little girl's face, she had already won the public's sympathy before she had opened her mouth.'

The young actress was caught up in the euphoria of that jubilee spring, fêted and spoilt in a town where the great exhibition of industry and art erected in the Prater grounds, at the fabulous cost of eighteen million gulden, was attracting visitors from all over the world. There was an orgy of spending. Since the defeat of France in the Franco-Prussian War of 1870, Vienna had taken the place of Paris as the most important stock market in Europe. A free market encouraged mushroom companies and private banks to spring up overnight, and everyone from the archdukes to the smallest shopkeepers indulged in a fever of gambling. In their splendid palaces on the Ringstrasse Austria's new millionaires, many of them immigrants from the ghettoes of eastern Europe, introduced an oriental opulence into the old Habsburg capital. Though the doors of the *Erste Gesellschaft* (the First Society), the great feudal families who gathered round the throne, remained hermetically closed to any outsider, the *Zweite Gesellschaft* (the

Second Society), which represented all that was gayest and most amusing in the capital, welcomed the advent of the so-called *Finanz-Barons*, who owned the best horses, hired the best music, and gave the best balls in their palaces decorated by Makart.

One of the phenomena of Vienna society in the 1870s was the domination of Hans Makart, a painter who was not so much a great artist as a great showman, transforming the banalities of a completely materialistic society into a glorious dream world peopled with medieval knights, renaissance princes and voluptuous odalisques. He was a master at the pageants and processions which celebrated the jubilee year, and visitors to Vienna paid hundreds of gulden to be admitted to the fantastic parties at his studio on the Gusshausstrasse. Every aspiring hostess had at least one room done up *à la* Makart, with gilded mirrors, rosewood furniture and peacock feather fans; everyone who was in fashion had a plumed hat *à la* Makart, and Katharina Schratt would have been no exception. We can picture her supping at Sacher's after the theatre, wearing one of those sumptuous velvet hats which shadowed her laughing eyes, eyes which promised so much, though it did not take her admirers long to discover that 'the little Schratt girl' had no intention of becoming seriously involved in any serious romance. Laube kept her hard at work, watching over her with a strict fatherly eye, trying her out in various parts till he discovered that her natural bent was for comedy. Disregarding her prettiness he exploited her defects, the big feet which contrasted with the lovely arms and hands; the boyish stance; the deep voice with the rough edges; and the clear, mocking laughter. No one could be at once so droll and so enchanting, so provocative and pert.

Her development as an actress passed almost unnoticed. The brilliant jubilee spring had ended in disaster: the opening of the World Exhibition coincided with a depression on the stock market and the exposure of fraudulent companies. Depression spread to panic. There had been heavy speculation on the exhibition, but a wet spring made it impossible to finish the new buildings, and exhibits and restaurants in the Prater meadows were bogged down in the mud. Those who had gambled their savings were faced with ruin, and as always it was the small investors who suffered most, and who turned against the promoters and financiers they held responsible for their losses. There was a wave of suicides, an atmosphere of despair and gloom, and the theatres played to empty houses. But by September the light-hearted Viennese had reverted to their natural optimism.

It was a warm and sunny autumn. Johann Strauss was once more conducting his concerts in the Volksgarten, and the crowds stood on the Ringstrasse to see the Emperor drive by with his royal visitors. They came in droves and Franz Josef never spared himself. Each one of his guests, from the Crown Prince of Germany to the obscurest of Balkan princes, was personally conducted round the exhibition. Some of them, like the Shah of Persia, with his bejewelled retinue and pink-maned horses, provided better entertainment for the crowds than the exhibition itself. But for the poor Emperor it was a terrible year. The stock exchange crash had affected him personally. The proudest and most honourable of men had seen his own brother, the Archduke Ludwig Viktor, involved in a fraudulent company, and his chief adjutant, Count Folliot de Crenneville, so deeply in debt that he was forced to hand in his resignation. Nevertheless the Emperor continued to carry on with his duties in his correct and selfless manner, comforted by the presence of his wife, who in these moments of crisis always rallied to his side, and for all her dislike of crowds and public ceremonies was present at every function throughout the year.

One of the last official dates in the court calendar of 1873 was a gala performance at the Stadttheater. It had been generally assumed that in view of its popular success *Das Käthchen von Heilbronn* would have been chosen for Their Majesties' first visit to the theatre. Laube's decision to stage an entirely new production of Shakespeare's *The Taming of the Shrew* was received with considerable surprise and criticism. It was a part which was usually given to a mature actress, redhead or brunette. To give it to a twenty-year-old blonde and allow her to play it without a wig inevitably led to protests of favouritism from the protectors of the other ladies of the company. But the Shrew was to be one of Katharina Schratt's greatest roles, in which she proved herself the subtlest and most accomplished of comediennes. Shakespeare's Katherine directed by Laube was no screaming termagant, starved and bullied into subjection, but a mischievous, envious and capricious girl who, in spite of her exasperating ways and violent temper, was sufficiently fascinating to make Petruchio feel that it was not only the money which made the battle worth while. Nor in the last act did anyone in the audience believe that Katherine had become a submissive, mouselike creature, ready to be her husband's slave; as interpreted by Katharina Schratt, she was a woman who enjoyed being dominated by her man but was at the same time triumphant in the knowledge that she had won his love.

The curtain fell on a storm of applause. Katharina Schratt was called back time after time. Never had a sophisticated gala audience shown such enthusiasm. The Schratt girl was a sensation, and even those who had previously supported Dingelstedt now admitted that Laube was still the greatest of all directors. Their Imperial Majesties summoned him to their box to congratulate him on the evening's performance, but he was disappointed when neither the Emperor or Empress said a word about the young actress he had made into a star. '*Es war sehr schön, es hat mir sehr gefreut*' ('It was very beautiful and gave me much pleasure') was the classic phrase with which the Emperor showed his appreciation of the various gala performances, concerts and exhibitions he attended throughout the year. He was probably too tired, and the Empress too bored, to pay much attention to what was happening on the stage. But Their Majesties' indifference was barely noticed by Katharina Schratt. For Heinrich Laube had praised her tonight for the first time, calling her 'his little bird of paradise' and telling her she had no rival on the German-speaking stage.

2

Laube's 'Little Bird of Paradise'

For three years the Stadttheater kept playing to full houses and Katharina Schratt affirmed her popularity with the Viennese public. The photographers on the Kärntnerstrasse exhibited her picture in their windows and autograph hunters gathered round the stage door, but Laube's backers were short of cash. The stock exchange crash of 1873 had lasting consequences and they kept urging the need for economy, which interfered in the grandiose projects of a director who had become ever more intransigent over the years. Finally it came to an open break, with Laube handing in his resignation and accepting what at the time appeared to be a splendid offer from America. In loyalty to Laube, Katharina Schratt followed his example and left the Stadttheater at the height of her success, accepting an offer to appear as guest artist at the German Court Theatre of St Petersburg. The Russian capital had a large and prosperous German colony and both the imperial family and a considerable proportion of the aristocracy were partly of German blood, which assured visiting artists of large, enthusiastic audiences.

The spirit of adventure, a curiosity for new horizons, and the temptation of a salary such as she had never earned with Laube, took Katharina Schratt to Russia. It was a new and exciting world for a girl of twenty-three, familiar with the plays and novels of the great Russian masters. Here was no closed society, no *Erste Gesellschaft*, and the popular Austrian actress was welcomed into the great marble palaces on the Neva and showered with gifts of an oriental magnificence, of which Mama Schratt would have been the first to disapprove. But the other side of Katharina's nature, that of a cosy, middle-class Viennese, who is never happy far from the *Steffel*,* made her just as homesick among the splen-

*In Viennese dialect, the steeple of St Stephen's Cathedral.

dours of St Petersburg as she had been in Berlin. No sooner did she hear that Laube was back at the Stadttheater after a disastrous American tour, in which a dishonest agent had embezzled most of the funds, than Katharina turned her back on the opulence and glitter of the Russian capital and rejoined her old mentor. But Laube's return may not have been the only reason. Before leaving Vienna, her name had been linked with that of the actor Alexander Girardi – a rumour which, in view of the fact that Girardi happened to be the most celebrated comedian of his day, was widely publicized. He represented to the Vienna of his day what Maurice Chevalier did to a later generation in France. Chevalier's famous boater may even have been inspired by Girardi, who made that form of headgear so fashionable in the Vienna of the 1880s that it was known simply as a 'Girardi'.

The most lovable and beloved of actors, he was the friend and *alter ego* of Johann Strauss and interpreter of some of his most successful operettas. His romantic attachment to Katharina Schratt, had it ended in marriage, would have made them the most popular couple on the German stage. It began in the summer of 1878, but unfortunately the following spring brought Nicholas Kiss von Itebbe to Vienna, and this dark and handsome Hungarian in his romantic Honved uniform swept Katharina completely off her feet, embarking her on a tempestuous love affair ending in a disastrous marriage. Outwardly she appeared to be making an excellent match. Her fiancé came from a family of well-to-do landlords from Temèsvar and moved in the fashionable circles of the Austrian capital, but there was wild blood in the Kisses. The grandfather had been condemned to death as a general in the revolutionary forces of 1848 and had had his estates confiscated by the crown. The two grandsons, who had been given back their properties, spent their revenues in Vienna, and many of their fertile acres were gambled away at the Jockey Club. Katharina, who only a few years before had had the good sense to refuse to marry a young Count Coronini on the grounds that she did not want to tie herself for life to a man who kept her out of his winnings at cards, now fell irrevocably in love with a far greater spendthrift than poor Coronini had ever aspired to be.

After a whirlwind courtship they were married in the late autumn of 1879 and moved into a splendid fourteen-room apartment on the Gumpendorferstrasse, where Kiss, who was an experienced man of the world, initiated his young wife in all the social graces, making her into the perfect hostess, whose dinners at Hietzing were later so appreciated by both gourmets and connoisseurs. As a proud Hungarian he refused to allow her to continue with her theatrical career, and for the time being Katharina was sufficiently under his spell to accept his word as law. Laube never forgave her defection, and her relations with the one man who might have made her into a great actress ended with her marriage. She missed the stage and her old friends. Nicholas spent most of the day either at the Club or on the racecourse, and with time on her hands she indulged in the delicious pastime of spending money without stopping to think that for the first time in her adult life she was without means of her own and that her father's handsome dowry had gone to pay her husband's most pressing gambling debts.

By 1880 she was pregnant, and the birth of a son, Anton or Toni as he was soon called, brought the added expense of a nursery, layettes from Paris, an English nanny – nothing was too good for Katharina's baby. Financial worries led to quarrels and mutual recriminations over extravagance, added to which Nicholas Kiss was jealous and possessive and Katharina, who had been fed on admiration since she was a child, was subjected to violent scenes if she as much as smiled at any man. By the time their son was barely two years old, the situation had become intolerable. The great romance had degenerated into sordid squabbles and the couple agreed to separate. Nicholas Kiss hurried off to Budapest just as the bailiffs moved in, leaving his wife to face their creditors alone. Her parents, who had suffered severe losses from the stock exchange crash, could do little to help beyond offering her a home, but Katharina had travelled too far to settle down to a bourgeois life in Baden, and she decided to return to the stage. It was not easy to make a comeback after an absence of over three years. Laube had retired, the Stadttheater was closed, the rigid rules of the Burgtheater refused admittance to any actress who was financially in debt, and none of the other theatres could offer a salary which would solve the problems of a young woman burdened with nearly thirty thousand gulden worth of debt.

A fortuitous offer from the German theatre in New York gave her the chance to escape for the time being from a situation sufficient to daunt even someone of her sanguine disposition. Leaving Toni with her parents, she embarked for New York, where she landed in January 1882 publicized by her promoters as 'the German Bernhardt', a title she herself would never have presumed to claim.

The German theatre was situated in the unfashionable Bowery district, but enthusiastic reviews of 'Miss Schratt's performance' of Cyprienne in Sardou's *Divorçons* (*Let's Get Divorced*) brought the habitués of Broadway flocking to the Thalia Theater. A leading critic who complained of the 'lack of novelties' in the New York theatre wrote:

> There is one exception, the Thalia Theater where I saw *Divorçons* very elegantly presented on the stage and more perfectly played than it would have been in any up-town house. The acting is to be credited to Miss Kate Schratt, a favourite from Vienna, and Herr Basserman, a leading man from Berlin, who were simply perfect in their roles as a flirting wife and sensible husband. Distant as the old Bowery now seems from the height of fashion, it is now crowded nightly with some of the best people of New York. The public will go anywhere to see a good show.

There is a photograph of Katharina Schratt taken against a snowy landscape in New York which shows her in a feathered hat and satin gown with fur-trimmed cloak and muff, but, in spite of the sophistication of her dress, looking so incredibly youthful that it is difficult to envisage her as a woman of thirty with a broken marriage behind her. The little round face with the strongly marked eyebrows and determined chin has none of the look of the fashionable leading lady. She is still true to herself, the simple girl from Baden whose spontaneity and charm conquered the New York public as she had conquered her audiences in Berlin, Vienna and St Petersburg. Only the language barrier prevented her from becoming a Broadway star, and the warmth and friendliness of her American admirers, many of them of German origin, helped her to regain the confidence she had lost in the past year. Some of these solid, shy young men offered her marriage, and there may have been moments when the thought of all the difficulties that awaited her in Vienna tempted her to send for Toni and remake her life in America.

But those moments never lasted for long. Dominating all was the determination to have Toni brought up as a Hungarian gentleman who would inherit his estates unencumbered by debt. It was an ambition which, for the time being, seemed impossible to realize and one that only a woman of exceptional courage and optimism would ever have contemplated. Katharina Schratt's love for her son was now the leitmotiv of her life. The mother took pride of place over the artist. Respectability became almost an obsession with her. To assure that respectability she was willing to make the sacrifice of remaining tied to a man who to the end of his days knew how to capitalize on the situation.

Her relationship with her estranged husband remains ambiguous. Her adoration for Toni, who resembled his father in both character and appearance, shows that her affection for Nicholas Kiss was not entirely dead and that in spite of all her disillusions he still had a place in her heart. When he finally settled down to work and entered the consular service, a decision for which she was largely responsible, it was she who found the money to pay his debts and who throughout the years tried to promote his career, though the highest rank to which he ever attained was that of Consul in Algiers. He was welcomed to her house whenever he came on leave, and not even her closest friends ever heard her say a word of criticism against him. She never felt any bitterness towards the husband who, through his carelessness and selfishness, had destroyed whatever passion she was capable of. However warm and affectionate in her friendships, however loving, she never allowed another man to dominate her life. She had numberless flirtations, a few discreet and circumspect affairs, but no one ever made her forget her responsibilities as Toni's mother, least of all the man who was to give her a place in history.

She was thirty years old when she returned to Vienna to face her creditors and recapture her public. Success had come so easily to her in her youth when she had been the spoiled and cherished

Käthi Schratt, Laube's 'bird of paradise'. But the Austrian public is notoriously fickle, and during her absence new faces had appeared on the Vienna stage. The insuperable barrier of thirty thousand gulden worth of debts still barred the way to her ultimate goal, which was to become a member of the Burgtheater, where Frau Kiss von Itebbe could take her place among the various titled members of the company and enjoy the privileges of a court actress. To bring her name back into the limelight she went on a tour of all the provincial cities. In the spring of 1883 she was appearing at the Municipal theatre of Czernovitz where the District Commissioner at the time was a young Count Kielmansegg, one of the many Hanoverians who after the war of 1866 had entered the Austrian service, in which he was destined to make a brilliant career.

In his memoirs Count Kielmansegg devotes a chapter to Katharina Schratt, whom he saw for the first time in 1872 when she was making her stage debut at the Stadttheater. Even then he was struck by her vivid personality and the natural quality of her acting. The only things which to his critical eye detracted from the charming ensemble were the big feet in the white stockings and tight shoes. But when they met again in Czernovitz the experienced actress had long since learned to camouflage her defects. Katharina Schratt at thirty was even more alluring than as a girl. The young District Commissioner was flattered when she enlisted his help in procuring her favourable notices in the local press. No critic was too obscure to be ignored, for every review would be added to her collection of newspaper cuttings which she hoped to present to Director Wilbrandt of the Burg.

Count Kielmansegg throws an interesting light as to how Katharina Schratt won her way into the Burgtheater. His account of her first meeting with Franz Josef is very different and also far more credible than the one in Count Corti's *Life of the Emperor*, or in the preface of Baron Bourgoing's carefully edited letters of the Emperor Franz Josef to Katharina Schratt. Neither of these authors makes any mention of who paid up the debts which enabled the actress to get into the Burg. Both seem to have accepted the version given to them by her son Baron Anton Kiss and perhaps also by Frau Schratt herself who, in her dignified old age when she was immortalized as the *gnädige Frau* of Schönbrunn, may not have wanted to recall the days when she got into the Burgtheater through the help of a Jewish banker and his friends.

Laube's backers had been mostly Jewish financiers and Katharina had many ties with the rich and important banking world. As the wife of Nicholas Kiss she had entertained most of the prominent figures of the *Zweite Gesellschaft*, and among the most prominent and influential was the President of one of Austria's biggest mining companies, the Alpine-Montan Gesellschaft. Edward Palmer was a convivial, elderly bachelor with a large apartment on the Kolowratring, where he enjoyed entertaining pretty actresses and also ladies of a more dubious character. He was popular with the smart young men about town who could count on his discretion when they borrowed his apartment for their illicit rendezvous, and even the Crown Prince Rudolf was not above making use of this amiable Jew, for his recent marriage to an inexperienced Belgian princess had in no way cured him of his bachelor habits.

Palmer had been an admirer of Katharina Schratt since the early days of her marriage and was a frequent guest at the Kiss apartment. He and Katharina had recognized in one another a capacity for friendship such as was rarely found in their materialistic society. He for his part was probably more than a little in love with the charming young woman who later showed such courage in adversity. When she returned to Vienna she went to him for help. He gave it generously and freely, without imposing any conditions or presuming to become the 'rich protector' which many men in his position might have insisted on. But Palmer's wealth was not unlimited and he had already too many commitments to take upon himself the full payment of her debts. Therefore he opened a subscription fund among their friends to which he himself contributed the largest sum. There is no greater proof of Katharina's popularity, both as an actress and as a woman, than that the large amount of twenty-three thousand gulden was collected in a few weeks.

Seven thousand gulden had still to be found, and according to Count Kielmansegg it was then that Palmer addressed himself to his good friend Baron Mayr, who administered the private funds and revenues of the imperial properties. Mayr, who was himself an assiduous theatre-goer, was asked to intervene with the Emperor on behalf of a brilliant young actress whom Director Wilbrandt was anxious to acquire for the Burg.

Franz Josef had little time or interest for the theatre, but he looked upon the Burgtheater as a family concern for whose welfare he was directly responsible. Katharina Schratt may have made little impression on him as an actress, but he recalled the audience's enthusiasm at the gala performance of *The Taming of the Shrew*. Having little knowledge of the arts, he relied on the judgement of those whom he trusted in such matters. One of them was Baron Mayr, who had no difficulty in persuading the Emperor to help an aspiring Burgtheater actress out of his private funds. Franz Josef, who never handled money, had so little idea of its value that he was as willing to part with fifty thousand gulden as with five hundred. Parsimonious, almost frugal, in his personal habits, he lived in spartan discomfort in the midst of a prodigal court.

By the beginning of 1884, Katharina Schratt had achieved what six months before would have seemed impossible. She had become a member of the Burgtheater, though she had still to wait for three years to obtain the coveted title of *Kaiserliche und Königliche Burg Schauspielerin*, with all the privileges attached to what was virtually a royal appointment. It was natural that her first audience with the Emperor should be in order to thank him for his act of gracious condescension. On this occasion she appears to have been so overcome with nerves and so intimidated by the pomp and grandeur of the setting that she forgot every word of her carefully worded speech and, finding herself face to face with the Emperor, could only stammer, 'Oh dear, Your Majesty, what I was going to say was so beautiful and it is now gone clear out of my head.' These words, spoken in her pretty Baden-Viennese dialect, were so natural and so utterly devoid of affectation that Franz Josef's kind blue eyes crinkled in amusement, for here was someone completely different from the usual court actresses with their airs and graces and finely modulated accents. His smile dissipated her fears, and when she left the royal presence the adjutants on duty noted that the audience had lasted far longer than the customary two and a half minutes.

Count Kielmansegg heard this story from Edward Palmer, to whom Katharina Schratt must have told it at the time. According to the other version, as related by Baron Bourgoing, the actress had her first meeting with the Emperor when she came to him as a supplicant on behalf of the Kiss family who were trying to recover the income from properties forfeited after 1848 and only given back in recent years. Katharina was far too intelligent to identify herself with a case which, her friends would have told her, had little chance of success; moreover, among the papers inherited by Anton Kiss and hitherto unpublished are a few rough copies of extracts from his mother's correspondence with the Emperor that are particularly important as the originals have never come to light and in all probability have been destroyed.

One of these drafts shows quite clearly that the Kiss family only tried to use Katharina Schratt as an intermediary when she was already on friendly terms with the Emperor. In an undated letter the actress begs to be excused over a matter

> ... for which I am not responsible. On coming home from Schönbrunn after a walk with Your Majesty I was waylaid by my brother-in-law, Elemér Kiss, whom actually I have hardly ever spoken to before. He told me he had to see me on urgent business which also concerned my son, and that on the following morning he was to have an audience with Your Majesty to ask for reinvestigation into the events which had impoverished his family. He wanted me to accompany him because of Toni. Naturally I declined. I can imagine Your Majesty's horror had I suddenly appeared. You would have thought you were seeing a ghost.

In another undated draft written probably a few weeks later, the actress encloses the document which Kiss's brother 'gave me a few days ago. I have been so bold as to permit myself to do this, but as far as I can make out it seems very longwinded and unclear.' This appears to have been all that Katharina was prepared to do on behalf of her husband's family. The petition was dismissed by Franz Josef on the advice of the Hungarian government and further attempts made by Elemér Kiss to reopen the matter were equally unsuccessful.

When Baron Bourgoing edited the Emperor's correspondence with Frau Schratt, Anton Kiss was still living as a retired Legation

Counsellor. On the one hand he had profited and on the other he had suffered from his mother's relationship with the Emperor. He had been spoiled and indulged, not only by her, but also by Franz Josef, who when he was still a child allowed him favours denied to the highest in the land. Educated at the élite Theresianum College where he was said to have been popular with the boys, he had nevertheless on more than one occasion been the victim of a jealousy and a vindictiveness which did not hesitate to strike the mother through the son. Anonymous letters written to a child of twelve are not likely to be forgotten. In Toni's case it seems to have aroused an exaggerated loyalty to his father and an inordinate pride of his Hungarian ancestry. While according to Katharina's colleague, the famous actor-director Hugo Thimig, her son had a snobbish dislike of her connection with the stage.

Both Toni and his mother, who lived for nearly forty years after she had retired from the Burgtheater, may have been responsible for spreading the legend of the beautiful supplicant appearing before the Emperor to plead the cause of her persecuted family. But had this been the case Franz Josef would never have been so interested. What appealed to him was that the 'brilliant actress' described by Baron Mayr was in reality a shy young country-woman who spoke in a Baden dialect and had stage-fright in his presence. Curiosity took the Emperor to the Burgtheater to see Katharina Schratt perform for the first time in Birch-Pfeiffer's *Dorf und Stadt*, in which she played the part of an innkeeper's daughter, looking enchanting in Black Forest costume and acting with such verve and humour that Franz Josef, who rarely relaxed, was delighted and amused. In the long and lonely winter months when the Empress was on her travels, he gradually got into the habit of visiting the Burgtheater for an hour or two whenever he had a free evening, and by chance these evenings always happened to be when Katharina Schratt was playing the lead.

3

'The Unforgettable Hours at Frauenstein'

One of the most brilliant events of the Vienna carnival was the *Industriellenball*, which by permission of the Emperor was held in the great *Redoutensaal* of the Hofburg. It was one of the rare occasions on which the various societies mixed and the Emperor and the archdukes had the opportunity of meeting the wives and daughters of the bourgeoisie. The Empress was never present and most members of the aristocracy came unattended by their wives. But the banking world and industry, the legal world and the stage were fully represented, and the prettiest women in Vienna were to be seen at the ball. The ladies of the Burgtheater were among those who were privileged to sit on the high dais and be presented to the Emperor.

It was at the *Industriellenball* of February 1885 that Franz Josef met Katharina Schratt for the second time, and engaged her in a conversation which everyone noted to be particularly animated. Eye witnesses recall that she was looking her loveliest that evening, wearing a low-cut white satin gown and a corsage of jasmine and roses, and it seemed as if the Emperor was loath to leave her side.

Life had been kind to Katharina in the past year. Free from debt, with a handsome, if not exorbitant salary, she could afford to have Toni living at home and maintain an establishment which her mother, who was now a widow, considered to be extravagant, but which she regarded as her due. She had recaptured the hearts of her Viennese public, and what was even more to her credit, had ingratiated herself with her colleagues at the theatre. Both Hugo Thimig and the actress Rosa Albach-Retty, who died in 1980 at the age of 103, remember her as *ein lieber Kerl* (a good fellow), a term which is more often applied to a man than to a woman, and denotes a generous, warm-hearted nature devoid of meanness and of petty spite.

Following in her wake was a train of admirers, such as the loyal and devoted Palmer, and the three dashing Baltazzi brothers, Hector, Aristide and Alexander, who with their open purses, superb horsemanship and marriages into the Hungarian aristocracy had succeeded in crashing their way into a society which would not normally have accepted people of their dubious Levantine origins. There was the actor Alexander Girardi, now at the height of his fame, collaborating with Johann Strauss at the Theater an der Wien. But the most fascinating of all her admirers was the celebrated Count Hans Wilczek, a character belonging to the Italian Renaissance rather than to the Vienna of the 1880s. He was at once an explorer and an art Maecenas, a liberal and a humanitarian, who in the Austro-Prussian War of 1866 had enlisted in the ranks in order to experience and make known the hardships endured by the ordinary soldier. Today he is remembered as the founder and first president of the Austrian life-saving society, and as the creator and owner of Kreuzenstein, a perfect replica of a medieval castle, filled with treasures collected from all over Europe.

Wilczek was already approaching fifty when he met Katharina Schratt. He had been married at the age of twenty to a beautiful Venetian and had a large number of children and grandchildren. His love affairs were legion and he was still considered to be irresistible to women. But his romance with Katharina Schratt is incorporated in the family legends, and appears to have been more serious and to have lasted longer than any of his other affairs. It is associated not with Kreuzenstein but with Moosham, another castle he acquired as a ruin and restored for his own use, but one where he never brought his family until many years later.

Here in the Carinthian woods flowered a relationship of which all too little is known. It was only after Wilczek's death that old retainers showed his children the rooms where Katharina Schratt and her little boy came to spend the summer months. Toni Kiss remembered staying at Moosham as a small child, and being entranced by the shining suits of armour and the hunting trophies on the wall. But his mother was not given to betraying confidences. In the eyes of her admirers her discretion was perhaps the most appreciated of all her attributes.

There is so much we would like to know. How long did Katharina's love affair with Wilczek last before it settled down to a friendship sufficiently close to arouse an Emperor's jealousy? Nor was Katharina Schratt the only reason for the Emperor's jealousy of Wilczek. The young Crown Prince Rudolf had an enormous admiration for the liberal-minded aristocrat whose political views were diametrically opposed to those upheld by his father's hidebound entourage, and many of the Jewish philosophers and scientists whom Rudolf called his friends were introduced to him by Wilczek. The Count's influence was entirely beneficial. As he influenced Rudolf, so he influenced Katharina Schratt, who started to take an interest in culture and politics. Under Wilczek's guidance she began to collect antique furniture and to frequent museums and art galleries. But their greatest bond was a love of nature, a passion for mountaineering, which she kept up till late in middle age, and of which the Emperor, who was himself a keen mountaineer, always appears to have disapproved. It makes one wonder whether Wilczek was sometimes her companion on what Franz Josef called 'those hazardous and unnecessary expeditions'.

There must have been a time when Katharina was in love with Hans Wilczek, or had she been too hurt and too unhappy in her marriage to let herself become too deeply involved with a man who belonged to a completely different world and had so many other commitments? Their romance dates from the early 1880s and her regular visits to Moosham appear to have ended in 1885, when, after a successful season as guest artist at the Kurhaustheater in Ischl, she rented for the following summer a house on the Wolfgangsee.

Her performances at the Kurhaustheater were among the best she ever gave. Alexander Girardi was her leading man and Raimund's famous comedy *The Spendthrift* (*Der Verschwender*) was the perfect vehicle for their talents. Even Hugo Thimig, who was not usually one of her admirers, wrote: 'Kathi gave of her best in the part of Rosl. She was fresh, pretty and delightful.' The Emperor, who always spent his holidays at Ischl, must have gone to the theatre on more than one occasion but there is no record of their meeting, nor does he appear to have made any attempt to get in touch with Katharina Schratt since the night of the *Indus-*

triellenball. But in the past year his visits to the Burgtheater had become so regular that the actress now permitted herself to smile at him from the stage, and her colleagues, who had been so benevolently inclined in the beginning, began to show the first signs of jealousy. The management's decision to include Katharina Schratt in the select company of actors who were to perform at Kremsier was probably not so much on account of her former visit to St Petersburg, but because she was already known as His Majesty's favourite actress.

Everything changed at the Kremsier meeting of 1885, and it changed largely because of the Empress who that evening suddenly realized that her husband was still capable of emotions she could no longer feel. In the first years of her marriage Elisabeth had been so jealously possessive of Franz Josef that she resented it if he as much as looked at another woman. Her dislike of her mother-in-law, the formidable Archduchess Sophie, was largely based on jealousy. She had resisted all Sophie's efforts to make her conform to court etiquette, to appear in public even when she was pregnant and thereby disfigured in her own eyes. The whole business of childbearing was distasteful to Elisabeth, for each time she feared it might mean the loss of her beauty, the one thing she cherished above all else. Conjugal life became ever more irksome to her, and in spite of his adoration, Franz Josef, who was a normal, full-blooded young man, began to console himself with other women. He was not always careful in his choice. In 1861 matters came to a crisis when the Empress caught a mysterious illness to which no doctor would give a name but for which the Emperor was generally thought to have been responsible. This was followed by her flight to Madeira, and the relationship between husband and wife becoming so taut that Elisabeth could not bring herself to be under the conjugal roof for more than a few weeks at a time.

Austria's defeat by Prussia in 1866 brought her back to Vienna, reminding her of her duties to her husband and her country. The birth of their younger daughter Valerie put the seal to their reconciliation – a reconciliation with political implications. When Austria's fortunes were at their lowest ebb, the Hungarian statesmen Julius Andrássy and Franz Deák saw that the moment had come for their two countries to forget the wounds inflicted in 1848 and to make peace. And it was Elisabeth, loving Hungary far more than Austria, who persuaded her husband to come to terms with men whom he had formerly condemned as rebels. The Historic Compromise or *Ausgleich*, which created the dual monarchy and gave Hungary full autonomy in all her internal affairs, was the Empress's contribution to the Empire, after which she retreated once more into her world of fantasy, cutting herself off from her family and her responsibilities.

All the love she had left to give was centred on her youngest child, Valerie, whom she overwhelmed with a stifling, possessive adoration. She had still a certain affection for her husband, and a certain gratitude. If asked whether she loved him she would probably have replied in the affirmative. When hunting in England she still found time to write, begging him to join her for a few weeks and not to be such a slave to duty. On her return from one of her Mediterranean journeys she would have been miserably disappointed not to find him waiting for her at Miramare, the castle near Trieste which had formerly belonged to his brother Maximilian, the ill-fated Emperor of Mexico. Franz Josef's selfless, uncomplaining love was accepted as her due, and in a flash of truth she admitted that 'life would have gone badly for me, had I not become an Empress'. There were times when she realized how little she gave her husband in return, and felt a certain remorse. It was on one of these occasions that she thought of Katharina Schratt as an amusing and agreeable companion to cheer the Emperor in his loneliness. It would never have crossed Elisabeth's mind that her husband might end by falling in love with the pretty actress. Love was for the young and the beautiful, walking in Elysian fields, not for a crotchety, ageing Emperor with crows' feet round his eyes. She had known of and ignored the stories of women being secretly brought into the Hofburg, richly rewarded for their services and then dismissed. But no woman of the first society could ever claim to have been the Emperor's mistress, nor would Elisabeth ever have tolerated such a situation any more than she allowed any of the archduchesses who deputized in her absence to be treated with the full honours due to a reigning sovereign – a curious trait in a woman who affected to despise all pomp and protocol.

In the year 1885-6 the Empress stayed longer than usual in Vienna, for her daughter Valerie was growing up and a series of small *Hofbälle* were being held in the Hofburg to which only her daughter's closest friends and young men attached to the court were invited. The Empress made an effort to put herself out for her young guests, but she was too beautiful and too remote to do anything other than intimidate them; Franz Josef on the other hand, who enjoyed the company of the young, was at his most charming and relaxed, so that they came home to their parents saying that the Emperor was by far the easier to get on with. Elisabeth also accompanied her daughter to the theatre, but whereas she had hitherto only visited the Burgtheater when Sonnenthal or Tewerle were appearing in Shakespeare, she now took her to see Katharina Schratt performing in *Dorf und Stadt*, and was just as charmed as Franz Josef by the warmth and spontaneity of her acting.

One of the kindest things Elisabeth ever did was to encourage a friendship which without her assistance might never have existed. Coming to the throne at the age of eighteen, Franz Josef had had little time for friendships. His mother had taught him to believe that no one in his entourage must ever become indispensable: 'An Emperor should be able to change his ministers as easily as he changes his gloves.' His own brothers stood in awe of him. His only son had become more or less a stranger, and not even his Prime Minister, Count Taaffe, the affable bohemian aristocrat of Irish origin who had been the companion of his youth, would never have dared intrude into his private life.

It required Elisabeth's intuition and imagination to pave the way by commissioning the court painter Heinrich von Angeli to execute the actress's portrait as a present for the Emperor. Von Angeli was a conventional and accomplished artist who followed in the tradition of Winterhalter by confining himself to portraits of royalty and the aristocracy, and it was immensely flattering for the young actress to be included amongst his sitters. Not until the picture was nearly finished was Katharina told for whom it was intended.

On 20 May 1886 she was sitting to von Angeli for the last time, chatting in her artless fashion on the current gossip of the day, on

Girardi's enthusiasm for his part in Johann Strauss's forthcoming production of *The Gipsy Baron*, on the costume she was going to wear at Princess Metternich's charity ball – when the artist informed her that Their Majesties were coming that morning to view the finished picture. He was surprised to find her terrorized at the idea of meeting not so much the Emperor as the Empress, and begging to be allowed to leave before they arrived. But the carriage was already at the door, von Angeli was running down the stairs and Katharina, overcome with shyness, found herself curtseying to a woman whom she later described as having the most beautiful face she had ever seen.

Apart from a brief meeting at the Archbishop's palace at Kremsier, she had only seen the Empress from across the footlights or driving in an open carriage down the Ring – an apparition rather than a human being. But now Elisabeth was smiling at her with that bewitching smile which woke golden glints in the brown eyes, and the voice which addressed her was so soft and caressing it was hard to believe that it could ever utter a command. It was impossible to envisage her as a woman approaching fifty. The hair piled high under the little bonnet had still the warm lights of youth; the figure revealed by the clinging gown, for the Empress never followed the fashions, was that of a young girl. Only the skin showed the first signs of age, weather-beaten from long days on the hunting field and at sea, and no beauty remedies could dispel the faint tracery of lines round the mouth and eyes.

Yet for all her amiability – and the Empress was at her best with artists, admiring the portrait and praising both the painter and the sitter – Katharina Schratt found her far more intimidating than the Emperor. In front of Elisabeth the spoilt and fêted actress felt as clumsy and inadequate as the youngest of the guests at the *Hofball*. She never got over this feeling, even after the Mayerling tragedy had brought them together with the Empress treating her as a friend on whom she could unburden her responsibilities.

No one could meet Elisabeth without falling under her spell. Even her ladies-in-waiting, soured and embittered by years of devotion to a mistress who, in her colossal egotism, had little regard for their feelings as ordinary human beings, were nevertheless still willing to waste their lives in her service, and the actress whom she singled out by her kindness and attentions was only too ready to worship at the shrine of the Queen Empress. But the very nature of the friendship fostered by Elisabeth was to make it impossible for Katharina Schratt to love the Emperor without criticizing his wife for her coldness and neglect. She was herself too normal to sympathize with the moods and obsessions of the Wittelsbachs, and on more than one occasion Franz Josef defended his wife in his letters to his friend: 'Once you really know her you will understand what a really wonderful person she is.' It was only after Elisabeth's death that Katharina Schratt was to realize how much she owed the Empress when, bereft of her protection, she found herself exposed to all the calumnies and petty humiliations of which a jealous court was capable.

Never had von Angeli been so flattered by the Empress as during that visit to the studio. Her gracious condescension went to the lengths of inspecting all his works, thus leaving the Emperor free to talk to Frau Schratt who, before long, was chatting to him without any sign of timidity or nerves. In her company Franz Josef, who was usually so unapproachably polite, was as relaxed as if he was talking to one of his daughter's friends. This spontaneous youthfulness appears to have been the secret of her magic; words and laughter bubbled out, irrepressible and unrehearsed. It was a quality which had nothing to do with looks, though at thirty-two Katharina Schratt was still exquisitely pretty and desirable, with the plump and rounded freshness of the type most likely to appeal to an elderly man whose wife had not gone to bed with him for over eighteen years.

By the end of the morning Katharina must have been aware that something had happened which was to change the whole course of her life. The Emperor had enquired about her plans for the summer, and she had told him that she had taken a house in the Salzkammergut on the Wolfgangsee, whereupon he replied that he would come over and visit her from his summer villa at Ischl. She did not take this seriously until just before leaving when he asked her the address of the house where she would be staying, and again she had the feeling that this visit had been deliberately planned and that events were moving out of her control.

Two days later came a letter with a small parcel delivered by the court jeweller. In his letter the Emperor, signing himself 'your devoted admirer' wrote, 'I beg you to accept a small token as a sign of my grateful thanks for having taken the trouble to sit for the portrait by von Angeli. I must tell you that I would not have permitted myself to ask of you this sacrifice, and therefore my pleasure over this cherished gift is all the greater.' The small token was a magnificent emerald ring, sufficiently large to impress even an actress who was used to expensive gifts. But what touched Katharina far more than the ring was the simplicity and modesty of the wording. Two weeks later on 6 June came a second note, in which the Emperor begged to be excused for troubling her again and asked for details as to when she would be leaving Vienna and on what date he could be sure of finding her at Sankt Wolfgang. In his precise, bureaucratic fashion, Franz Josef asked her to reply to the following questions. What was the name of the house, which he had stupidly forgotten? How long did it take to walk there from Sankt Wolfgang? And would she already be in residence at the beginning of July, or only later? This time the Emperor's letter was signed 'your devoted Franz Josef', and was the beginning of a correspondence which was to last for nearly thirty years. Alas, most of the letters from Katharina appear to have been destroyed, but judging by the few rough copies which survive, she must have been a fascinating correspondent full of wit and humour, with a mixture of childishness and commonsense which entranced the Emperor.

How many copies of her first letters must have been corrected and rewritten! How many friends must have been consulted as to the proper way to address an Emperor! But in the end she probably wrote in her own natural fashion, telling him that she was going to Karlsbad towards the end of June and would be at Schloss Frauenstein after the first week in July.

She had barely arrived, and the trunks were still in the hall, when a messenger appeared at the door, bringing a letter from the Kaiser Villa to say that unless she had any objection His Majesty would be calling on her the following day at eight-thirty in the morning. The hour would have been surprising if Katharina had not already been informed of the Emperor's matinal habits, and in an unguarded moment, with the wish to please, had told him that she herself was an early riser and loved getting out in the early morning air. The Emperor excused himself for visiting a lady at such an unheard-of early hour, 'but I already know that you are up and about at that hour, and it is the one time when my duties permit me to leave here'. Katharina Schratt was to know Franz Josef for twelve years before she had the courage to confess to him that her nerves could no longer stand the strain of those early visits. It was one thing for the Emperor, who went to bed at eight or nine in the evening and got up at dawn, but it cannot have been easy for a popular actress who enjoyed her social life, her supper parties after the theatre, to be fully dressed and at her best at seven or eight in the morning, ready to entertain the Emperor with the latest gossip of the town.

Schloss Frauenstein, which lies above Sankt Wolfgang, was more of a villa than a castle, whose charm lay in its setting, the surrounding woods and meadows and the view over the lake. It was reached by a small path leading up from the village, where Franz Josef left his carriage to walk up the hill on this sunny July morning in 1886. It was an exciting and novel experience for him to be visiting an actress in her home. Wearing the local Tyrolese costume, the huntsman's leather breeches and thick socks, he was indistinguishable in appearance from any other elderly gentleman on his summer holiday. But there was not a person on the road who did not recognize his Emperor, for Franz Josef was more beloved in these regions than in any other part of his Empire.

Katharina Schratt prided herself on being a good housekeeper. She was known for the delicious food she gave her guests, but Franz Josef had announced his visit on a Sunday and she was at her wits' end as to what she was to offer him for breakfast. The cook was in tears as the shops had been shut on Saturday. She had run out of her best cigars, and His Majesty was known to enjoy a smoke in the morning. But the smiling hostess who welcomed her Emperor at the gates of Frauenstein showed no signs of stress, and within a few moments Franz Josef was ensconced in a comfortable armchair, with Katharina talking to him as if she had known him all her life, opening out to him a world of which he knew so little, the gay, brilliant world of the 'second society', regaling him with the intimate gossip of the Burgtheater, the international gossip of the casino at Karlsbad. Witty imitations and trenchant comments on critics and directors had the Emperor laughing as he hadn't laughed for months. And then suddenly she changed and became the proud young mother, presenting her six-year-old son and confiding to him that her greatest ambition was to have Toni educated at the Theresianum College.

Breakfast, so modestly offered and eagerly accepted, was superb. Even the mediocre cigars seemed excellent when smoked in the company of a delightful young woman who for a brief hour had made him forget the despatch boxes waiting for him on his writing desk at Ischl. That Sunday morning of 9 July 1886 was the first of a series of visits which Franz Josef referred to as 'those unforgettable hours at Frauenstein.'

4

The Wittelsbach Inheritance

Every year on 18 August the Emperor's children gathered at Ischl to celebrate their father's birthday. It was an occasion on which even the Empress made an effort to be present. But every year it became more painfully apparent that it was generally regarded as a duty rather than as a pleasure, and Franz Josef must have thought back with nostalgia to those happy birthdays of his boyhood when his parents still lived in the old Villa Eltz, before his mother had built and given him as a wedding present the large and pompous Kaiser Villa.

The Empress hated Ischl, which reminded her of her mother-in-law. She was not on good terms with either of her older children, having never taken any interest in Gisela, who at eighteen had married Prince Leopold of Bavaria and was now the mother of a growing family: nothing depressed Elisabeth more than to be reminded of her grandchildren. Rudolf had fallen out of favour when, on a visit to England, he had dared to criticize her behaviour and her friends. She could not bear her daughter-in-law, whom she called 'that clumsy Flanders mare', and for all his infidelities Rudolf was sufficiently chivalrous to stand up for his wife against his mother's cruel sarcasm. Valerie was the only one who tried to introduce an element of gaiety into her father's birthday. But even her efforts were unsuccessful, for in this summer of 1886 the Empress was still haunted by the tragedy of that cold Whit Sunday night when her cousin King Ludwig of Bavaria was found drowned in the shallow waters of Lake Starnberg.

Elisabeth was in Bavaria at the time, staying across the Lake at Feldafing, and she remained haunted by the thought that Ludwig had been trying to reach her in his desperate attempt to escape from his keepers. The King, who had brought so much beauty into a pedestrian world, who had identified himself with Richard

Wagner, the greatest musical genius of his age, had been called insane and locked up like a common criminal, and the man who had signed the warrant of arrest had been Gisela's own father-in-law, the Regent of Bavaria. When Elisabeth was still a normal young woman she had looked upon her cousin as an eccentric boy, to be mocked and humoured but never to be taken seriously. She had been as angry as her mother when he had jilted her young sister Sophie only a few days before the wedding. But in the past few years, when her approaching menopause had intensified the latent family instability, she had begun to feel a growing affinity with a cousin who also lived in a world of fantasy, raising his fairy castles on inaccessible mountain heights, and communing with the ghost of Marie Antoinette in a miniature Versailles built on a Bavarian lake. Her brothers called King Ludwig mad, and said that his follies and extravagances were ruining his country. Her mother, who had never forgiven him over Sophie, accused him of having unnatural vices. But the simple people had loved him, and stories of the beautiful swan prince were already incorporated in their legends. No one spoke of the doctor whose strangled body had been found lying beside him in the mud of the Starnberg Lake.

Elisabeth's hysterical reaction to her cousin's death was such that for the first time her children began to question her sanity. On the evening after she had received the news, Valerie came into her room to find her lying stretched out on the floor, sobbing and praying to 'the great Jehovah, the god of vengeance, the god of hope, the god of wisdom'. Her daughter's terrified screams brought her back to her senses, and in a piteous fashion Elisabeth told her that she had been tormenting herself in trying to understand the inscrutable ways of God and the retribution in another world. Small wonder if Valerie preferred her father's quiet, undemonstrative affection to these frightening and at the same time pathetic scenes. But she was too loyal to discuss her mother with either her brother or her sister, and was embarrassed when they asked her searching questions to which she did not know how to reply. Gisela was a normal, sensible young woman, who would have liked to help her mother but was treated with an icy reserve and held responsible for her father-in-law, the Regent's, treatment of the King, while Rudolf, whom Ludwig had loved as a brother, had only to come into the room for his mother to burst into a flood of tears.

The Emperor was the only person who refused to admit that his wife was in any way abnormal. At a time when Vienna could boast the best neurologists in the world, and Wagner-Jauregg was experimenting with new methods for the treatment of the insane, the Empress's doctors appear to have found no other cure for her nerves than to send her from one watering place to another, which, combined with the rigid diets she inflicted upon herself, made her even more nervous than before.

Nevertheless she made the effort of coming to Ischl for the Emperor's birthday, a gesture for which he was touchingly grateful, happy to drive with her through the flower-decked streets, cheered by the loyal inhabitants waving their black and yellow flags. But what touched him even more was the interest she showed in Katharina Schratt, going out of her way to shield her from gossip, accompanying her husband on a visit to Frauenstein, and encouraging Valerie to collect photographs of the actress as a present for her father. All this kindness and generosity on Elisabeth's part may have been a way of placating her conscience and of giving herself more freedom for the future. By the end of August she had already left with Valerie to resume her aimless travels across Europe. Gisela and her family returned to Munich. Rudolf, already afflicted with a venereal disease which he knew to be incurable, unhappy in his public and his private life, disliked and distrusted by his father's entourage, returned to Vienna to an existence with which he was becoming increasingly dissatisfied and bored.

The Emperor remained alone, with the visits to Frauenstein 'the only rays of light in my otherwise dreary life'. He spent little more than a month at Ischl, during which time he cannot have seen Katharina Schratt more than a dozen times. But in that short time she succeeded in winning both the confidence and love, though he hardly dared to call it by that name, of a shy, reserved man, who till now had never confided in anyone or loved anyone except his wife. The breakfast room at Frauenstein was an Armida's bower, where an elderly Emperor allowed himself to be seduced by a young woman who made no attempt to seduce him, but whose art lay in being completely natural. Time and again we read in Franz Josef's letters, 'I feel so happy, so much at ease in your company.' She was a woman who, chameleon-like, could adapt herself to the needs of every man, and what Franz Josef needed most of all, something he had never had since his boyhood at the Villa Eltz, was the cosiness, the *Gemütlichkeit*, which every Austrian claims as his birthright.

Out of this *Gemütlichkeit* flowered a friendship so intimate and tender that by the end of the summer, when they said goodbye at the crossroads of Sankt Wolfgang, Katharina Schratt knew that from now on she would have to accept duties and restrictions that were alien to her character. She would be constantly reminded of phrases which had hitherto played no part in her vocabulary, such as 'watch out', 'take care', and 'guard your tongue'. At first she thought mainly of Toni's future, of her own career, and the glittering prospect of an Emperor's friendship. But now she found herself thinking not so much of herself as of that pathetically lonely man, so desperately in need of human companionship. To her surprise she found herself missing his early morning visits, his charming, old-fashioned courtesy and genuine concern for her and her little boy. In one of his first letters he was already writing, 'Your good name and reputation are sacred to me.' His sense of honour would never allow him to visit her in her apartment in the Nibelungengasse, only a few minutes' walk from the Hofburg. What was permissible in Ischl was impossible to contemplate in Vienna. Rather than transgress these rigid rules of conduct, the Emperor accepted his lonely, cheerless life, in which circumstances allowed him to see Katharina Schratt only from across the footlights of a theatre, at a public ball or in the Hofburg chapel, where actresses of the Burgtheater were privileged to attend mass on Sundays.

Franz Josef never knew the sacrifice which it meant for Katharina to have to get up in the dark on a cold winter's morning, and after a late-night performance walk or drive down the Ring for seven o'clock mass. Yet her presence in the gallery seemed to afford him pleasure, and sometimes he would hurry back into his room so that out of his window he could have a glimpse of 'her dear familiar figure walking across the square'.

The only other place where their two worlds met was in the gardens at the palace of Schönbrunn, where the Emperor, with his passion for fresh air and his healthy disregard of the weather, would sometimes go and walk between one and two in the afternoon. And during the next few months these occasional encounters in the snowbound gardens of Schönbrunn provided the only opportunity for the Emperor to exchange a few words with a woman who was constantly in his thoughts, and to whom he wrote,

> I need not tell you how often I think back to those wonderful hours at Frauenstein, for anyway you must know it. Seeing you the other day in the theatre made me feel quite sad, though naturally I was glad to be there. But how different from those other days, which were so wonderful for me. I have not thanked you enough for your many kindnesses, so allow me to do so now from a full heart.

Like most actresses, Katharina Schratt was superstitious, and Franz Josef's valets and adjutants must have been amused to find four-leafed clovers pressed into his wallets and cigar cases, and lucky charms dangling from his watch and chain. The gratitude with which he thanked her for the little gifts which the actress sent on his name-day and at Christmas shows an ever-growing affection and longing for her company. He wrote from his Hungarian castle of Gödöllo,

> Your pictures with the four-leaved clover adorn my bedroom in Vienna. Your calendar with the inscription *'Dieu Vous Garde'* is here on my desk, and I used your cigar case at the autumn shoots where it brought me good luck. I also have it here, but do not use it for fear of losing it. So you see your gifts remind me all the time and everywhere of the dear giver.

She in return received pearls and diamonds which, by the time of the old Emperor's death nearly thirty years later, had become a collection of such value that when the Austrian currency crashed at the end of the First World War Katharina and her dependants were able to live in comfort for the next twenty years by selling only a part of her jewels. The sale of one piece, a diamond dragonfly which she left to a niece, paid for the restoration of an apartment house destroyed by the Russians in the Second World War.

Franz Josef did not confine his gifts to jewels. In the carnival month of 1887, the man who is so often accused of having been a heartless bureaucrat wrote one of the most charming and sensitive letters that anyone in his position could send a woman to whom he was offering financial help. Katharina was notoriously extravagant and the hard lessons learnt in her early married life had in no way cured her of her habit of overspending. The Burgtheater actresses had to supply their own clothes, except when they appeared in historical and theatrical costume, and there was considerable rivalry among the younger ladies as to who had the most elegant wardrobe. The Emperor appears to have been aware of Katharina's money difficulties when he sent her what he called 'a small contribution', but which was in fact a considerable sum, 'to help towards the cost of your attire.' He wrote:

> I regard you as a distinguished and talented woman, but I am not quite convinced of your financial talents, and this may serve me as an excuse. I can also say to you, for your peace of mind, that I give my children for their birthdays and saints' days gifts of money. They find it more practical. So I hope, my dear madam, that you are not offended. This financial transaction remains strictly between us, and when you cheer me again with one of your letters you must not mention it at any time. The gratitude is all on my side.

To identify the actress with his daughters was the most delicate of compliments, and in response Katharina called him her guardian angel and worried what she could do to make him happy. An excerpt which survives from one of her first letters reads, 'At times I think I am dreaming and all this cannot be happening to me.' But Katharina Schratt was not a dreamer by nature. She was essentially a realist, and in this winter of 1886-7 her career as an actress was causing her considerable concern. She still continued to attract large audiences, and was considered one of the most popular actresses of the Burg, but she no longer received the rave notices which she had had at the time of her début under Heinrich Laube. One has only to compare the enthusiasm with which the critics hailed her performance in *The Taming of the Shrew* when Laube presented it at the Stadttheater in 1873, and the tepid, even hostile reviews she received eleven years later when she played the same part at the Burgtheater. The influential *Neue Freie Presse* wrote on this occasion:

> Her voice is too dry and brittle for the part. She is lacking in the light touch, the flexibility and feminine grace which makes even capriciousness seem charming and shrewishness appear attractive. This being the case, the sudden change to sweetness is difficult to conceive, and her performance on the whole was not a great success. It would seem as if Frau Schratt were a disappointment to the Burgtheater.

Katharina's sensational ovation when she appeared in the same part in a gala performance in 1873 had been due to the very qualities which the critics now denied her. Were they at fault, or had she lost the magic which Laube had managed to instil into the young actress he had made into a star? Director Wilbrandt appears to have taken notice of the critics. For the next two years none of the big Shakespearean roles was given to Frau Schratt, who continued to have great success in folk dramas and light comedies. But her ambition was not satisfied, and she felt that others were being favoured at her expense. One of her chief rivals was the beautiful Stella Hohenfels, married to Baron Berger, an influential figure in the Burgtheater management. The two actresses had entered the Burg in the same year, and Stella was not only the darling of the critics but also received considerable publicity on account of what were supposed to be her illustrious and mysterious origins. Both actresses made use of hired claques to swell their applause, till Director Wilbrandt issued a rule forbidding them. Katharina considered that Stella Hohenfels was being unfairly promoted, and in the autumn of 1886, only three years after she had been admitted to the Burg, she was already having a direct confrontation with the management.

One would have thought she would have spared the Emperor the list of her grievances. Franz Josef was not only given a word-for-word account of her interview with Wilbrandt, but was actually asked to intervene on her behalf. That Katharina Schratt should have dared to ask this of the Emperor, and in so doing jeopardize their entire relationship, shows how sure she was of his affections and leads us to believe that those 'wonderful hours at Frauenstein' were not confined to cosy chats over the breakfast table. The fact that the Emperor complied with her request, and acted in a manner which was in every way contrary to his principles, is a far greater proof of his devotion than all his material gifts. When Katharina wrote to him in one of her gloomiest moods, telling him that her interview with Wilbrandt had had no success, and adding half reproachfully that so far no one had done anything to help her, he replied,

> I had wanted to speak to Baron Bezecny [the manager] on your behalf, but did not dare to do so, acting on the principle that until now I have never interfered in the scheduling of the plays and the casting of the roles. For I have always believed that the theatre is there for the public and not for me. Also I have no great opinion of my understanding of these matters. Apart from this I fear that my protection might bring you into a false light and harm you rather than be of use to you. But now for your sake I will try and take the next opportunity to speak to him on your behalf.'

A few days later he wrote again,

> Just a few lines to inform you that yesterday I spoke to Baron Bezecny about your affairs. Whether it was of any use I do not know, but at least he seems to be well disposed towards you and seems inclined to carry out your wishes. He complained a great deal about the Director's hard head and obstinacy (this remark remains between us), and thinks that among the plays which have been taken on from the former Stadttheater, and which are going to be produced by the Burg, there will be some excellent parts, suitable for you.

The Emperor added, with his usual modesty, 'I only hope that my intervention will be of some use.'

Two months later Katharina Schratt had the satisfaction of being chosen to play the role of Portia in *The Merchant of Venice*. It was a part she undertook with considerable trepidation, and the Emperor's unexpected visit on the first night made her so nervous that she almost forgot her lines. Franz Josef was quick to reassure her, 'I am sorry my presence was disturbing. But it in no way affected your performance, and gave Shakespeare no cause to be restless in his grave. I had not meant to go to the theatre that night, but was drawn again to the dear old house just in order to see you.'

She was all he had to cheer him in those lonely months of 1887 when the Empress was away on her travels and his country was going through a crisis which nearly brought war with Russia. Bulgaria, the most backward of all the Balkan states, had become the focal point of European politics ever since the statesmen who had gathered round the congress tables of Berlin had divided what had formerly been a Turkish province into Eastern and Western Rumelia, the former still remaining under the Sultan's rule and the latter becoming a semi-independent principality under Alexander of Battenberg, a morganatic cousin of the Tsar. Alexander's father, a Prince of Hesse and brother of the Tsar's mother, had fallen into disfavour with the Russian court by marrying his sister's Polish lady-in-waiting, who on becoming his wife had been created Countess of Battenberg. Franz Josef had given him a commission in the Austrian army and his sons were later made Princes of Battenberg; one of them marrying a daughter of Queen Victoria.

Alexander, the second of the Battenberg brothers, was only twenty-two when the statesmen at Berlin picked upon him as a suitable candidate to rule over a backward, brigand-infested country of which he could not even speak the language. Officially Bulgaria or Western Rumelia was still a vassal state paying lip-service to the Sultan, but it was the Tsar and not the Sultan to whom Prince Alexander owed his throne, for the Russian monarch hoped to find in his young cousin the perfect puppet prince to administer a country which Russia looked upon as a natural sphere of influence for pan-Slavist propaganda. Russian officers and advisers were sent to help in training the new Bulgarian army and in recruiting civil servants. But before long it became apparent that the Battenberg Prince had no intention of becoming a tool of Russia, and was more inclined to follow the advice of the patriot Bulgarian leader Stefan Stambouloff than that of his dear cousin. When in 1885 Eastern Rumelia threw off the Sultan's yoke and declared its union with the principality, Alexander had the courage to defy the dictates of Berlin by declaring himself Prince of 'a united Bulgaria'.

The world waited on the reactions of the Sublime Porte. But Sultan Abdul Hamid, who realized that the survival of his ramshackle empire depended largely on the great powers quarrelling among themselves, resigned himself to the loss of a rebellious province and watched with a certain amusement the perturbations of Austria, whose occupation of Bosnia and Herzegovina had given her a stake in the Balkans, and the angry reactions of Russia. Prince Alexander had not even troubled to consult his cousin on an action which upset the whole balance of power in the Balkans, and in protest the Tsar recalled both officers and advisers, leaving Bulgaria with a half-trained army with which to face its hostile neighbours. Serbia was the first to attack and it was generally thought that Bulgaria was doomed. But, led by their German Prince, the people fought like lions, and within a few weeks the Serbs were totally defeated and the Bulgars had invaded their territory. Alexander was the hero of the day and all that the powers could do was to rob him of his victories by forcing him to accept peace terms maintaining the status quo. But the Tsar, who already had his eye on Bulgaria's Black Sea coast, had no intention of leaving a popular hero to rule in Sofia. On 9 August 1886, at a time of year when the rulers of Europe were on holiday, when statesmen were drinking the waters in Karlsbad and Bad Homburg, when Franz Josef was at Ischl and Queen Victoria at Balmoral, a dozen men paid by Russia abducted the Prince from his palace and drove him down to the port of Rustchuk on the Danube, where he was put on board a yacht and taken to a Russian station in Bessarabia.

But this time the Russians had gone too far. An attempt by their agents to set up a provisional government, on the grounds that the Bulgars were not fit for constitutional rule, brought rioting and bloodshed to the streets of Sofia, and the people, under their leader Stefan Stambouloff, demanded the return of their prince. European reaction was equally violent. Ministers returned to their posts and armies were mobilized. Both Queen Victoria and the German Emperor wrote personal letters to the Tsar, while in Vienna the anti-Russian party, led by the Archduke Rudolf and the former Foreign Minister Count Andrássy, inveighed against the pusillanimous policy of the Ballhausplatz and clamoured for a war with Russia. Public opinion forced the Russians to capitulate, as the diary of Walpurga Paget, wife of the British Ambassador to Vienna read:

The Russians have got frightened, and on the express wish of the German Emperor have let Prince Alexander go. He is now on his way back to Sofia. His journey through Austria, Hungary and Rumania has been a triumph and now he is more popular than ever. The Russians are always much too clever, but I fear will make us pay some day for the slap in the face they have just received.

Walpurga Paget was right in her prognostications, for the Bulgarian triumph was short-lived. The Battenberg prince, who returned to his capital of Sofia after having been a prisoner for no more than a few weeks, was very different from the ardent young man who had saved his country the year before. The hardships he had suffered in prison had broken him in mind and body, and to the consternation of his government he declared that he could only continue to rule with the approval of Russia who had been the first to give him his crown. The Tsar refused to accept the olive branch, thereby destroying all hope of reconciliation, and Alexander abdicated, to the sorrow of the Bulgarian people who had grown to love their foreign prince. A last attempt by the pro-Russian party to seize control ended in failure, with the Russian commissioner, Baron Kaulbars, having to be protected from the fury of the mob. A regency was set up by Stefan Stambouloff and the Bulgarian throne was again available to any ambitious prince with a sense of adventure. But candidates were thin on the ground. Both Waldemar of Denmark and Charles of Romania declined an offer which had the sanction neither of the Sublime Porte nor of any of the great powers, and was actively opposed by Russia. But in the last days of June 1887 the young Prince Ferdinand of Saxe-Coburg, who was staying in Karlsbad at the same time as Katharina Schratt, showed her a telegram which offered him the Bulgarian throne, and the actress, whose sense of adventure was as great as his own, said without hesitating, 'And of course, monseigneur, you are going to accept'.

5

Intrigues in the Balkans

Of all the spas of Europe, none was more fashionable and cosmopolitan than Karlsbad, a pleasant little Bohemian town not far from the German frontier and equally accessible from Vienna and Berlin. During the summer season you might come across Prince Bismarck or the Prince of Wales drinking the waters at the Schloss Brunnen, or meet King Milan of Serbia dragging his gouty legs on his way to the Casino. Strolling down the Alte Wiese you might run into the actor Adolf Sonnenthal or the millionaire Baron Hirsch, who had made a fortune in Balkan railways and was now proud to lend of his millions to the Crown Prince Rudolf and the Prince of Wales. And in the coffee houses under the lime trees you could always be sure of hearing the latest political gossip and the newest international scandal.

When Katharina Schratt arrived at the Schloss Hotel in the last days of June 1887 she was pleasurably surprised and also somewhat embarrassed to find that she had suddenly become someone of importance whose acquaintance foreign diplomats were eager to cultivate, and whose doings the journalists were anxious to report. Everyone seemed to know of her friendship with the Emperor, though she had seen so little of him in the past ten months. There were times when she despaired of ever breaking down that iron discipline which would never allow him to follow his natural instincts or transgress his rigid moral code to the extent of visiting her for a cup of coffee. Their meetings were still confined to occasional walks in the gardens of Schönbrunn. His reserve was such that he sometimes avoided her on the rare occasions when they did meet at a charity performance or a public ball. There is a pathetic letter written by Franz Josef on the morning after the Concordia Ball, at which Katharina was, as usual, surrounded by admirers, and the poor Emperor did not dare to approach her

[... for fear of having to break through all the people surrounding you, with everyone watching either with or without their opera glasses, and all the press Jews hanging around waiting to snap up every word one says. Alas I was not sufficiently bold to come near you, but I was longing to do so. Besides what could we have said to each other in the crowded Redoutensaal? I am so accustomed to your kindness, to be able to chat to you confidentially and that would hardly have been possible. I feared you might be angry that I did not try to speak to you.

But Katharina was quick to reassure him. Where another woman would have wished to parade her illustrious conquest, she on the contrary affected to be more anxious than the Emperor to prevent any form of *Tratsch* (gossip).

Living in his splendid isolation, Franz Josef could easily ignore the petty slanders and jealousies to which ordinary mortals were subjected, and Katharina was the first to repeat to him the gossip which others would not have dared to mention. In his noble, unworldly fashion he maintained that 'as there is nothing wrong in our friendship, I see no need to hide it'. His only concern was that her reputation and good name should not be compromised on his account. He considered it acceptable to be seen with her in public in the gardens of Schönbrunn and to visit her at Frauenstein and later at Hietzing, but utterly impossible for him to visit her in her third-floor apartment in Vienna. The only time he came to the Nibelungengasse was on the occasion of her mother's death in 1896 when he wrote to Elizabeth, 'I felt it only right to pay a visit to the "*Freundin*" [friend] in order to express my sympathy, but I assure you that this visit to the Nibelungengasse will not be repeated.' These lines were written when he had for the past six years been visiting Frau Schratt at her house in Hietzing, a house bought on account of its proximity to Schönbrunn, where the actress spent most of the spring and summer months, with the Emperor visiting her almost daily for an early breakfast before their morning walk.

What is extraordinary is that this middle-class woman from Baden should have understood and sympathized with all these restrictions and taboos, while maintaining her independence and never allowing the Emperor to dictate to her, either in her habits or her choice of friends, some of whom did not always meet with his approval. One of these was Prince Ferdinand of Saxe-Coburg Kóhary, whom Katharina met in Karlsbad in the summer of 1887 and who became a lifelong friend.

It was a momentous summer for the twenty-six-year-old Prince, who was about to exchange the pampered life of a brilliant dilettante for the hazards of the Bulgarian throne. Outwardly no one could have appeared a more unsuitable choice than this slim-waisted, golden-curled young man, with a high-pitched, drawling voice, whose mother, Clémentine of Orléans, a daughter of King Louis Philippe of France, was reputed to be one of the cleverest and shrewdest princesses in Europe. It was her restless ambition which was generally thought to have been the driving force in getting her son to accept the dubious honour of becoming Prince of Bulgaria. Otherwise it was hard to conceive why a rich and highly educated prince should choose to go and risk his life in a brigand-infested country when none of the powers was prepared to recognize his claims and, in the likely event of his new subjects assassinating him in a few months, not a single foreign warship would be sent in protest to the Black Sea.

Russia was implacably hostile to any candidate other than one of her own choice, and no one was prepared to go to war with Russia on account of Bulgaria. Prince Bismarck had stated categorically in the Reichstag that it was a matter of complete indifference to Germany who sat on the Bulgarian throne, or what became of that country. 'Not for Bulgaria's sake will we suffer anyone to cast a lasso round our necks and drag us into a quarrel with Russia.' This speech was aimed at the anti-Russian party in Austria and also served as a warning to France who, by fostering the ambitions of Russia, hoped to stage a revenge for the humiliating defeat of her army at Sedan. Though Franz Josef was as much in favour of peace as Prince Bismarck, he nevertheless resented the tone of this speech and demanded an apology from the elderly German Kaiser. Neither Franz Josef nor his Foreign Minister had the slightest intention of becoming involved in Bulgaria. Austria had done little to help Alexander of Battenberg, who was personally sympathetic to the Emperor, so Franz Josef was hardly likely to help a Coburg, a member of a family which

was profoundly antipathetic to him. The mad ambition of Charlotte, his Coburg sister-in-law, had encouraged his brother Maximilian to embark on the ill-fated Mexican adventure; Rudolf's
Coburg wife, the Archduchess Stephanie, had not even been able
to produce a son and her jealous scenes were driving her husband
to drink and dissipation. Her father, King Leopold of Belgium,
was a man whose character and morals he despised and, from what
he had heard of Ferdinand, he did not seem to be any better than
the rest of the family. Having inherited vast estates in Hungary
from a paternal grandfather, Count Kóhary, he had had the privi-
lege of serving in the Austro–Hungarian army, but had in no way
distinguished himself. And in a letter to Katharina Schratt the
Emperor referred with contempt to '*le petit Ferdinand*'.

None of his fellow princes, including his Orléans cousins, appears
to have had a very high opinion of Ferdinand's talents. On hearing
of his nomination, the most illustrious of his relatives, Queen
Victoria, telegraphed to her Prime Minister Lord Salisbury: 'I
hope there is no truth in respect of Prince Ferdinand of Coburg as
a candidate for the Bulgarian throne. He is totally unfit, delicate,
eccentric and effeminate, and it should be stopped while there is
still time.' The following day she telegraphed again: 'It is important that it should be known that I and my family have nothing to
do with the absurd pretensions of this foolish young cousin of
mine.' Nothing could have been more crushing than the old
Queen's reply to the Princess Clémentine, when the latter confided
her hopes and ambitions for her beloved Ferdinand. 'My dear
cousin. I received your letter, I must confess with some astonishment. Knowing how much you love your son, I am astonished
you have ever considered this proposal. In your place I would be
thankful if it were dropped.' But in the eyes of the Princess
Clémentine any throne was better than none, a belief which appears
to have been shared by her son.

While drinking the required number of goblets of mineral
water at the Schloss Brunnen and taking the daily walk prescribed
for the cure, Katharina Schratt listened to the ambitious plans of
a young man who in the years to come would bring a little
country on the edge of Europe to the forefront of the political
stage. She knew little about Bourbons and Saxe-Coburgs, but

during that fortnight in Karlsbad she saw enough of Prince Ferdinand to realize that underlying the effeminate manner was a
cold and brilliant brain, possessing the qualities which would later
enable him to overcome obstacle after obstacle, to charm, cheat
and double-cross, fighting his opponents with their own weapons.
Naturally she was flattered by his attentions – any vain and pretty
woman would have been pleased to have Prince Ferdinand as a
cicisbeo. Her sense of drama delighted in the intricacies of Balkan
politics, which were more like a Strauss operetta than anything in
real life. In her long and artless letters, which told Franz Josef so
much he had hitherto ignored, were endless references to the
Coburg Prince. Ferdinand on his side appears to have been one of
the first to realize that the Emperor's feeling for Katharina Schratt
was far more than a passing infatuation, and that in the future she
might prove to be a valuable friend, both to him and to his new
country.

Franz Josef was inclined to disapprove of the actress's friendship
with the Coburg prince, whose presence in Bulgaria could only
make further trouble, for he was hardly likely to succeed where
the popular Alexander Battenberg had failed. In thanking Frau
Schratt for one of the lucky charms she was so fond of giving him,
the Emperor wrote on a note of exasperation, 'I hope that this
talisman together with your prayers will serve to protect us from
war and from misfortune, in spite of the efforts of your Bulgarian
friend.' But Ferdinand was to surprise the world by displaying
both courage and statesmanship and succeeding in circumventing
all Russian attempts to prevent him from reaching Bulgaria.

At dawn on 9 August 1887 he left his Austrian castle of Ebenthal
and, travelling in the greatest secrecy, boarded a second-class
carriage of the Orient Express at Marchegg, which took him as
far as Orsova on the Danube. Here, by the so-called Iron Gates,
the narrow defile of granite rock through which Trajan's legions
passed on their way to the conquest of Dacia, Ferdinand and his
little party of elegant gentlemen, who in their panama hats and
pearl grey gloves looked strangely incongruous in that wild, romantic setting, boarded a small steamer of the Austrian Lloyd
Company which was to take them as far as the Bulgarian frontier.
Stefan Stambouloff, the kingmaker, was waiting to receive them

on the same yacht which the Russian Tsar had originally presented
to his Battenberg cousin and on which, only a few months ago,
conspirators in the pay of Russia had kidnapped the Prince and
abducted him to Bessarabia.

By the time Prince Ferdinand had embarked for Bulgaria,
Katharina Schratt was on the way to Frauenstein. From Karlsbad
she had written to the Emperor:

> A letter from Your Majesty does me more good than all the
> Sprudels and Schloss-brunnen in the world. Every morning on waking
> up my first glance goes to a certain picture of which there are only
> five copies in existence, and my first thoughts are of the dear and
> revered original. In this manner I begin my day in the happiest fashion
> and hurry off to the springs to drink my prescribed number of goblets.

No wonder she felt elated, for the Emperor's longing for her
company is revealed in every one of his letters. 'You cannot
imagine how happy I will be to see you again, for the three weeks
since I spoke to you last seem to have lasted for ever.' A glimpse
of her at the races, driving down the Ringstrasse or crossing the
Michaelerplatz on her way to the theatre brought moments of
happiness to an otherwise lonely day. Never had he felt so depressed as during the past year, in which the Empress had spent no
more than a few weeks at home. The villa built in the game reserve
at Lainz, meant to be a home for their old age, had failed in its
object. What was intended to be a simple country house had in
the hands of court officials and royal architects turned into a cross
between a French *château* and a resort hotel. Franz Josef found it all
too grand for his simple taste; he was always frightened of spoiling
things. His daughter Valerie thought that all the marble reliefs and
bronze-chased fireplaces were depressing. But Elisabeth was delighted with the vast gymnasium fitted with every kind of appli-
ance, including the inevitable weighing machine on which she
weighed herself three times a day. No court architect could spoil
the wonderful view out of the windows, the terrace one had only
to cross in order to find oneself in the middle of a forest. But the
house which the Empress in the first flush of her enthusiasm for
classical Greece called the Hermes Villa saw her for no more than
a few weeks, and the saddest thing of all was that it was in the
comparative solitude of Lainz that husband and wife discovered

how little they had to say to one another. The Emperor was the kindest and most chivalrous of men, but his temper had not improved with age, and there were times when his wife's poetical meanderings irritated him beyond endurance. Hearing her philosophize on the emptiness and futility of life, and quote Heine by the hour got so much on his nerves that he would become curt and almost rude, whereupon she would weep on Valerie's shoulder and complain that her father was impossible to live with.

Their chief quarrels were over Valerie. This daughter, for whom the Empress had an obsessive adoration, had fallen in love with her cousin Franz Salvator of the dispossessed Tuscan branch of the Habsburgs, a young man who had little to recommend him beyond his impeccable lineage and his undeniable good looks. Though Elisabeth was inconsolable at the thought of losing her daughter, she was at the same time doing all in her power to encourage a romance which would keep her in Austria and still under her control. The Emperor, who recognized her underlying selfishness, had other plans for Valerie. The heirs apparent of Saxony and Portugal were coming that winter to Vienna, both with the intention of asking Valerie's hand in marriage, but if he dared to suggest that either of them would be a better match than a penniless cousin his wife would respond with tears, complaining about either his cruelty to Valerie or her own lonely and unhappy future. It can hardly have been pleasant for him to hear the woman he had spoiled and cherished all his life saying quite openly that life would be utterly worthless to her once Valerie had left her.

That summer Elisabeth spent no more than a few days in Ischl, and Franz Josef was alone for his few weeks of holiday. There were chamois to hunt in the mountains, and in nearby Sankt Wolfgang was a charming young woman whose only thought was to see him happy and content. Few places are more romantic than Sankt Wolfgang which lies in the heart of the Salzkammergut, with the shining steeples of the church of Sankt Gilgen reflected in the lake, and the balconies of the celebrated White Horse Inn dripping their geranium petals on the water. On fine summer days visitors to the inn would see the Emperor and Frau Schratt being rowed across the lake by a farmer's wife from Frauenstein. Even when it rained, as it did so often in the Salzkammergut, the Emperor and the actress would be seen walking down the hill, she chatting as gaily as always, with her fresh little face smiling up at him from under the umbrella. She had so much to tell him, all the gossip of the Burgtheater, where Director Wilbrandt's resignation had caused endless intrigues over the choice of his successor. There was turmoil among those whom Katharina nicknamed 'the gods of Olympus'. Sonnenthal was Jupiter, and Charlotte Wolther was Juno, while Stella Hohenfels (Diana) was pulling every string of her bow to get her husband nominated as the new director. Franz Josef, who until now had taken little interest in the theatre, was highly amused by it all and took part in criticizing anyone whom he felt might be a potential rival to his friend.

But even more fascinating than theatre talk was the latest news from Bulgaria. Throughout the summer of 1887 Ferdinand kept Frau Schratt fully informed of his adventures and tribulations. His arrival in his new country had been fraught with difficulties. A loyal and courteous address to his liege lord the Sultan had had no other response than a summary order to leave the country immediately. Abdul Hamid may have grown indifferent as to who ruled in Eastern Rumelia, but he had no intention of giving Russia an excuse for bringing her ships back into the Dardanelles. None of the foreign consulates, with one exception, put out their flags when Prince Ferdinand made his state entrance into his capital. The one exception was that of Austria, for he had deliberately chosen to enter Sofia on 18 August, the Emperor's birthday, a trick which made even Franz Josef laugh when Katharina Schratt repeated to him what his Foreign Minister had not dared to mention. But in spite of all the setbacks and humiliations, the complaints to Frau Schratt of the primitive conditions of his country, the lack of comfort in the former Battenberg palace and the execrable food, Ferdinand showed that he intended to stay on in Bulgaria with or without the recognition of the great powers. And by the end of the summer Franz Josef was writing to Katharina, 'Your Bulgarian friend is showing himself to be truer than I would have thought him.'

The Emperor affected to be jealous of her new admirer (who called himself her 'brotherly friend'), 'but I am flattered to hear that you keep him waiting in replying to his letters, while you write to me so diligently'. Some of the news supplied in the Prince's letters was very useful to Franz Josef, and his ministers were surprised to find the Emperor so well informed on the situation in the Balkans.

It was during this summer of 1887 that the Emperor's friendship with Katharina Schratt reached a degree of intimacy it would never have attained if Elisabeth had remained at home. Whatever has been written to the contrary, and Katharina Schratt in her old age was the loudest in her denials, it is difficult to believe that there were not certain moments when Franz Josef's iron discipline broke down and their relationship overstepped the tenuous bounds of an *amitié amoureuse*. From Ischl he writes to Frau Schratt begging to be excused for not having thanked her sufficiently for his birthday present, 'but I was still bemused over the wonderful things that have been happening to me'. And when those 'glorious weeks' were over and he was back at Schönbrunn on his way to the autumn manoeuvres, he sent her a sad little note: 'It is not more than eight days since I saw you, yet to me it seems an eternity, so quickly does one grow used to happiness.'

But what Katharina Schratt had still to learn was that Franz Josef no longer thought he had any right to happiness, and was prepared to go back to the old routine of visits to the theatre, their chance encounters, and the cold walks in the gardens of Schönbrunn, with only their letters to kindle the embers of a few treasured memories. Nor was he the most gifted of letter writers. He himself was painfully conscious of his limitations: 'I am a very dull fellow, and you must find my letters terribly boring.' He never wrote without recording the exact reading of the barometer, regaling her with detailed accounts of the army manoeuvres, and the number of roebuck and wild boar shot down at each of the imperial shoots.

On hearing that the Emperor was to attend a shoot in the neighbourhood of Eisenerz, where her aunt was married to the local pharmacist, Katharina was sufficiently bold to suggest a meeting, to which he had the inevitable reaction:

I am writing in haste to beg of you not to come to Eisenerz, even if you should get some leave which you yourself consider to be unlikely.

My gentlemen attendants all know you, and there will be several
press Jews hanging around to report on the shoot. People would only
say you have followed me there and there would be a lot of unnecessary talk. Also I would find it painful to be near you and perhaps not
to be able to talk to you at all. Forgive me for making these remarks,
and please do not be angry with me.

Far from being angry, she was contrite and full of self-re-
proaches. She was always having scruples in those early days, and
in those few scraps of letters which have survived and which must
have been so difficult to write, we read: 'Please, please forgive me,
Your Majesty, if as usual I have been too cheeky and too bold.'
And he replied: 'You can never be too cheeky or too bold for my
taste. You do not know what good it does to a man in my position
to have someone as frank and as open-hearted as yourself to talk
to.' He was grateful she was not annoyed at having been stopped
from going to Eisenerz,

> You can imagine how happy I would have been to see you and
> perhaps to have had a chance of speaking to you. But it was just as
> well I did not have this pleasure. Instead I consoled myself by looking
> across at the pharmacist's house which is situated at the bottom of the
> garden of the house where I am staying, and as always my thoughts
> were with you.

Was it by accident or design that in the same letter Franz Josef
broached the subject of Toni's education. Katharina's highest ambition was to get him into the Theresianum, but it would not have
been easy even for a Burgtheater actress to have her son admitted
to a school originally founded by the Empress Marie Therese for
the sons of officers and civil servants, and now one of Vienna's
most exclusive colleges. In his modest, unassuming fashion, the
Emperor wrote: 'From your last letter I see that you would like to
get Toni into the Theresianum. We must discuss the matter next
time we meet, and perhaps I can be of some help to you.' In the
autumn of 1888 Toni Kiss was enrolled as a pupil of the Theresianum, and at the same time his father became a member of the
Kaiserliche Königliche (Imperial and Royal) consular service, with a
posting as Vice Consul in Tunis.

Katharina Schratt had no longer any family or financial worries to distract her from her career, which in the years 1887-9 saw her firmly established as one of the leading ladies of the Burgtheater. She might lack the dramatic power of a Charlotte Wolther, or the poetic quality of a Stella Hohenfels, but as the critic Hermann Bahr described her, 'She was the average man's ideal, a Melusine with the kitchen ladle in the hand.' She was both seductress and housewife, earthy and sophisticated, as much at home in a folk drama as in one of those light, drawing-room comedies which figured so largely in the repertoire of the Burg. Looking through old programmes, one comes across the name of Katharina Schratt starring in many plays adapted from the French, such as Claude Ohnet's *The Iron Master*, Eugène Scribe's *Fairy Hands*, and Octave Feuillet's *The Impoverished Nobleman* – light, elegant trifles of the kind to please the frivolous taste of the Burgtheater public, who still looked upon the satire of a Nestroy with suspicion and labelled Grillparzer as a revolutionary. The successful young Austrian dramatists imitated the French, and some years were to pass before a medical student called Arthur Schnitzler turned his talents from medicine to the stage, exposing the Austrians to themselves, unmasking their superficial frivolity to disclose the *Weltschmerz* of a dying empire. Had she been born ten years later, Katharina Schratt would have been the perfect Schnitzler heroine, the prototype of the Viennese '*süsse Mädel*' (sweet girl) he immortalized on the German-speaking stage. But the Emperor might not have approved of her playing the heroines of Schnitzler; as she once complained to a friend, 'His Majesty always likes to see me playing ladies.' And parts were not lacking which gave the opportunity of wearing ravishing costumes which, in certain newspapers, received almost as much notice as her acting.

The needs of her theatrical wardrobe added to the already astronomical sums of her dressmaker's bills, and she was growing to depend more and more on the bills of exchange enclosed in the Emperor's letters. Franz Josef wrote writing to her from Hungary,

Now that I am to be allowed to act as your Finance Minister, the next time we meet in Schönbrunn I should like to ask you one or two questions regarding your wardrobe. Do not be frightened, I am not going to make you any reproaches, but I would like you to answer me as frankly as possible, so that there should be no secrets between us.

It was difficult for Katharina to be honest about her finances; they were always in such a state of chaos that she did not know how much she owed. The answer she gave on this occasion appears to have been unsatisfactory, for a few days later, on 6 February 1888, the Emperor, who meanwhile had been to Vienna and returned to Hungary, wrote again,

> Enclosed is the sum I promised you, and I beg of you to let me know immediately if it is not sufficient. Forgive my harping on the same subject, but I have your interests so much at heart, and I am so anxious to put your finances in order that I am prepared to risk being considered both unpleasant and a bore. You must not have any debts, or what comes to the same thing, leave your bills unpaid for so many months. I have been making out a list of expenses you have had to incur this winter. Your various costumes for the theatre, your new dress for the *Industriellenball*, and another one for tonight, must add up to a considerable sum, which will be a fresh drain on your exchequer. I will be infinitely grateful if you will write to me here the exact amount you need, which will then be placed immediately at your disposal. Now you will say, 'He really is an impossible fellow', but that is a judgment I am prepared to put up with. Nor am I unduly worried, for I know that at heart you are really quite fond of me.

No one could fail to have been touched by the sweetness and generosity of this letter, and Katharina Schratt reacted in her warm, impulsive fashion. Carried away by a sense of gratitude, the feeling that she was giving him all too little in return, inspired by a love that was akin to hero worship, she wrote Franz Josef a letter which in the years to come he was to read and re-read a hundred times, consoling him in the darkest hours, and reminding him in his loneliness that there was one natural human being who really loved him for himself. Alas, there is no draft or copy of what must have been an enchanting letter, in which Katharina Schratt in the fullness of her heart offered to become the Emperor's mistress. But she wrote without taking into account the mysterious influence which Elisabeth exercised over her husband, which kept him still worshipping at an empty altar. And in the autumn of 1887 the Empress was again at home.

6

Friend or Mistress?

At court the general opinion was that the Empress had come back to put an end to the Emperor's growing infatuation for Frau Schratt. But for the time being Elisabeth was concerned with very different matters. She had come home to placate her husband and prepare him for the future; once Valerie was married she intended to retire from the world and live out the rest of her life on a Greek island. Throughout October she had been sailing the Ionian Seas in appalling weather, causing the maximum discomfort to her attendants and the maximum inconvenience to the Greek royal family, who had had special roads laid out on barren islands to enable her to pursue a new-found passion for archaeology.

The man responsible for this passion was the Austrian Consul in Corfu, an ageing Hellenist called Baron Warsberg, whose collection of essays entitled *Odysseische Landschaften* had become the Empress's bible. Both the officers of the *Greif* and the miserable, seasick ladies-in-waiting detested this pedantic scholar who went into ecstasies over every crumbling ruin, but no one dared to poke fun at him in front of the Empress, who hung on his every word, and in the stormiest seas forced the captain of the *Greif*, the oldest and most unseaworthy of all the imperial yachts, to cast anchor in dangerous harbours, or to take her out in a small cutter so that she might pick a bunch of withered flowers on beaches from which Odysseus had set forth on his ill-fated journeys. Had Franz Josef foreseen the disastrous influence the Baron and his *Odysseische Landschaften* would have over his wife, he would have had him instantly dismissed from the service. As it was he wrote to Elisabeth with his usual resignation, 'I cannot think what you find to do for four days on Ithaca, but the main thing is that you should be well and content and this seems to be the case.' He can hardly have appreciated a poem she sent to him, dedicated to 'the kingdom of

Odysseus', and it was wounding to feel that she was happier wandering round the Greek islands with an obscure consul than being at home with her family at Lainz, in the villa he had built her with so much loving thought.

But now at last she was coming back, and Franz Josef wrote, 'How happy I am that tomorrow will see an end to those expeditions in the cutter, and those dangerous excursions into troubled Albania. But I shall only be at peace when I know you are safely home.' After a stormy voyage the fragile Empress arrived in blooming health, while her attendants were all in a state of collapse. Even Baron Warsberg confided in his journal that 'the exhaustion exceeded anything I have ever experienced on my travels in the east, and these were not devoid of exertions'.

The family reunion took place at Gödöllo, the country estate which the Hungarian people had given to their beloved Queen for the part she had played in bringing about the Historic Compromise. The report of a few isolated cases of scarlet fever had been sufficient to keep Elisabeth away from Vienna for fear of infecting Valerie. She always preferred staying in Hungary, and for the first weeks after her return put herself out to be charming to her husband, reducing him to his usual state of subjugation.

Vienna society, which was so avidly gossiping over the Emperor's extraordinary infatuation for a Burgtheater actress, would have been astonished to hear that in his letters to his wife Franz Josef never failed to mention his meetings with Frau Schratt, who is referred to under the pseudonym of the '*Kriegsminister*' (the Minister of War). In a letter addressed to Corfu we read: 'I went walking in Schönbrunn with the *Kriegsminister*, who was in very good spirits and had many interesting things to tell me.' A few days later he wrote again: 'At one o'clock I met the *Kriegsminister*. On the day before she had had a great success at a charity matinée held at the Opera House, in which she appeared in a tragedy by Anzengruber, written in the Austrian dialect. The newspapers were full of praise.' Elisabeth on her side would send affectionate messages to the *Kriegsminister*, and shortly after her return Franz Josef informed Frau Schratt that he had been dining alone with the Empress and Valerie on St Catherine's Day, 'and was quite astonished to see champagne glasses set out on the table, as we usually do not permit ourselves the luxury of this wine, where-upon the Empress informed me that she had ordered the champagne so that we could drink to your health, which was done most heartily. This was really a very pleasant surprise.' How the actress must have laughed, and possibly cried as well, at the touching simplicity of the richest monarch in Europe treating champagne as a luxury, whereas it flowed like water in the gay, spendthrift society of the theatre world.

Elisabeth's charming mood lasted no more than a few weeks. The approach of Christmas, which coincided with her fiftieth birthday, reduced her again into a state of despair. The whole of her family, with the exception of her parents who were too old to travel, were coming to Gödöllo to celebrate what for her was an occasion for mourning, and she had invited Baron Warsberg to help her endure these painful festivities, without stopping to think what an alien element he would be in an exclusively family gathering. Both Franz Josef and Rudolf took an instant dislike to him, while the Wittelsbachs, in the full tide of a family reunion, completely ignored him. Elisabeth, however, maintained that the Baron was the only person worth talking to, and encouraged him to recite long passages from Homer in front of a hostile audience. The delighted Warsberg already saw himself as her intimate confidant, writing in his journal, 'Her Majesty is enchantingly kind, and perhaps no one has ever stood in such a close relation with her. I am afraid however that this favour on her part does me harm in other quarters.' However conceited he might be, he could not fail to observe a certain coolness on the part of the Emperor, who would have been cooler still had he realized that during this visit the Empress had instructed Warsberg to look out for a villa on Corfu with a view to renting and eventually buying it.

The family Christmas which Franz Josef had been looking forward to for so long was completely spoiled, and he consoled himself in taking his guests out hunting with a pack of hounds which were kept in the neighbourhood, and in shooting wild duck in the Danube marshes. Hardly a day passed without him writing to Frau Schratt. But on returning with the Empress to Vienna early in the new year, he heard that Toni Kiss was laid up with chickenpox and, owing to Elisabeth's fear of infection, he was to be deprived for three weeks both of meeting the actress and of receiving her letters. In the past year he had grown so dependent on her company that Toni's very mild attack of chickenpox was regarded by the Emperor as a major tragedy.

By 11 January 1888 he was already counting the days since he had spoken to her: 'The fourteen days since we met seem endless. I am in a constant state of agitation that you might still catch Toni's rash.' Four days later he was writing again: 'It is dreadful for me to hear so little of you, and to have to do without the letters which make me so happy. Will this frightfully long quarantine ever end? Since days I hear nothing of your movements, and therefore am very much alarmed. I do not even know if I am any longer in your thoughts.'

It was the height of the Vienna season, rendered more brilliant than usual by the fact that the Empress was again at home. The British Ambassador's wife, Walpurga Paget, who met Elisabeth at a court dinner, noted in her diary: 'The Empress is back, enchanted at being thinner than ever, the gold and silver stuffs in which she is encased, not draped, look as if they covered a being scarcely human in its fantastic attributes of hair and line.' But all those who saw Elisabeth even when she was putting herself out to be pleasant had the impression that she was living on a completely different planet and had no real interest in matters of this world. No one was more conscious of her growing detachment than Franz Josef, who after one of these court dinners would retire to his room and cheer himself by re-reading the letters which Katharina Schratt had written him since the beginning of their friendship. He assured her, 'It is the most pleasant occupation, for they are so charmingly written, and in their chronological order evoke such lovely memories.'

Meanwhile the court physician, Dr Widerhofer, was instructed to keep him informed on the progress of Toni's illness, and the doctor, who was famous for his discretion, must have been secretly amused at the interest His Majesty was taking in Toni's chickenpox. At last the quarantine was over, and the fifty-seven-year-old Emperor wrote to Frau Schratt: 'If I were not so old, and had not got a cough, I would shout with joy at the thought of seeing you again.' And neither cough nor old age could prevent him from meeting her for a walk in the snow, where like a shy young lieutenant he told her: 'Perhaps the ground will be sufficiently slippery to permit me to take your arm.'

This was the season of the public balls which each in turn was honoured by the Emperor's presence, and where every ambitious lady of the 'Second Society' aspired to be presented. Protected by what he called his 'nimbus', Franz Josef made the rounds, courteous and amiable with all, infinitely polite and infinitely remote, all the while searching for the friendly smile, the laughing eyes of the one person who interested him in the room. On the morning after the *Industriellenball* he was writing to Katharina Schratt: 'Thank you for manoeuvring so ably at the ball, and thus giving me the great pleasure of being able to speak to you. You were so surrounded by brilliant company that I am sure I spoke a lot of nonsense.'

He had only time for one visit to the theatre to see her perform again in a popular comedy, *The Goldfish*, and to take a last walk in Schönbrunn before he was recalled to Budapest to cope with the claims and pretensions of Magyar politicians, who refused to admit the rights of any minorities other than themselves. Even the Empress's company could not compensate for the worries and frustrations of these weeks in Hungary. For the past twenty years Franz Josef had honourably tried to abide by the terms of the Historic Compromise, only to be forced time after time into an untenable situation by men who cared nothing for the Empire but only for Hungary. Elisabeth, who always sided with the Magyars, had neither sympathy nor understanding for the problems which beset her husband. And gradually the Emperor fell into the habit of confiding his difficulties to Frau Schratt, who, with little knowledge or experience of world affairs, nevertheless counted many journalists and even ministers among her friends, and was surprisingly well informed on the political situation. But it was not so much her intelligence as her warmth, and a lovable childishness in her character, which attracted Franz Josef.

In one of the few scraps of her letters which survive we read: 'I wish I were a magician, to cast a spell and inflict a little wound on the tongues of every one who dares to speak ill of Your Majesty, or causes you the slightest annoyance.' She has a picture of the castle at Budapest by her bed and wishes to know exactly 'where Your Majesty's room lies, so that my thoughts can fly in at the window and be with Your Majesty at all hours of the day. ... How happy I would be to sit quietly by Your Majesty's writing desk. I would not disturb in any way but perhaps occasionally I would be allowed to hand you a pen or blot one of your papers.'

No wonder the Emperor waited anxiously for these letters, which introduced an element of gaiety into the gloomy castle overlooking the frozen Danube, where Elisabeth insisted on speaking nothing but Hungarian and the round of social duties was even more exacting than in Vienna. 'Nerves and irritation make me very grumpy,' he confessed. And one day the Empress told him quite openly that she was sure he would rather 'be a porter in the Nibelungengasse than reign as King of Hungary'. In repeating his wife's remark to Katharina Schratt, the Emperor adds, 'and in a sense she is not far wrong'.

Never had Franz Josef admitted so frankly how much he missed the ordinary comforts of family life, and Katharina Schratt's instinctive reaction was to reply by offering him all the affection she had to give. The famous *Gedankenbrief* (letter of thoughts), which the Emperor treasured throughout the years and must have destroyed shortly before his death, can only be judged by his reply and the few mutilated drafts of letters Katharina must have written in moments of remorse and fear at having presumed too far, and appearing in the light of a '*böse Verführerin*' (a wicked temptress).

She was not throwing herself at the Emperor's head when she offered to become his mistress. It is even doubtful whether she really wanted to, for Toni and her position as Toni's mother were what counted in her life even more than her career. It was probably a gesture dictated by tenderness and generosity rather than by passion. But she can hardly have expected a reply which was at once a declaration and a renunciation of love. Still addressing her by the formal title of *Gnädige Frau* (my dear madam), the Emperor wrote, what for him must have been one of the most difficult letters he had ever had to send.

Today to my great delight I received your nice long letter. The enclosed one which you call your letter of thoughts made me enormously happy, and if I did not know that you are always truthful with me, I would find it hard to believe, especially when I look into the mirror and my old wrinkled face looks back at me. It will be very difficult for me to answer these letters, which are so well reasoned and so charmingly written. Nor do you leave me much time, as you seem to want an early reply. I am being asked to express my sentiments, though surely you must know that I adore you, or at least you must suspect it. This feeling has been growing in me ever since I was fortunate enough to know you. So now we have both said what is on our minds, and that is all to the good. But there it must remain and our relationship must be the same in the future as it has been up to the present – that is, if it is to last, and it must last, for it makes me so very happy. You say that you will control your feelings, and I shall try to do the same, though it will not always be easy for me. But I will do nothing wrong. I love my wife and do not intend to abuse her confidence and friendship for you. As I am too old to be a brotherly friend, permit me to be your fatherly friend and treat me with the same kindness you have shown me up to now. Your letter of thoughts will be one of my most precious treasures, and as proof of your affection I only hope that you will always keep for me the place I occupy at present in your warm and spacious heart.

After writing of other matters the Emperor ends his letter: 'Please do not be angry with what I have written, for you know that I worship you, but in the future I must not say this any more.'

'I worship you' were words Franz Josef had never said to anyone other than Elisabeth, and should have been sufficient to reassure Katharina Schratt on whatever scruples she may have had for having dared to put on paper 'thoughts that had better been left unsaid'. She wrote:

I keep making myself reproaches over the 'letter of thoughts'. Not that I wish to retract a word of what I have written, for that would be to deny the truth. Only I am so afraid that Your Majesty might misjudge my words, and see me in the light of a scheming seductress, and that would be terrible for me.... A copy of the offending letter is by me now, like so much of what I write to Your Majesty it would never have passed the Imperial Censors, and perhaps that would have been just as well, for I still keep worrying about it.

This rough draft, which has no date, must have been part of a letter to which the Emperor replied on 18 February:

So you still have qualms that I might regard you as a wicked woman and be angry – as if such a thing were possible. You are indeed so beautiful, so good and so beloved, that you could well become dangerous to me. But I shall always remain strong and since I have your letter of thoughts and know your feelings I am not only happy but also put at ease. Frankness is always best, even if it is not always quite correct. Also I am now protected from that silent jealousy which has all too often plagued me.... The offending letter has already been read and re-read, I do not know how many times.

Everything that concerned her was of interest to him. The progress of Toni's education, the plot of a new play she was rehearsing at the time, and the state of her health, whether it was an ordinary cold or her monthly menstruation. He was constantly referring to what he called '*die stille Woche*' (the quiet week), when it was not unusual for a spoilt actress to plead sickness and spend a couple of days in bed. In this respect Frau Schratt appears to have made full use of her privileges. In between excessive bouts of energy, performances twice a day, followed by a supper or a ball, and getting up early on the following morning to attend seven o'clock mass, she would then retire to her bed, exhausted and suffering from depression, the '*Weltschmerz*' so prevalent at the time.

Katharina was by nature strong and robust, but there can be little doubt that the equivocal nature of her relationship with the Emperor, the restrictions it placed on her ordinary way of life, and the insecurity of her position with the Empress, combined to react on her nerves. Franz Josef's reply to her 'letter of thoughts' made it clear that their friendship depended entirely on Elisabeth who, with her capricious and unstable nature, might at any moment turn against her, causing a situation the Emperor would never have the courage to confront. Yet Katharina felt no jealousy of the woman who was also her sovereign, and who later in a strange way she grew to love. The only criticism she ever allowed herself was on account of Elizabeth's neglect of the Emperor.

There is an old Austrian tradition that on 1 March violets are sold in the streets and given to friends, and for the second year running Katharina Schratt sent violets to the imperial family in Budapest. Judging by Franz Josef's letter of thanks, it would appear that no one other than Frau Schratt had thought or perhaps dared to send flowers to their sovereign.

> You should have seen how the Empress and Valerie rejoiced at your delightful gift and how surprised and touched they were that you should also have remembered them this year. But to tell you the truth, which I always do, I was so shameless that I was already hoping the violets would arrive today, and when the box was brought in I knew at once that it came from you. The flowers are quite fresh and smell gloriously.

Two days later the Empress and her daughter left for England and the Emperor was again alone, so that Katharina sometimes wondered if Elisabeth would have cared if Franz Josef had taken her for his mistress. But the Empress's behaviour on her return in May, when Katharina was invited to visit the imperial couple in their villa in the Lainzer Tiergarten, an invitation given by the Emperor in his wife's name, showed her that they were far closer than she had thought, and that Elisabeth would never have received her had she believed the scandalous rumours circulating round the court.

No first-night nerves could equal the actress's shyness when she drove up for the first time to the gates of Lainz, to find the Emperor and Empress already waiting to bring her by foot to the villa; Elisabeth, charming and relaxed, leading her through the forest, warding off the wild deer with her lace parasol, stopping in the gardens to pick her the first roses; Franz Josef somewhat stiff and embarrassed, but happy to show her their home. It was the first of many afternoons the three were to spend together in Lainz and Ischl and Schönbrunn, and it was probably the only time when the chatty, witty actress was completely tongue-tied from fear and unable to do justice to the delicious iced coffee and cream cakes the Empress had specially ordered for her. That night she stayed awake worrying about what impression she had made upon Elisabeth, but Franz Josef was quick to reassure her:

> I am most sincerely sorry that you had a sleepless night after your visit to us the day before yesterday. In spite of the tea and iced coffee I slept better than for a long time. You can set your mind completely at rest about the impression that you left behind here. The Empress

has spoken repeatedly about you most favourably and affectionately, and I assure you that she is very fond of you. If you were to know this splendid woman more intimately you would certainly be filled with the same feeling.

By the end of the summer Elisabeth was no longer referring to Katharina Schratt as the *Kriegsminister* but as *die Freundin*, (the friend) whose rich and varied life made her such enchanting company. And Katharina Schratt could boast of her friendship not only with the Emperor but also with the Empress. Nevertheless Franz Josef's reply to her letter of thoughts had had its effect, making her all the more determined to preserve her independence and never to let him interfere with her friendships, which was not always easy, for the Emperor was both jealous and exacting. She made no secret of the visits of Count Wilczek, the letters of Prince Ferdinand, and her rides in the park with the Baltazzi brothers. But she was careful never to praise her friends too much: 'Your Majesty knows that there is only one person who interests me at all, and that is your dear beloved self.'

She was truthful but not too truthful, and the Emperor was not told of the rich presents given her by certain wealthy admirers. Nor would he have enjoyed the tone of some of her letters to Prince Ferdinand, in which she addressed him as 'Your Royal Highness, My Dearest Friend'. Franz Josef was even more jealous of her reputation than of her friends. He disapproved of her going riding with the wealthy Baltazzi brothers, now popular and well-known figures in the sporting world.

The actress, who was very vulnerable to criticism, took umbrage when the Emperor asked her whether she was acquainted with Hector Baltazzi's wife, and he excused himself for causing her unnecessary distress:

> I had no real reason at all behind my question as to whether you knew Frau Baltazzi, but as you seem to have decided not to go riding regularly with her husband I can just as frankly tell you that I prefer it so, for in the first place I am not at all easy in my mind as to whether the horses he would give you to ride would be safe enough.... And then there is something else, which I ask you to keep to yourself: Hector Baltazzi, though I myself occasionally talk to him and even the Empress formerly saw a good deal of him and his wife, does not

have an entirely correct reputation in racing and in money matters, so that there was a time when he could no longer appear on English racecourses. I do not know the situation exactly and I should not like to injure him, therefore I beg of you not to repeat my remarks.

The Emperor ended this letter with a jest over a possible duel: 'as of course I could give him no satisfaction in the Prater meadows, even in the dim light of dawn'.

Little did Franz Josef foresee that in less than a year he would be depending on Frau Schratt and her friendship with the Baltazzis to help him in solving the greatest tragedy of his life.

7

An Uneasy Alliance

On 15 March 1888 Franz Josef was writing to Frau Schratt 'I cannot be tomorrow morning at Schönbrunn because at eleven o'clock I have to attend a funeral service for the old German Kaiser, to be held at the Protestant church on the Gumpendorfer-strasse, and as I have never before taken part in such a service I do not know how long the affair will last.' In these few laconic words Franz Josef wrote of a former enemy whom expediency had made into an ally and whose death marked the end of an era.

The future was unpredictable, for the ninety-year-old Wilhelm's successor was a dying man. The liberal-minded Kaiser Frederick, from whose reign so much had been expected, was in the last stages of cancer, unable even to utter his coronation vows, and behind his mild and noble figure was the aggressive, bombastic shadow of his twenty-eight-year-old son, impatiently waiting for the throne.

Neither in this letter to Frau Schratt nor in any other does Franz Josef mention the ugly demonstrations which took place in the streets of Vienna on the eve of the old Kaiser's death, when members of the new 'pan-German party', led by George von Schönerer, broke into the office of the Jewish-controlled *Wiener Tagblatt*, because the paper had announced the news before it was officially released. The Prime-Minister Count Taaffe, whose policy was never to worry his master with unnecessary unpleasantness, may have deliberately prevented these reports from reaching the Emperor, for Maurice Szeps, the editor of the *Neue Wiener Tagblatt*, was an intimate friend of the Crown Prince Rudolf who was known for his pro-Jewish sympathies. But what the Emperor ignored must have been known to Katharina Schratt, who lived in a predominantly Jewish world, where the activities of George von Schönerer were causing considerable concern. Schönerer, who was a small landlord with a seat in Parliament, was a fanatical demagogue, virulently anti-Semitic, who believed in the Teutonic myth and the greatness of the German people, and looked for leadership to the Hohenzollerns rather than to the Habsburgs.

In her drawing-room in the Nibelungengasse, where she entertained most of the leading men of the day, Katharina Schratt must have heard almost everything that was going on in Vienna. But one wonders how much of it was repeated to the Emperor, or whether, like Count Taaffe, she also believed in sparing him unnecessary unpleasantness. She herself had no anti-Jewish prejudices; the first time we hear of her intervening on behalf of a protégé was on account of an old Hungarian rabbi whose two sons had been arrested for embezzling. Since she had a kind and credulous nature, her protégés were all too often scoundrels, and the Emperor had to tell her that after studying the reports he had unfortunately come to the conclusion that the two sons of the honourable rabbi were such great rogues that a pardon for them was quite impossible.

The German nationalist demonstrations, followed by Schönerer's arrest and trial, aroused great interest in a town where anti-Semitic feeling had been growing over the past years, ever since the stock exchange crash of 1873 for which the Jewish finance barons had been held responsible. The upper classes, with the exception of the Crown Prince and a few enlightened intellectuals like Count Hans Wilczek, had always been anti-Jewish. Even the tolerant and humane Franz Josef is quoted in his daughter's diary as having said, 'Of course one must do everything to protect the Jews, but is there anyone who really likes them?' But whatever he may have said in confidence to his daughter, in public life the Emperor was the first to honour any outstanding Jew. And the renaissance in art and literature, the enormous progress made in the medical field, in the last decade of what is known as the *Franz-Josefzeit*, were largely due to the Emperor's protection of the Jewish minorities in his Empire.

The raid on the offices of the *Neue Wiener Tagblatt* was only the first of the riots and demonstrations staged by the pan-Germans in 1888 – a year which saw the completion of the Ringstrasse, with the inauguration of the Maria Theresa monument in the spring and the opening of the new Burgtheater in the autumn. The first was a brilliant patriotic ceremony, attended by all the members of the imperial family including the Empress, with the newspapers dedicating long panegyric articles to the glory of the Habsburgs. It was an occasion on which Elisabeth aroused considerable criticism by appearing in a plain brown dress, when all the ladies of the 'First Society' were wearing their smartest spring toilettes. Pauline Metternich remarked that 'the Empress was dressed like a maid in her Sunday best', but Elisabeth was indifferent as to what Princess Metternich or anyone else might say. Her dress was in a sense a protest against all public ceremonies, at which she appeared only under duress.

Very few members of the imperial family knew of the ugly scenes which had taken place on the previous evening on the Ring, when the news of the verdict of Schönerer's trial brought a crowd of his supporters out into the streets, protesting against the severity of the sentence which condemned him to four months of imprisonment, and the loss of his title and seat in Parliament. Excited youths, wearing the black, red and gold colours of the Hohenzollerns, paraded down the Ring, shouting anti-Jewish slogans and singing '*Die Wacht am Rhein*'. There were clashes with the police and traffic was brought to a standstill. A court carriage taking the Crown Prince Rudolf back to the Burg was caught up in the traffic jam. It must have been a traumatic experience for the Prince, who in his youth had been the idol of his people, to hear this vulgar and hysterical abuse of the men who were his friends. Though strict censorship prevented any written attack against a member of the imperial family, several papers both at home and abroad had already criticized 'a certain highly placed person who was in the hands of the Jews'. And in his nervous and depressed condition Rudolf must have felt that some of the slogans shouted in the streets were being personally directed against him.

On the morning of the inauguration of the Maria Theresa monument the Crown Prince looked so wretched that the Empress, who rarely noticed such things, asked him if he was feeling ill. But mother and son had become so estranged that Elisabeth would have been the last person in whom Rudolf would have confided the doubts and fears which had assailed him in the past years. The Empress was not entirely responsible for the lack of communication between herself and her son. Neither trusted the other, for both recognized in the other the same instability of character and fatal indiscretion which, in the early days of Elisabeth's married life, had antagonized so many of her friends and well-wishers, and in Rudolf's case made the Emperor's ministers warn him not to trust the Crown Prince with secret documents which might find their way into the hands of the foreign press. Rudolf's tutor Count Latour had been the first to note that his pupil had far more talent than character, and that the most serious of his defects was a lack of courage, a quality which both his parents possessed to a superlative degree.

In June Franz Josef was writing from Budapest to Frau Schratt of having to attend another Protestant funeral service, this time for the poor Kaiser Frederick who had died after a reign of only ninety-nine days, 'a tragic destiny, though the end must have come as a relief'. Franz Josef had never been in sympathy with the liberal-minded Frederick, whereas his wife Victoria, who was the eldest daughter of Queen Victoria, was one of the few crowned heads whom Elisabeth regarded as a friend. The Empress's instinctive reaction was to pay the widow a visit of condolence, a suggestion turned down by the Emperor on the grounds that her health would not stand the strain. Others maintained that it was not so much the Emperor as his Foreign Minister Count Kálnoky who, in view of the notoriously bad relations between the new Kaiser and his mother, advised his master that a visit of this kind would meet with the disapproval of the Prussian court. Prevented from making a spontaneous gesture of affection, Elisabeth was compelled to be involved in the German state visit in the autumn, a visit which was a far greater strain on her nerves.

The Empress's dislike of Kaiser Frederick's son, Wilhelm was as nothing compared to the antagonism he aroused in Rudolf who was his exact contemporary and in the interests of the German alliance always had to keep up the illusion of friendship. The death of Kaiser Frederick had spelt the end to his political hopes, for Frederick and his English wife would have given a new orientation to German politics. There would have been closer ties with England, friendly overtures to France leading perhaps to the return of

Alsace-Lorraine, and Austria-Hungary would have had a strong ally to support her against Russian aggression in the Balkans. Above all it would have meant the end of Bismarck's hegemony over central Europe. But now Bismarck's pupil was on the throne – a vainglorious, aggressive and self-confident *Junker*. Everything had gone well with Wilhelm. He had a large family with four sons and had inherited a great and prosperous Empire at the age of twenty-nine. In comparison Rudolf saw himself as a miserable failure, broken in health, suffering from an incurable venereal disease, unhappily married with no male heir to give security to the throne, spied on and distrusted by his father's ministers, and with a father who at the age of fifty-eight was still in the prime of life and likely to reign for many years. The events in Germany now provided the last drop in an already overflowing cup of bitterness, frustration and despair.

Franz Josef who, in a life full of political vicissitudes, had learned to bow before the inevitable, was prepared to accept Wilhelm II as his new ally, and to show him the same scrupulous loyalty as he had shown his grandfather. But he disliked receiving orders in his own house, and Wilhelm's refusal to visit Vienna at the same time as his uncle the Prince of Wales very nearly led to a diplomatic incident. The Prince, who was a frequent and popular visitor to Austria and, despite the difference in their ages, an intimate friend of Rudolf, was due to attend the September manoeuvres and take part in some of the imperial shoots. By staying over for the German state visit, he had hoped to have the opportunity of meeting his nephew on neutral territory. But the German Ambassador Prince Reuss had the unpleasant task of informing Count Kálnoky that the presence of the Prince of Wales would be *non grata* to his imperial master. And the situation was only saved by the Prince who, with the tact which was to serve England so well in the future, announced his intention of leaving Vienna on a round of visits. Rudolf was the first to invite him to his shooting lodge in Transylvania, writing in a letter to Stephanie, 'I am delighted to have Wales as a guest. If I had to invite Wilhelm it would only be in order to arrange a discreet little shooting incident which would despatch him out of this world.'

Very few of these political controversies are to be found in the

Emperor's letters to Katharina Schratt, though by the autumn of 1888 their relationship had reached such a degree of intimacy that he occasionally allowed himself to poke fun at his royal guests. From the September manoeuvres in Croatia he wrote:

> The reception given me by the local population was very heart-warming, and the manoeuvres went off splendidly in gorgeous weather. We did a lot of riding, and by trotting and galloping I did my best to keep away from the Prince of Wales, but I could not manage it. The fat man was always at my heels, and held out quite unbelievably. Only he got very stiff and tore the trousers of his red hussar uniform, which must have been very uncomfortable for him as he was wearing nothing underneath.

Edward was no stranger to Frau Schratt, for at Karlsbad he had made it his business to meet the lady who had infatuated the austere Franz Josef. But Katharina was a home-grown product, not likely to attract the sophisticated Prince of Wales.

That summer the Emperor's holiday at Ischl had been curtailed by a series of royal visits, but was compensated by the presence of the Empress, who was in a particularly gracious mood and went out of her way to facilitate his meetings with 'the friend'. To while away the time, which hung heavy on her hands, Elisabeth took elocution lessons from Katharina's old instructor Alexander Strakosch, and invited two of her colleagues from the Burgtheater to give poetry readings at the Kaiser Villa. An excursion up the Jainzen, which was Elisabeth's favourite mountain, was spoiled for Katharina by having to compose a poem to be inscribed in what the Empress called her 'Jainzen book'. The actress, who had no talent as a poet, produced two little verses freely adapted from the well-known satirist Wilhelm Busch, redeemed by a charming dedication addressed to 'the Princess who is by the Muses kissed'. Elisabeth, who fancied herself as a poet, was delighted, and Franz Josef was happy over 'the friend's' success. Katharina, who was immensely flattered by the Empress's condescension, wrote to a colleague in Berlin:

> People say the Empress is frigid, but with me she speaks in the frankest possible manner, telling me many things that seem to me as incomprehensible as they are touching. She certainly has rare qualities,

among them her still enchanting looks. If these have perhaps been somewhat affected by her many sad experiences and disappointments, it has also served to make them more expressive.

But Katharina never really felt at ease with Elisabeth, and she confessed to the Emperor that, however much she tried, she was still as frightened by her as when she met her the first time. How could one be natural with a woman who one moment would be confiding in one the most intimate secrets of her life, and a few hours later greet one with barely a smile? Even her beauty was unnerving, and there were times when Katharina saw the Emperor gazing at his wife in such humble adoration that she wondered what part she had to play in this strange *partie à trois*. But on seeing them more often she grew to understand that Franz Josef was never at ease with his wife, and that one of the reasons he came so often to Frauenstein was in order to spend a few hours as an ordinary human being. He enjoyed hearing of the local village life, of the church fair at Sankt Gilgen at which one of the farmer boys had forced her to dance and, after treading on her toes, had slapped her on the back and assured her that she 'danced fine'. Franz Josef only wished he could have been there to see her dance 'so fine', instead of attending a gala dinner for the Portuguese King and Queen.

Katharina Schratt left Frauenstein at the end of the summer of 1888. The owners had refused to renew the lease and she may also have thought it wise to move nearer to Ischl, where the Villa Felicitas had been put at her disposal. It was neither as pretty nor as romantically situated as Frauenstein, but it had the advantage of being within walking distance of the Kaiser Villa. Meanwhile the Emperor was becoming ever more dependent on her. When Toni went to school for the first time, he sent greetings to the little Theresianist, 'whom I wish I could see in his uniform'. On the eve of the German Emperor's visit he was at the Burgtheater to watch her perform for the last time in the 'old house'. 'I spent a peacefully happy evening, seeing you look so wondrously beautiful. Thank you for wearing my diamond swallows in your hair.'

By now he was so involved in her career that he was even ready to listen to her complaints, 'for everything that concerns you is of interest to me, and speaking your mind will surely do you good'. Her complaints were directed chiefly against Sonnenthal, who was acting as provisional director of the Burgtheater and who, being a far greater artist than Katharina Schratt, was not prepared to humour her just because she was the Emperor's friend. Her requests for extra leave were refused, younger actresses were allowed to appear in parts she regarded as her own, performances as a guest artist at summer theatres were curtailed, and if she complained of being given too little work his answer was to present her with a schedule in which she had to perform for six consecutive evenings. 'I see we are to have a regular Schratt week,' wrote Franz Josef. 'Is it a punishment or a reward?'

There were numerous quarrels caused by her championship of weaker colleagues. Some of the Emperor's sarcastic remarks at the expense of Austria's most eminent actor show how much Franz Josef was under her influence. On one occasion he wrote: 'Jupiter was present and as affected as ever. But I really should not say this to you, for it is contrary to discipline and the respect you owe to your chief. I hope you will keep my unseemly remarks strictly confidential.' He never dared to praise one of her rivals; of Stella Hohenfels he wrote: 'I fear Diana [Hohenfels] will be angry with me for having left during the first scene in the last play. But to put it bluntly "*Das ist mir ganz wurst*"' (Austrian slang for 'I couldn't care less').

By now Katharina had learnt not to ask the Emperor to intercede on her behalf; he did not think it was in her interest to do so. Such advice as he gave her was 'to beseech you to moderate your temper, to be more conciliating and not make so many scenes which are unworthy of your noble character'. But Katharina was a fighter by nature, and her independence and refusal to submit to any form of injustice were the qualities he was most ready to admire.

She was at the centre of the controversy raging round the new Burgtheater which opened in the autumn, and was being bitterly attacked by both the public and the press. It was a handsome and imposing building, a mixture of the fake renaissance and baroque which characterized the Ringstrasse architecture of the 1880s, and its faults of construction were due not so much to the architect

Karl Hasenauer as to the constant interference of court officials who knew nothing either of architecture or of the stage. The result was a roof which was far too high, with appalling acoustics, and a heavy ornamental dome which obscured the view for both the gallery and the upper tier of boxes. The actors, who were attached to their old theatre on the Michaelerplatz and had never wanted to leave it in the first place, were in despair. Many of them were frightened that their voices would not carry over into the vast, echoing auditorium. All the money spent on the splendid marble foyer, the grand staircase with the frescoes by Gustav Klimt, the new curtain painted by the artist Joseph Fux in which Charlotte Wolther was portrayed as tragedy and Katharina Schratt as comedy – all this could not hide the fact that the new theatre was a failure.

Her colleagues brought their complaints to Katharina in the hopes they might reach the Emperor's ears. In his memoirs Hugo Thimig pays tribute to her courage, reporting a conversation she had with the Emperor on the subject of the new theatre.

When Franz Josef asked her if she liked it, she replied: 'Well, Your Majesty, you like it, so no one dares to speak against it.'

'What do you mean, I like it? – I don't like it at all.'

'But Your Majesty, it is your fault that it is so high. It is you who wanted the *Logengang.*'

'I never wanted any such thing,' he declared.

But Katharina Schratt insisted: 'That is what people are saying, Your Majesty.'

Thimig adds that 'these must have been the first words of truth the Emperor has heard in regard to our unfortunate theatre'.

Barely a year later her colleagues persuaded Katharina Schratt to present in their names a petition to the Emperor asking for a small theatre to be built as an annexe to the new one, in which to stage the one-act plays and intimate drawing-room comedies which had always been part of the tradition of the old theatre. Franz Josef was evidently in sympathy with the actors, and would have been prepared to accede to their demands but for the fact that he did not want to offend the Lord High Chamberlain, Prince Hohenlohe, who had been mainly responsible for the new theatre and who, when the matter was broached, is reported to have said:

'If Your Majesty builds another theatre, it is as good as saying that the present one is unusable and I am publicly labelled as an idiot.' Eight years later the Burgtheater was closed for six months in order to carry out the necessary alterations, after which the company, who by now had got used to the larger stage, could pride themselves on having one of the finest theatres in Europe.

The new theatre on the Ring, which was to have its gala opening during the German state visit, was not ready till a fortnight later. After taking the Kaiser on a tour of the unfinished theatre, Franz Josef wrote to Katharina: 'I was yesterday at the new Burgtheater with Kaiser Wilhelm, and saw the beautiful curtain by Joseph Fux. Your portrait was not recognizable, but that of Toni is a better likeness.' One's heart goes out to the eight-year-old schoolboy whose loving parent had him portrayed as a cupid gambolling at her feet. Small wonder Toni Kiss grew up disliking his mother's connection with the stage.

Franz Josef's letters during the German visit tell nothing of his personal reactions to the young Kaiser, who was already behaving as if Germany was the senior partner in the alliance, allowing himself to criticize the inefficiency of the Austrian infantry during the manoeuvres, disregarding the fact that the Crown Prince Rudolf was inspector-general of the infantry. Rumour has it that he went so far as to suggest, in the presence of both the Emperor and the Empress, that the Crown Prince should be replaced by a professional general, and that Elisabeth was so outraged by his tactlessness that she pleaded a headache and left the room. A further example of his indiscretion was in presenting the Prussian Order of the Black Eagle to the Hungarian Prime Minister Count Tisza and ignoring the Prime Minister Count Taaffe, who had angered his Prussian Majesty by his support of the Czech minorities in Bohemia. The Kaiser may also have known that Taaffe had given special orders to keep Schönerer's followers off the streets, and had banned all pan-German demonstrations during his visit.

But all that we read in Franz Josef's letter to Frau Schratt is that

> ... the festivities of the recent days have been safely survived. At dinner yesterday I gave my toast, of which I was extremely nervous, but luckily without breaking down and without prompting. And now I have only to accompany my guests this afternoon to Mürzsteg, and it

The Empress Elisabeth of Austria

The Emperor Franz Josef of Austria

The actress Katharina Schratt, whose *amitié amoureuse* with the Emperor lasted for over thirty years

Katharina on a professional visit to New York in 1882

Katharina as the Emperor first saw her in 1885, as an inn-keeper's daughter in the play 'Dorf und Stadt'

A studio portrait of Katharina

Katharina as a mature actress in a play by Franz von Schönthan

The Emperor Franz Josef in military uniform

Crown Prince Rudolf of Austria, who died in a suicide pact with his mistress Mary Vetséra, at Mayerling

King Ferdinand of Bulgaria whose close friendship with Katharina aroused Franz Josef's jealousy

Count Wilczek with whom Katharina
had a longstanding love affair

Alexander Girardi, celebrated
actor and admirer of Katharina

Alexander Baltazzi, friend of Katharina and uncle of Mary Vetséra

Burgtheater, Vienna; the controversial new theatre opened in 1888

Hofburg Palace, Vienna, residence
of the Imperial family

Toni Kiss, Katharina's son by her husband Nicholas Kiss von Itebbe

Franz Josef and Katharina at Ischl, the Emperor's summer home

looks to me as if it will be the same abominable weather that has plagued us for several years on our autumn hunts in the mountains.

During his long reign Franz Josef had endured too many royal visits to allow himself to be upset by the brashness of a young man who had not yet learnt to behave as a sovereign and a gentleman.

For Elisabeth the German visit had been a torture, and she had made no effort to conciliate or please. The British Ambassador's wife gives a picture of her arriving at a gala concert at which the heat was intense: 'wearing a last winter's dress, trimmed with fur, which looked agonizing'. Others might criticize, but the Emperor was grateful for her presence. She had been particularly nice to him during the past months, even going so far as to invite Katharina Schratt to visit her in the Hofburg. In transmitting her message, Franz Josef told the actress, 'How glad I shall be to show you from inside my room the very window to which you have so often had the kindness to direct your glance from outside.'

But by the middle of October the Empress was already on her way to Corfu where Warsberg had rented her a villa, and her disconsolate husband was writing: 'I am in very low spirits at the thought of your departure for the distant south, and your long absence, especially after our recent meeting which was so happy and so harmonious. You were particularly charming and sweet, for which I again send you my thanks. Think often of your boundlessly loving and lonely little one.' The letter is that of an adoring husband, but in the same week he was writing to Katharina Schratt, from whom he had not heard for several days:

> From one courier to another I hoped for a letter, and longed for it as a ray of light in my very harassed and unpleasant existence. But each morning I have been disappointed. I hope the answer is a simple one, either that you find writing irksome to you, which would be quite understandable, or that you do not want to disturb me during the hunting, which is less understandable, for you must know by now that your dear letters are infinitely precious to me.

8

Impending Disaster

Was it the growing agitation over the Hungarian defence bill, or the stirring of new political forces among the masses, which caused the sleepless nights of which Franz Josef complained in his letters to Katharina Schratt, or were more personal issues at stake? He writes of 'his harassed and unpleasant existence', but his worries may have been caused not so much by politics as by the files of the secret police concerning the subversive activities of the heir apparent. Franz Josef, who was fond of his son, did not want to have him watched by the police. But Count Taaffe had irrefutable evidence that the Crown Prince was in direct contact with the Hungarian extremists who were plotting to sabotage the defence bill with a view to obtaining a separate army for Hungary. The fact that one of their leaders, Stefan Karolyi, was a shooting friend of Rudolf's did not justify the letters in which the Crown Prince sympathized with the opposition and spoke in contemptuous terms of his father's ministers. Rudolf even went so far as to criticize the old Archduke Albrecht, commander-in-chief of the army, and the only one of his relatives whom the Emperor really admired. The Archduke for his part had little sympathy for Rudolf, whom he accused of neglecting his duties and of being too friendly with his cousin Johann Salvator, whose restless ambition made trouble in every regiment in which he served. But the most dangerous of all was the Crown Prince's almost pathological dislike of the new Kaiser, and the anti-German articles which kept appearing in both the *Neue Wiener Tagblatt* and the foreign press, of which he was said to have been the author.

Certain aspects of Rudolf's private life may have been kept secret from his father, but Franz Josef must have known of the venereal disease from which his son had been suffering for the past two years, and which at times affected his eyes to such an extent that he was unable to go shooting, one of the few interests father and son had in common. But whereas with the Emperor it was a love of the sport, with the Crown Prince it was the joy of killing, and there was an unfortunate incident at one of the imperial shoots, when Rudolf, who was always ready to aim at anything within range, whether they were his own or his neighbour's birds, only just missed shooting his father by wounding the loader who was standing behind him. The Emperor was furious both on account of Rudolf's lack of sportsmanship and because he knew how much the story would be exaggerated once it had made the rounds of the Vienna clubs. This incident caused further strain in the relations between father and son. However much he may have wanted to ignore it, Franz Josef cannot fail to have noticed the tragic decline in both Rudolf's appearance and morale. But when his daughter-in-law, terrified out of her wits after her husband had asked her to prove her love by joining him in a suicide pact, came running to the Emperor for help, all she received was a polite rebuff. She was told not to give way to idle fancies, that Rudolf was probably doing too much, and that it was her duty as his wife to see that he stayed more at home – as if poor neglected Stephanie could have any influence over a husband who had lost all sexual interest in her, and still kept his bachelor quarters in the Hofburg, of which she was never allowed to pass through the door.

Another woman from a very different world tried to give the police the same warning. Mitzi Kaspar, who was an ex-dancer and had been Rudolf's mistress for several years, was a gay, light-hearted Viennese who had laughed at the Crown Prince when he first suggested her joining him in a suicide pact, which was to take place at the Husarentempel at Mödling, a monument dating from the Napoleonic Wars and a favourite spot for romantic trysts and unhappy lovers' suicides. It was only when Rudolf kept harking back to the same subject that Mitzi began to take him seriously, and decided to go to the chief of police and tell him that the Crown Prince was mentally ill and on the verge of a nervous breakdown. It was a brave action on the part of a woman of Mitzi's reputation, to beard the formidable Baron Kraus. And had the Baron had more imagination he would have taken her warning seriously, instead of treating Rudolf's threat of suicide as the idle talk of a neurotic, the kind who in every emotional crisis talks of suicide and never carries it through. All he did was to get Mitzi to sign a declaration for the police records, and warn her that she would be liable for prosecution if she ever divulged a word of the matter to anyone else; not a very pleasant way to treat a young woman who, out of loyalty to the ruling house, had done what she considered to be her duty.

Either from obtuseness or from pride, Franz Josef refused to admit that his son was a neurotic, in the same way that he would never admit that his wife was mentally unbalanced. Her doctors confined themselves to stating that Her Majesty had too much imagination and was too highly strung to stand the slightest shock to her nervous system, and her reaction to her cousin Ludwig's death had proved them to be right. So now there was a conspiracy of silence in Elisabeth's entourage, to prevent her from hearing of Rudolf's disorderly life and growing addiction to morphine and alcohol. But a more loving mother would have noted and worried over the physical deterioration of her son, which was apparent to the most casual observer. Elisabeth, however, was too taken up with Valerie's impending engagement, and her own plans for the future, to spare a thought for the sick, unhappy Rudolf.

In Corfu Baron Warsberg had found her the house of her dreams: a rose-coloured, colonnaded villa, dating from the days of the Venetian occupation, with wooded terraces falling down to the sea – an enchanting house, if only she had been content to leave it alone. But, encouraged by Warsberg, she saw herself as a goddess of mythology, living in a Phaecean palace, and the modest Villa Braila turned into the Achilleon, a tasteless Germanic construction dedicated to Achilles, who was the Empress's latest hero. It was a southern replica of the Hermes Villa, and in the end it cost even more. To prepare her husband for the shock of this new expenditure, Elisabeth wrote long and affectionate letters home, sending back cases of fruit of which one was to be given to *die Freundin*, who, 'if she wants to make me really happy, should send me a good autographed photograph of herself in a leather frame from Rodecks'. Elisabeth's friendship for Katharina Schratt appears to have been quite genuine at the time, and later in the year she asked her Hungarian companion, Ida von Ferenczy, to allow the Emperor and the actress to meet in her apartment, which though in the same building as the Hofburg was not actually part of the palace.

Ida, who may be said to have been the Empress's closest friend, had come into her life as a young girl whose burning enthusiasm for the Hungarian cause and hero worship of the patriot leader Count Andrássy had won Elisabeth's heart. For the past twenty years she had been her most intimate companion. Even when separated, Elisabeth wrote every day to Ida long and loving letters which were curiously immature for a woman who had already suffered and experienced so much. The fact that Ida's lack of noble quarterings prevented her from ever gaining an official position at court was an added advantage in the Empress's eyes, and while Marie Festetics, Elisabeth's Hungarian lady-in-waiting, accompanied her on all her journeys, little Ida remained at home watching over her interests, looking after her favourite animals, keeping her in touch with Hungary and with Andrássy. The Emperor was grateful to Ida for her devotion to his wife, and accorded her the same privileges as if she had been attached to the court.

There was never any suggestion that the meetings in Ida von Ferenczy's apartment consisted of anything more than a friendly chat over a cup of coffee. Elisabeth's kindly gesture was also a constraining one, and Katharina Schratt felt more at home in the gardens of Schönbrunn than in these rooms where pictures of the Empress looked down from every wall. In the following year she acquired with Franz Josef's consent a house at Hietzing, only a few minutes from Schönbrunn, where she could entertain him in her own home.

In Elisabeth's absence, Franz Josef's only distraction was the Burgtheater, and he told Katharina Schratt, 'You make me specially happy when you write to me of the theatre. This may not be very high-minded of me, nevertheless it is true.' Adolf Sonnenthal had resigned and Franz Josef hastened to inform his friend that Förster was the new Director of the Burg. 'I hope that he will be a kind and a more obliging chief for you, but not a more affectionate one, for that I should not like.' To which Katharina replied, 'The fact that the first news of Förster's appointment should be given me by Your Majesty is a sure sign of good luck for the future. But what made me particularly happy, so happy that I shall never *never* forget it, is what Your Majesty wrote about not wanting him to be more affectionate.'

The Emperor, who until a few years ago had taken so little interest in the theatre, was now anxious to have her opinion on the acting of Sarah Bernhardt who, during his absence in Hungary, was having a triumphal season at the Burgtheater. Katharina was full of admiration for her French colleague and went to see her act both in Sardou's *Théodora* and *Tosca*. In an extract from one of her letters we read:

> Now comes the theatre news. I went twice to see *Théodora* both on the Friday and the Saturday, and in my opinion the play is far better and more interesting than *Tosca*, that is if the part of *Théodora* is well acted, and it can only be acted by Sarah Bernhardt, for whom the play was originally written. If Juno [Wolther] could hear me saying this she would murder me as easily as Théodora murdered her Andreas.

Katharina was on the whole a generous admirer. Even when quarrelling with Sonnenthal she could still be moved to tears by his King Lear, and young newcomers to the Burg could always count on her encouragement and help. But for both the directors and the management, the Emperor's favourite must have presented somewhat of a problem. 'I hear that efforts are being made to give you new roles, more in accordance with your wishes,' wrote Franz Josef, 'so I hope there will be a rosy future for you at the Burgtheater, and if you are happy then I shall be happy too.' But before long Katharina was finding fault with the new director for not giving her enough work.

> I have not seen Dr Förster yet. I called in at his office the other day but he had just left. I have very little to do at present unless there is a last-minute change in the repertoire. Not that I am so mad keen to act with Your Majesty not being in Vienna. And even if you were in Vienna and I was given the choice of being together with Your Majesty or of acting in front of Your Majesty, I should not hesitate in choosing the former. But alas that does not happen very often. And when I am acting it gives me a warm agreeable feeling to know that Your Majesty is out in front. But this is just what the gods [the management] are trying to prevent.

There were times when even the Emperor got tired of her complaining, and she promised that 'from today I will stop my lamentations'.

> Yesterday I made myself continual reproaches that in letting myself go over the conditions prevailing at the Burgtheater I was allowing myself to be influenced by my mood at the moment, and Your Majesty might have got the impression that I was a very discontented person. In the theatre as in everything else one cannot always suit oneself. There are bad days and good days, and at times the bad days last longer and the good days seem shorter. Then inevitably one becomes nervous and overstrained. The pinpricks and the nagging are taken too seriously and sometimes one loses control. But it all adjusts itself in the end. What I dread most of all is that Your Majesty should think I am dissatisfied. How could such a thing be possible when my life is so utterly transformed and everything around me has changed to such an extent that it seems almost like a dream and I keep asking myself, 'Can this really be true?' Even if I spent the whole day on my knees in thanking dear God and my beloved guardian angel [*Oberengel*] for all that he has given me, even then it would not be sufficient, so please, please do not be cross with me.

Life had certainly changed for Katharina Schratt. As she herself said, 'Sometimes it does not seem quite real.' And in the last months of 1888 she found herself being drawn into the gathering elements of a drama for which she had never been rehearsed. The Emperor's criticism of the Baltazzis had in no way put an end to Katharina's friendship with them. If she did not ride with them any more in the Prater, it was probably because she had lost her enthusiasm for riding which for her had only been another way of trying to lose some weight which, with the approach of middle age, was giving her considerable concern. Among the papers she bequeathed to Toni Kiss are several photographs of the Baltazzi brothers, and in particular of Alexander, with whom she appears to have been the most intimate. He was a convivial bachelor with all the charm and exuberant vitality which characterized the family, and had enabled his sister Helene Vetséra, who could never have been described as beautiful, to have many influential lovers and to get her daughters invited to all the most exclusive balls. The elder girl, who was plain and serious, gave her mother very little hope of success, and all her ambitions were centred on the seventeen-year-old Marie, known as Mary, for in Vienna it was considered smart to be anglophile and anything English, whether English horses, English grooms or English names, were the fashion. Mary was a fascinating, bewitching little creature whose education had largely consisted in the art of pleasing men; women might say that she was fast, that she had a bad figure with a short neck and an overdeveloped bosom. But there was hardly a man who did not come under her spell, and the Duke of Braganza, one of the most eligible young widowers in Vienna, was said to be hopelessly in love with her.

No one in the family took it seriously when Mary became infatuated with the Crown Prince Rudolf. There was not a girl in Vienna who had not been in love with him at some time or another. But Mary had inherited her mother's push and drive. She waylaid the Prince at the races and at exhibitions, and bombarded him with passionate, adoring letters. Before long it came to her uncles' ears that Rudolf was discussing the little Vetséra girl with his friends, talking of her in a somewhat disparaging fashion, and they suggested to their sister that it might be a good thing to change the girl's ideas by taking her on a trip to England. But Mary returned from London as infatuated as ever, and a sudden interest in her studies made her teacher suspect that she must be in love with a cultured man who expected her to talk of other things than racing and social gossip.

In a pamphlet in which Baroness Vetséra later tried to exonerate herself and her family from the vile defamation to which they were being subjected, she made the mistake of over-emphasizing her innocence. She pretended that she knew nothing of her daughter's affair with the Crown Prince until a few days before her disappearance from the house she searched her room and found some compromising letters. But several months earlier Mary Vetséra had been seen going into Edward Palmer's apartment on the Ring, which the complacent banker was always ready to put at the disposal of the Crown Prince, and after a family council her uncles decided it was time for the Emperor to be informed of his son's affair with a seventeen-year-old girl. It was not easy for anyone in their position to approach Franz Josef in order to tell him what Count Taaffe was determined he should not know. The only one among their acquaintance who had access to the Emperor was Katharina Schratt who, through her friendship with the Baltazzis, thus became involved in the tragedy of Mayerling which, with the passing of ninety years, still remains a mystery.

One of the Baltazzis, in all probability Alexander, visited the actress at her apartment in the Nibelungengasse a week before Christmas 1888. But only a few days later Toni Kiss came home for the holidays with measles, and it was not until three weeks later that the court physician allowed Frau Schratt to see and to communicate with the Emperor other than by telegram. A delicate matter concerning the Crown Prince could hardly be conveyed by telegram, so it was not until the middle of January that Franz Josef was in possession of information which had been in the hands of his secret police for the past two months, and of which Katharina Schratt had known for several weeks. Most of the letters and documents relating to these days have been destroyed. Two years later, when Katharina brought a lot of adverse criticism on herself by taking part in a ballooning expedition with Alexander Baltazzi, Franz Josef, who was justifiably annoyed, wrote: 'I have never objected to your associating with Alexander Baltazzi, because that would have been ridiculous. On the contrary, I was thankful that in that way I learnt from you so much that it was important for me to know during a difficult time.'

But during the Christmas celebrations in the Hofburg, while Katharina remained in quarantine, Franz Josef was still in complete ignorance of his son's affair with Mary Vetséra. Rudolf, Stephanie and their little girl were present on this occasion, giving the impression of a united family, though the Crown Prince was already secretly contemplating divorce, not for the sake of Mary Vetséra but in order to be rid of a jealous and nagging wife. Christmas was particularly festive this year, for Franz Salvator was present for the first time as Valerie's official fiancé. Even Elisabeth appeared to be happy, for Rudolf had pleased her by giving her for her birthday eleven of Heine's autographed letters, which Maurice Szeps had procured for him in Paris. The Emperor was less pleased; for Rudolf and his mother to proclaim their admiration for the revolutionary Heine in front of the whole court was only adding fuel to the gossip over the Crown Prince's subversive activities.

In her diary the Empress's lady-in-waiting, Marie Festetics, relates a curious incident which is said to have taken place that evening when Valerie, overcoming her customary shyness with her elder brother, threw her arms round his neck and asked for his blessing. Whereupon Rudolf, who was never very affectionate towards the young sister who had all their mother's love, replied in the gentlest of tones, promising that he would always look after her and her family. Then suddenly and unaccountably he burst into tears. This strange behaviour on the part of someone who usually affected a cynical indifference should have warned his parents that their son was on the verge of a nervous breakdown. But though both Emperor and Empress appear to have been much affected at the time, neither seems to have taken it very seriously, for Elisabeth left for Munich on the following day to present Valerie's fiancé to her family, while Franz Josef appears to have been more concerned over Toni Kiss's measles and the weeks of quarantine which would deprive him of both seeing Frau Schratt and hearing from her other than by telegram.

Now for the first time he addressed the actress not as '*Gnädige Frau*' (Dear Madam) but as 'My true and most beloved friend'.

> Permit me to use this title at the moment when your letter with its alarming news of Toni's illness has struck me like lightning out of a clear sky, and when the thought of the long impending separation makes me realize how deeply fond I am of you. Forgive this perhaps indiscreet outburst of feeling, but I am so very sad that I cannot see you for so long, and my only consolation lies in being able to express myself in writing.

In his new year greetings he asks her 'to continue to be as sweet and kind to me as you have been in the past, to be patient with me even when I am tiresome, and above all to love me just a little bit. Tomorrow perhaps you will give me a thought and say a short prayer for me, for God knows I need it.' To add to his worries Katharina fell ill with a bad attack of influenza, and the Emperor was terrified of her catching measles. 'Do be good and reasonable and follow the doctor's instructions. Sometimes you are really quite childish in not looking after yourself.' And while the Emperor was worrying over her health, Katharina was worried as to how she could impart certain information it was vital for him to know. The worry appears to have retarded her recovery, for it was not until 17 January that Dr Widerhofer pronounced her to be out of quarantine, and she was able to speak to the Emperor of the Baltazzis and their niece. Shortly after this Alexander Baltazzi appears to have been received in audience by the Emperor.

Franz Josef would have had little sympathy with either the Baltazzis or their sister. He remembered the Baroness as a scheming adventuress, married to a minor diplomat, who had pursued Rudolf in his early youth and had succeeded in getting him to go to bed with her. Her daughter had probably been educated on the same principles, and in all likelihood her mother had acted as procuress. But nevertheless he was furious with Rudolf for having been so foolish as to compromise a seventeen-year-old girl, who, whatever might be her reputation, was generally accepted in society.

There appears to have been an angry scene between father and son, in which the Crown Prince was ordered to put an end to the affair. Rudolf, who was a coward and frightened of his father, would certainly have complied had it not been for the unexpected complication of Mary's pregnancy, which she apparently succeeded in keeping a secret from her family but which now, in her terror of being abandoned, transformed her from a silly, infatuated girl into a lovelorn heroine, ready to die rather than to live without him. Rudolf's obsession with death had been growing in the past years. The hopelessness of his position, the restless ambition which could not stand the long years of waiting which lay ahead, the longing to escape from a loveless marriage, all contributed to the death wish nurtured both by his illness and by the incipient madness of his Wittelsbach inheritance.

Franz Josef appears to have confided to a certain extent in Katharina Schratt, for in a letter written on the morning of 27 January, in the evening of which he was to see Rudolf for the last time at a reception at the German Embassy, we read: 'My dearest friend, it was really too kind and sweet of you to write to me at night, even though you are tired and indisposed. Your dear lines reached me early this morning, and I thank you with all my heart for your concern.'

That evening at Prince Reuss's reception it was noted that the Emperor never addressed a word to his son. Both Baroness Vetséra and her daughter Mary were present at what was one of the most brilliant events of the Vienna season. Mary had never looked more beautiful, her blue eyes shining, her whole face aglow. As one of her fellow guests recalled, 'She was a reckless, triumphant beauty who barely bothered to curtsey to the Crown Princess.' But three days later there was hardly anyone in that room who would not willingly have believed that innocent little Mary was a murderess who had poisoned the Crown Prince.

9

A Tragedy at Mayerling

It was eleven o'clock at the Hofburg on the morning of 30 January 1889 – a morning like so many others. The Empress was having a lesson in modern Greek, the Crown Princess was with her singing teacher, and the Emperor was working in his study looking forward to the hour he was to spend with Frau Schratt, who in a few moments would be due at Ida von Ferenczy's apartment. Their last meeting had had to be postponed when she had suffered a relapse after performing in a draughty theatre. A walk in Schönbrunn had been cancelled and he had not seen her since the day when she had spoken to him of the Baltazzis and of Mary Vetséra. What she had hinted had in the meantime been confirmed. Rudolf had made no secret of his infatuation for the little Vetséra. But the Emperor knew enough of Rudolf's life to be concerned not so much by Mary Vetséra as by the fact that his son was not worthy of his great inheritance. His letter to the Pope asking for a dispensation of his marriage vows had been the letter of a coward, and the shame and scandal of a Habsburg prince denying both his religious and his dynastic duties had come as a shattering blow to a man as proud and rigid as Franz Josef. There were no witnesses to the last stormy scene between father and son. Only the Emperor's final words were overheard: 'Do what you will. I shall never permit a divorce.' And Rudolf had come out of the room looking deathly pale, his hands trembling so violently that he could hardly hold his gloves.

The previous night there had been a family gathering at the Hofburg, at which Rudolf had failed to appear. He had sent his apologies through his brother-in-law, Prince Philip of Coburg, who together with Count Hoyos had been guests at his shooting lodge at Mayerling. But the Emperor, who in a reign of over forty years had rarely missed a day's work, was not impressed by the excuse of a bad cold. Rudolf had absented himself because he lacked the nerve to confront him after their last meeting. There were many times when Franz Josef would have liked to discuss Rudolf's matrimonial troubles with Elisabeth – and never so much as now, when it was no longer the question of the failure of his marriage, but of his complete moral collapse. The doctors, however, were emphatic in declaring that the Empress must on no account be emotionally disturbed, and, failing the Empress, Katharina Schratt was the only person to whom he could unburden himself and who in her simple way knew how to strike the right note of sympathy and understanding. But by the time the actress had reached the Hofburg, Count Hoyos had arrived from Mayerling with the news of the Crown Prince's death, and by the irony of fate it was the Empress, so guarded and sheltered from the grim realities of life, who was the first member of the imperial family to be told of her son's death.

It was a day of terror and confusion, in which no one dared to ascertain the truth. Neither Prince Philip of Coburg nor Count Hoyos had been aware of Mary Vetséra's presence at the lodge. The servants and the fiacredriver Bratfisch, who had driven her out to Mayerling, had been sworn to silence, which explains the valet's unwillingness to force open the door of Rudolf's room when no answer came that morning to his knock. It was only after Prince Philip's return from Vienna, where he had gone to attend the family dinner, that orders were given to break into the room, where the guttering candles revealed the Crown Prince half sitting on his bed, a pool of blood on the floor, a mirror and an empty glass on the table beside him, and lying on the same bed the naked body of a beautiful young girl. The valet appears to have seen the revolver on the ground. But neither brother-in-law nor friend could face up to the terrible fact of suicide. It was so much easier to believe that Rudolf had been poisoned, for poisons such as cyanide which bring on haemorrhages could account for all the blood on the floor.

Prince Philip, who loved Rudolf like a brother, was so shattered by his death that he was incapable of action. Out of terror of doing anything wrong the shutters were left closed, the door of the death chamber locked, and Count Hoyos sent to Vienna to break the terrible news. Driving along icy roads to Baden, he arrived just as the Trieste–Vienna express was drawing in, a train which did not usually take on passengers at Baden. In order to convince the stationmaster of the urgency of his business, Hoyos had to tell him that the Crown Prince was dead. And in his nervous agitation he committed the first mistake, not only in saying he was dead, but in adding that he had been shot – knowledge he was later to deny. The stationmaster, who was a loyal employee of the Südbahn, of which the Rothschild bank was the principal shareholder, immediately telegraphed to the bank, with the result that the Rothschilds and their various connections through the foreign embassies heard the news before it reached the Hofburg.

There was further delay when Count Hoyos arrived at the palace, for in all that vast hierarchy of officialdom there was no one who wanted to take upon himself the responsibility of telling the Emperor. The controller of Rudolf's household consulted with the Lord Chamberlain, who said he had to consult with the Foreign Minister, and when the Foreign Minister could not be found then passed him on to the Adjutant General. Each courtier in turn evaded his duty, and in the end they all came to the conclusion that only the Empress could tell her husband. It was the controller of Her Majesty's household, old Baron Nopcsa, the gentlest and most retiring of men, who with the help of Ida von Ferenczy had to break the news of Rudolf's death to the mother who, absorbed in herself, knew nothing of her son's life and had till now ignored the very existence of Mary Vetséra. But that inner strength which came to Elisabeth in moments of crisis enabled her in those first moments not only to withstand the shock but also to support the Emperor. No one was witness as to what passed between husband and wife, but both seem to have been under the impression that Rudolf had been poisoned by his mistress, and both had the same instinctive reaction to hide the shameful secret from the world.

Meanwhile Katharina Schratt had arrived at the Hofburg to find the first crowds gathered in the Michaelerplatz, and to hear the first whispered rumours of something terrible having happened to the Crown Prince. Then rumour hardened into fact. In Ida von Ferenczy's apartment she learned that he was dead.

A maid told her that her mistress was with the Empress and asked her to wait. And she saw that there was another person in the room, sitting huddled in a corner, noisily sobbing. 'Where is my child, what have they done to her?' With growing horror Katharina realized that this miserable figure was none other than Helene Vetséra, divested of all her self-confidence and pride.

Helene Vetséra had not seen her daughter since the Monday morning when she had left the house to go out shopping with her friend Marie, the Countess Larisch. The Vetséras were very proud of their intimacy with this, the Empress's favourite niece and morganatic daughter of her brother Ludwig. Elisabeth had taken a fancy to the girl and petted and spoiled her, till there came the day when the ambitious Marie began to have designs on her cousin Rudolf. What began as a harmless flirtation developed into an affair, and she was quickly married off to the unattractive and insignificant Count Larisch, while her beloved aunt remained indifferent to her protests and her tears. Whether out of bitterness or a sheer love of mischief, Marie Larisch took upon herself the role of go-between in Rudolf's love affair with Mary Vetséra. Money may also have played a part for a young woman who was always in debt. A letter found after her cousin's death, which condemned her to perpetual banishment from court, mentioned large sums of money which were paid her in return for certain services. She not only introduced Mary Vetséra to the Crown Prince, but on more than one occasion accompanied her to his private rooms in the Hofburg and, when staying at the Grand Hotel, acted as an alibi when the lovers met at Edward Palmer's apartment on the Ring.

But Marie Larisch must have realized she had been playing with fire when on that Monday morning of 28 January she came out of a shop to find that Mary, whom she had left waiting for her in a cab, had disappeared, leaving her a note in which she admitted she was going with the Crown Prince to Mayerling and spoke openly of suicide. The Countess's immediate reaction was to go to the chief of police, but Baron Kraus, who was already acquainted with the Crown Prince's latest romance, had no intention of involving the police in a matter too delicate for them to handle, and Marie Larisch was left to break the news to Mary's mother. Neither appears to have taken the talk of suicide as anything more than the idle threats of a hysterical, love-sick girl, but both were terrified of the impending scandal. And when two days went by without any news of Mary, Helene Vetséra decided to invoke the aid of the all-powerful Prime Minister, Count Taaffe. But Taaffe's reaction was the same as that of the chief of police. Neither of them wanted to interfere in the affairs of the heir apparent, and perhaps earn his lifelong enmity. The Baroness was told that the only person who might be able to help her was the Empress, which brought her on this fatal Wednesday to Ida von Ferenczy's apartment to beg for her intercession.

Helene Vetséra had been too busy pushing her way into the higher echelons of society to cultivate her brothers' more bohemian friends, and Katharina Schratt, who was on such close terms with the Baltazzis, was barely acquainted with their sister. The two women hardly spoke as they sat in Ida's sitting-room waiting for the news they dreaded to hear. Then Ida beckoned from the door and Katharina followed her into a room where she was confronted by the Empress, a figure drained of all vitality and life, the face a mask on which the tears had frozen. In a voice so low as to be scarcely audible, Elisabeth said to her: 'You must go to him. You must try and help him. I can do nothing more.' And, taking Katharina by the hand, she led her across the corridor into her private apartments, where the Emperor was already waiting. And through her tears Katharina saw that in those few hours Franz Josef had become an old man, whose iron control for once had broken down, and whose eyes were red with weeping.

In invoking her help in this most terrible of family tragedies, the Empress gave Katharina Schratt the greatest proof of confidence and trust that any woman could give another. Her own reserves of strength were running out, and she felt Franz Josef needed someone from outside the family, someone sane and healthy who would help him to retain a normal grip on life. But the truth was to be so much worse than either the Emperor or Empress could envisage. It was only when Elisabeth told Valerie of her brother's death, and her daughter's first reaction was 'Did he kill himself?', that she began to realize how little she had understood her son. Vehemently she denied it in the same way as she continued to deny it when Stephanie, who had been the last to hear the news, spoke to her of Rudolf's obsession with suicide and of how on one occasion he had gone so far as to suggest that she should join him in a suicide pact. Elisabeth had never liked her daughter-in-law and now she almost hated her, as if Stephanie was in some way responsible for Rudolf's death.

For the first twenty-four hours both Elisabeth and Franz Josef were convinced that their son had been poisoned by his mistress, which explains Elisabeth's treatment of Helene Vetséra, when the unfortunate woman forced herself into her presence, throwing herself at her feet and crying: 'Give me back my child, whom the Crown Prince has taken from me.' Half pitying, half repelled, the Empress said: 'You need all your courage, Baroness, for your daughter is dead.' And as the truth sank in and Mary's mother lay sobbing on the ground, she added in a colder, harder voice, 'Also my Rudolf is dead', and the tone of the voice was such that for the moment even Helene Vetséra believed that her seventeen-year-old daughter had poisoned the Crown Prince.

Meanwhile Franz Josef remained with Katharina Schratt, who, having been the first to tell him of Rudolf's liaison with Mary Vetséra, was now the only one to whom he could speak openly of her presence in the lodge at Mayerling. There was no word of sympathy for the girl whom he believed to have killed his son. Her family would have to take their orders from the police, and at the same time be sworn to secrecy. No one must ever know that Rudolf had not died alone. The first official communiqué gave out that the Crown Prince had died of heart failure, and any newspaper which carried a different version was immediately confiscated.

The hidebound protocol which ruled the Habsburg court had prevented the Emperor from going to Mayerling as any ordinary father would have done. But perhaps even his indomitable courage might have failed him at the sight which confronted the court physician Dr Widerhofer, when the doors which Coburg and Hoyos had ordered to be locked were opened, and by the cold light of a winter's day he saw Rudolf's perforated skull where the bullet had gone straight through the head, the cracked mirror on the table beside him, the revolver on the floor and, lying on the bed, the beautiful young girl with the ugly, gaping wound on the left temple. To his horror the doctor noted she must have died six or seven hours before the Crown Prince. And all the way back to Vienna he kept wondering how he would ever bring himself to tell the Emperor what his integrity as a physician made it his duty to tell. But by the time he got back to the Hofburg the Emperor had already retired for the night and had left a message for the doctor to return at six o'clock in the morning. The day had not dawned when he was shown into the study where Franz Josef, who had obviously spent a sleepless night, greeted him with a gruff impatience so different from his usual courteous manner. 'Tell me everything, don't leave anything unsaid.' And the doctor, who was under the impression that the Emperor already knew of his son's suicide, tried to find some words of consolation by assuring him that His Highness had not suffered for a moment as the bullet had gone straight through the head.

Franz Josef interrupted angrily, 'What, are you talking about a bullet?'

'Yes, Your Majesty, the bullet with which His Highness shot himself.'

'It is not true, the girl poisoned him, you have got to explain yourself.'

And it was only after the doctor, whom he trusted implicitly, had given him a full account of what he had found at Mayerling that Franz Josef forced himself to face the truth which was too terrible to bear, and he broke down and sobbed as uncontrollably as any child. In those few seconds Widerhofer had not only broken his heart, but destroyed his pride. For added to the anguish of a father was a fear that Rudolf, descended from the Holy Roman Emperors, might be denied the right of a Christian burial. In his own fashion Franz Josef had loved his son, and the bitterest blow of all was that not one of the half-dozen farewell letters which the police brought back from Mayerling was addressed to him. There was only a letter for the Empress, in which Rudolf asked 'forgiveness of a father of whom I know quite well I am not worthy to be the son'. This letter, which was never published in full, contained the phrase 'I have no right to live, for I have killed', and in atonement he asked his mother to carry out what he knew to be poor Mary's greatest wish, to have them both buried together in the little church of Alland.

Did Elisabeth ignore the last wishes of her son? Or was the letter deliberately kept from her till all the complicated machinery of diplomacy had been set in motion, which would eventually enable Rudolf of Habsburg to be buried in the family vault in the crypt of the Capucin church? The fact that Mary Vetséra, far from having poisoned her son, had been an innocent victim appears to have been a matter of complete indifference to a woman wrapped up in her own grief. No kindly gesture was made to Mary's unfortunate mother who, on the day following her visit to the Empress, was seen by Count Taaffe and given to understand that it would be in her own interests to leave the country for the next few weeks. She was allowed neither to see her daughter nor to arrange for a decent funeral, for the presence of a second body at Mayerling was a secret which must at all costs be prevented from becoming known.

While the Crown Prince's body was brought back to the Hofburg to be embalmed and laid in state, with the wounds carefully concealed, while the heads of the foreign missions and the chief dignitaries of the Empire came to pay their last respects, Mary's body was thrown into a disused storeroom till late on the Thursday afternoon when the police sent for her uncle Alexander Baltazzi to identify her. And a physician with less integrity than Widerhofer carried out a hurried post mortem on the corpse, pronouncing it to be a case of suicide. Mary Vetséra might have been left to be buried in an unhallowed grave had it not been for the efforts of Katharina Schratt, in whom the Baltazzis now found a true and loyal friend. Katharina, who was extremely religious, was horrified at the way in which Count Taaffe and the police were treating Mary's family. She was the only one in those first few days who was in touch with both the Emperor and the Baltazzis. And though Franz Josef was still too stunned with shock, too filled with shame, to give a thought to the girl who had died with Rudolf, someone in his entourage must have listened to Katharina Schratt and been made to understand that in their bitterness and misery the Baltazzis could well refuse to play the gruesome role assigned to them by the police unless they were assured of a Christian burial for their niece.

Late on that Thursday night of 1 February 1889, nearly forty-eight hours after her death, the body of Mary Vetséra, dressed in a fur coat with a hat to cover up the head wound, was put in a carriage propped up by cushions and, seated between two of her uncles, was driven over a rough frozen road to the monastery of Heiligenkreuz where, following the visit of two highly placed court officials, the Abbot had been persuaded to provide a Christian funeral for what was categorically described as a 'suicide'. . . .

Alexander Baltazzi remained haunted throughout his life by the memory of that terrible drive in a jolting carriage, when with every jolt the corpse kept knocking against him and the absurd little hat kept falling off, revealing the ugly, gaping wound. It was past midnight when they arrived at the dimly lit monastery to find a roughly made coffin and a still unfinished grave and it was nearly dawn by the time they had left the windy, rain-drenched churchyard. In the funeral service there had been no talk of suicide. Someone, perhaps the Abbot himself, shocked by the behaviour of the police, had inserted the words 'Like a flower her life began, like a flower it was broken off'; spoilt, ambitious little Mary, who had died for love of a man who had only wanted her as a companion for suicide.

Alexander Baltazzi would not have spared Katharina Schratt the description of that gruesome drive and of the outrages committed in the Emperor's name. But Rudolf's grief-stricken parents could not be blamed for the terrible mistakes which were made in the first days when all the forces of autocracy allied to a rigid censorship were invoked to prevent the truth from leaking out. But the censorship did not extend beyond the frontiers, and after twenty-four hours the foreign press were all carrying in large headlines the story of suicide. Meanwhile Dr Widerhofer, who valued his professional integrity more than his position at court, had insisted on telling the truth in his post mortem. The only concession which he was willing to make, and which was perhaps also the truth, was to certify that on examining Rudolf's body certain conditions of the brain denoted a pathological disturbance which justified the supposition that His Imperial Highness had shot himself in a moment of mental derangement.

This medical report, signed by five physicians, represented Franz Josef's only hope of securing Christian burial for his son. By the evening of 1 February the papers carried the full report and in Rome the diplomatic battle with the Vatican had begun. Here the negotiations were fraught with difficulties. There was opposition in the sacred college, where that rigid doctrinaire Cardinal Rampolla was using all his influence to prevent the Pope from giving the necessary permission. And the proudest monarch in Europe had to wait in anguish before the necessary funeral arrangements could be made. Finally Leo XIII yielded to pressure not only from Austria but from her Catholic allies, and conceded the right for Rudolf of Habsburg to be buried among his ancestors. Only five days after his body had been brought back from Mayerling, the Lord High Chamberlain was already making the arrangements for the state funeral.

Throughout these days Elisabeth played no part in the efforts to rehabilitate her son. The magnificent control she had shown on the first day had broken down, and the depths of her despair were such as to make her family fear for her sanity. Dr Widerhofer's report referring to a 'mental derangement', which had come as a relief to Franz Josef, had had the opposite effect on his wife, reminding her of the medical report on her cousin Ludwig and making her believe that in some way she was to blame in having handed on to Rudolf her tainted Wittelsbach blood. In her unreasoning grief she forgot that Franz Josef was half a Wittelsbach and that the discipline and strength he had inherited from his Wittelsbach mother had enabled him to save an Empire in a time of revolution. Elisabeth was now convinced that both she and her son were mad, and at times she would speak and behave in such a way as to make her husband fear that the tenuous threads which still bound her to normality were on the verge of giving way.

How much of his misery did he impart to Katharina Schratt? Very few of his letters dating from these days survive. They shared the fate of all the other documents which relate to Mayerling. Neither in those published by Baron Bourgoing, nor among those which are still unpublished, is there any mention of the thorny negotiations with the Vatican. In the eyes of his father, Rudolf had died a coward's death. In private he is reported to have said, 'My son died like a tailor [*Schneider*].' *Schneider* is also the huntsman's term for a weakling, a stag who skulks in the undergrowth instead of coming out to fight in the open. But the legend of Rudolf had still to be preserved, and in writing to his fellow sovereigns Franz Josef never failed to refer to Rudolf as 'the best of sons and the loyalest of subjects'.

10

Our Poor Emperor

Katharina Schratt was not used to tragedy; she was rarely at her ease in a tragic role. But in the tenderness of her affection she succeeded in conveying to her afflicted sovereign the love and sympathy of the ordinary man in the street. Whereas in the eyes of the aristocracy Rudolf had disgraced his father and betrayed his class, the crowds who stood weeping outside the Hofburg mourned a beloved prince, and Katharina's greatest contribution to the Emperor in the darkest hours of his life was in enabling him to think of his son with pity instead of shame.

But the strain of those first days had overtaxed her strength. She was barely convalescent from influenza when she went to meet Franz Josef on that fatal Wednesday morning; by the end of the week she was again confined to her bed, from where she wrote the Emperor a letter, of which an extract still survives.

There are moments when words of condolence are meaningless. I know that only too well, and I will not even attempt to comfort Your Majesty with words. But the harshest of sorrows loses some of its bitterness in tears. So all I want to do is to weep with Your Majesty over the cruel destiny to which God in his unfathomable way has condemned us all. Your Majesty knows that in these tragic hours all my thoughts and feelings are with you, and I am only unhappy to be feeling so helpless, able to do nothing but weep and pray that the dear God may give Your Majesty the strength to stand up to this terrible ordeal.

Her influenza developed into a bad attack of conjunctivitis, for the following letter is dated four days later, on the morning after Rudolf's funeral.

I am not being disobedient or going against the doctor's orders. Though he will not allow me to go out before Friday or Saturday, I am nevertheless permitted to write a letter and I am not sure I would not have written anyway, even without his permission. I get feverishly restless at being so utterly useless and at not being able to do anything to alleviate my Emperor's grief. Yesterday afternoon I shut myself up in my room so that no one could disturb me, while I accompanied Your Majesty in my thoughts on that last sad walk to the church. In solitude I listened to the tolling of the bells coming from every part of the city, and I joined my prayers to the thousands of others, all praying for the poor Crown Prince, but together with my prayers for his everlasting peace went another special one, asking our dear and merciful God to preserve Your Majesty in health and strength for many years to come.

Franz Josef's gratitude to the friend who had stood by him and his wife in these first hours is expressed in a letter written on the morning of the funeral.

Only a few lines today, for you need not be told that in my inexpressible grief I think of you often and always with the deepest affection. Your true friendship and your comforting quiet sympathy were of great consolation to us both in these recent terrible days. The invitation to call on us yesterday came from the Empress, who is so glad to have you. I would scarcely have ventured to trouble you again . . . but now I have only to repeat a request, or rather a command, with which Frau von Ferenczy has already been charged, that you take good care of your health, obey the doctors in every way, and absolutely do not go out sooner than they allow. I hope you will soon be quite restored to health, and we shall have the longed for pleasure of seeing you with us. . . . Today I have before me the hardest task of all, of accompanying the best of sons, the most loyal of subjects, to his last resting place.

It was characteristic of Franz Josef to defend the memory of his son, even when writing to a woman who knew the whole truth of Mayerling and who in her own letters went no further than to refer to Rudolf as 'the poor Crown Prince'. Circumstances spared the Emperor the ordeal of a state funeral, for most of his fellow sovereigns, even including the German Kaiser who was not famous for his tact, had respected his wishes that the mourners should be confined to the family. Unfortunately the family included Stephanie's parents, the King and Queen of the Belgians, a couple whom the Empress disliked in ordinary times and whom now she could hardly be persuaded to see. She herself was too ill to attend the funeral, and stayed behind with Valerie while the Emperor went accompanied by his elder daughter Gisela, the one person in the family who had always been close to Rudolf since the days when they were two lonely children in the Hofburg, neglected by a mother who was rarely at home. Unlike Rudolf, Gisela had never suffered from this neglect and had grown up into a healthy, normal young woman, who at eighteen had married one of her Bavarian cousins and settled down to a happy family life. But not even Gisela ever had the courage to tell her father in what way their mother had failed them. Now it was too late, and all she could do was to support a proud old man on his tragic calvary. 'I bore up all the way,' wrote Franz Josef, 'it was only in the crypt that I could stand it no longer.' These words were spoken only to his wife and to Katharina Schratt.

Hemmed in by the Spanish etiquette of the Hofburg, he might never have known the extent to which his people took part in his sorrow had it not been for a letter written to Frau Schratt by one of his most faithful servants, a certain Baron Hawerda, who, as administrator of the Habsburg family funds, had come into contact with the actress and learned to appreciate both her loyalty and her tact.

In these tragic times I feel the necessity of pouring out my heart to someone on whose devotion to our sorely tried Emperor I can count as if it were my own. What I have only realized in the past few days, and which if he only knew would bring some measure of comfort to His Majesty, is the way in which his subjects from all parts of the Empire, coming from every walk of life, have identified themselves with his misfortune. But how should he know it, when he stands so high above us all? Those who would have the chance to tell him are too full of their self-importance, too little in touch with the ordinary people to inform him of what I am sure it would give him pleasure to hear. One must have walked through the Vienna streets as I have, and heard on every side, spoken in every language, and in the same heartfelt tones, the one phrase, 'Our poor Emperor'. One must have seen the teeming crowds, for once so strangely silent, converging on the Hofburg as if unconsciously wishing to draw nearer to the great suffering heart of their Emperor. One must have noted with what genuine feeling the people enquire after his health, or have read, as I have read, the thousands of letters which keep arriving from all parts of the country, and of which, alas, His Majesty is only shown the briefest and tritest of résumés, but where in many instances the very simplicity of the language is what would please him most.

What could be more touching than a letter received from a country district in Serbia, one of the smallest in the land, but which, in grateful memory of a fleeting visit once paid them by the Crown Prince, wished to show their loyalty and devotion to the throne? What could be more moving than an anonymous letter from Dalmatia, in which the writer begs the Emperor to dispose of the ill-fated island of Lacroma in view of the tragic destiny which overtook the last two owners?★ This may sound nothing more than an idle superstition, but what deserves to be appreciated is the concern it shows for the future of the Emperor and the reigning house. And this same feeling underlies all the numberless letters and telegrams, many of them addressed directly to His Majesty, which keep pouring in by every post, many of them coming from the humblest and poorest of his subjects; all of them expressing a devotion he does not even suspect. But perhaps I have already said too much, and am transgressing on state secrets.

This letter, carefully preserved among the Schratt papers, was certainly not written in vain, and Baron Hawerda was not the only one who, as the years went by, counted on Katharina Schratt to inform the Emperor of facts and abuses which might otherwise never have come to his notice.

On 11 February, five days after Rudolf's funeral, the imperial couple left for Budapest, and Katharina, who was by now re-covered, was invited to the Hofburg on the eve of their departure. The invitation came from the Empress, who in these days appears to have relied almost as much as her husband on her 'quiet sympathy'. Consumed with remorse, blaming herself for having failed her son, Elisabeth now tried to atone by devoting herself to her husband, refusing to leave him even when her agonizing rheumatic pains called for a warmer climate. Both the Emperor and her doctors hoped that a change of scene might help to calm her nerves. In Budapest she would be spared from hearing rumours which, in spite of all the efforts of Count Taaffe, were circulating round the Austrian capital. On 2 February a Munich newspaper had already printed the full story of Mayerling and of Mary Vetséra

★ Rudolf and his uncle, the Emperor Maximilian of Mexico, who was shot on the orders of the revolutionary Benito Juarez.

having died with the Crown Prince, and before the authorities could act clandestine copies of the paper were on sale in Vienna. Attempts to keep the Austrian people in ignorance of the truth had the fatal effect of encouraging the lowest and most scurrilous of gossipmongers. There were stories of Rudolf having been murdered by a group of Hungarian extremists, who had accused him of betraying their cause; of a jealous forester who had revenged himself on the Crown Prince for having seduced his wife. And the most libellous of all was a rumour which no one dared to voice aloud, of the heir apparent having been so deeply involved in treason that Count Taaffe, who had been informed that he and his mistress had gone to Mayerling, had staged what appeared to be a suicide but was in reality a political assassination.

There was genuine commiseration both in England and in France, where the Austrian Crown Prince had enjoyed considerable popularity on account of his liberal principles. Queen Victoria wrote to Lord Salisbury, 'The Prince of Wales has seen a friend of his from Vienna who is a great friend of the Emperor and knows all the details, which he gave to the Prince of Wales and which he says are too shocking to write. There is no doubt that the poor Crown Prince was quite off his head.' Franz Josef could only forgive his son by believing that he had shot himself in a moment of madness, but it was a subject which could never be mentioned in front of his wife, who was now tortured by the fear that she herself might end up mad and like her cousin Otto, King Ludwig's brother. Hope of her condition improving in Budapest proved a fallacy. The town where she had spent some of the happiest years of her life, and where Rudolf had been loved, only intensified her misery. The Emperor was also unhappier in Budapest than in Vienna, but his unhappiness stemmed from very different reasons. The furious debates in the Hungarian Parliament over the passing of the Defence Bill only served to remind him of his son's subversive activities, and of his friendship with the leader of the opposition, Count Stefan Károlyi, who was now doing his best to sabotage the bill by insisting that Hungarian regiments should have their orders issued in Magyar and be under separate command, measures calculated to disrupt the unity of the imperial army, which lay closest to the Emperor's heart.

Franz Josef's letters to Katharina Schratt from Budapest make sad reading.

> Our reception in Pest was better than I expected. The people at the station greeted us in silence, and even the crowds in the street were not as noisy as usual, so our horses could get through at a trot and the drive to the castle did not take too long. There were a few shouts of '*Eljen*' [Long Live] which pained the Empress, but I am glad to say that on the whole the Hungarians were more decorous and respectful than usual.

Living in seclusion up at the Castle of Buda, rarely venturing out into the street, the grieving Emperor was kept in ignorance of the fights and demonstrations in the town, and he wrote to Katharina Schratt, 'My presence here is useful and many people do me the honour of assuring me that if I were not here things would go still worse.' But his ministers could not prevent him from reading reports of the bitter quarrels in Parliament, and on 24 February he wrote:

> In Parliament things still go on very stormily, and what with the endless speeches the discussions over the Defence Bill are terribly slow. I must be both firm and patient, and if necessary one must even be ready for a clash. All these matters are painfully offensive at the present time and a proof of great rudeness and inconsideration, and vex me a lot. On the other hand they distract me and prevent me of thinking of sadder things.

On another occasion he wrote: 'I have no time to devote to my grief which is a good thing. Only the hours after going to bed are bad, also the waking up in the morning.'

There was little consolation to be gained from conversations with Rudolf's former gentlemen-in-waiting and with Dr Widerhofer, who had travelled down to Budapest to thank him for honours they had received.

> I spent over an hour with Widerhofer, talking over the whole sorrowful event, trying to find some reason, some underlying cause, but alas what is the use? There is no real purpose in going over it all again. But one can just think of nothing else, and talking at least gives a certain relief. Here I am going back on the same sad topic. Forgive me. But I know you will understand me. The time may come when one will have other thoughts.

To all outward appearances the Emperor remained the same. He was at his desk at five in the morning, he received his ministers and he gave the usual audiences. Only those who knew him well, like old Count Hübner who had served under him for nearly forty years, noted that after Rudolf's death Franz Josef was a different person, that 'when he was not talking, he gave the impression of someone who had been knocked on the head' and had not yet recovered from the shock. Nor would he ever be the same again. His love for his only son, and above all a fierce dynastic pride, had made of his reign a sacred mission, dedicated to the glory of the house of Habsburg. Now everything seemed meaningless. It was as if the mainspring of his life had gone and all that was left was an empty ritual, though the succession in the shape of Karl Ludwig and his sons made him more determined than ever to carry on for as long as possible.

Nor did conditions in the family contribute to raising his morale. Elisabeth did her best to keep him company, and in his chivalrous fashion he paid tribute to 'my wonderful wife who is only occupied by her concern for my welfare'. But she sank ever more into a state of apathy, and in a despairing mood he wrote from Budapest: 'I cannot tell you anything very interesting or amusing, for we live quietly, given over to our grief. It will prove very hard for the Empress to recover. Yesterday again she had a very melancholy day and wept a great deal at our little dinner for the three of us, so naturally also Valerie began to cry.' Poor Valerie was doing her best to distract her parents, accompanying her mother on walks, reading to her in the evening while her father fell asleep in an armchair. And all the time she was longing for her Franz, who was serving in the army and could only visit her when he was off duty. For the moment there could be no talk of marriage, as the very suggestion made her mother burst into a flood of tears.

The Emperor was also worried about Katherina Schratt, who had been suffering from chronic bronchitis ever since her attack of influenza earlier in the year. Though the doctors assured him there was nothing radically wrong, they nevertheless said that she was in need of warmth and sunshine and a complete rest, and recommended Meran in the Austrian Tyrol, which was renowned for its mild climate. But Meran was too dull for the pleasure-loving actress, who managed to persuade both herself and her doctors that the French Riviera would be far more beneficial to her health.

The Emperor wrote to her on her departure, 'For the time being think only of yourself. What you need above all is rest. I have had Forster instructed to grant you as long a vacation as you wish.' But what Katharina needed was not so much rest as distraction. Circumstances had plunged her into the midst of tragedy, involving her in the misfortunes not only of the Habsburgs but also of the Baltazzis. Alexander Baltazzi, who had loved his pretty niece, continued to haunt her doorstep and to inveigh against the cruelty and inhumanity with which the imperial couple had treated his sister. He was obsessed by the subject, and would not allow her to forget the horrible details of Mary's funeral, till there were times when she could not bear to listen any more. She longed for gaiety and relaxation, but Franz Josef, who would never begin to understand her mercurial temperament, spoke only of her need for rest. 'I hope you will use your leave to the end or even stay beyond it if you are still not completely recovered. I will take upon myself the official disagreeableness.'

For the Emperor to behave in a manner so utterly at variance with his character shows how indispensable the actress had become. His personal grief did not prevent him from worrying over her health to the extent of using his influence in the theatre to facilitate her leave, a form of interference to which he had hitherto been opposed. Small wonder if there was criticism among her colleagues when the supposedly ailing Frau Schratt was reported in the newspapers to have participated in the flower carnival at Nice, and to have been noted among the visitors to the casino at Monte Carlo. Though no manager dared to complain of the Emperor's favourite, neither Franz Josef nor Katharina was pleased when a role in which she had been promised the lead was given to a rival. For the first time since his son's death the Emperor started taking an interest in mundane matters, complaining that the actress who had got the part was not in his opinion either young enough or at all suited to the role. 'You see I am already turning to more cheerful topics, though from here I can report nothing but sorrow.'

With eagerness he awaited her letters, bringing him news of a world 'where life', as he somewhat wistfully remarks, 'seems to be a succession of pleasures and entertainments. . . . Mentone must be very agreeable, and according to descriptions in the newspapers the whole region must be paradise.' Katharina Schratt regaled the mourning Emperor with all the trivialities of social gossip, listing her admirers, many of whom had followed her from Vienna. There was a Baron Königswarther, who was being particularly *'aimable'*, and poor Franz Josef, who was only too ready to be jealous, commented, 'It sounds as if the charming Baron may have been too *"aimable"'*, but he added in his unselfish way, 'I am pleased you have found so many friends and are surrounded by a circle of admirers, which will put you in a good mood.'

The Riviera at the height of the *belle époque* must have been a very pleasant place for the pretty Viennese actress, known to be the Emperor's friend. Staying at the fashionable Hotel de Russie at Mentone, within easy driving distance of Monte Carlo, it was not long before Katharina was indulging in her irresistible passion for gambling. Franz Josef wrote:

> Less pleased am I to hear that you have been so often to Monte Carlo, but I am grateful and touched that you so openly confess your sins. So far you have not lost very much and you assure me that out of revenge against the God of Fortune you are not going back any more. But then you will start all over again and *'comme l'appetit vient en mangeant'* you will begin playing for higher stakes and end up by losing a lot of money. For in matters of finance you are hopelessly extravagant. Now I have finished with my scolding. No doubt you will be very cross with me and then you will naturally end by doing exactly as you please, which you have every right to do as I am not your tutor to mix myself up in matters which are none of my business.

But these letters, full of gaiety and sunshine, helped to dissipate the gloom in the Castle of Buda, and the lighthearted descriptions are strewn with *Maiglöckchen* (lilies of the valley), the charming Viennese expression for the kind of compliment which in itself is typically Viennese. 'I am sure that Your Majesty's censorship will disapprove on hearing that I sleep with Your Majesty's letters under my pillow at night, and though it may sound like *lèse-majesté*

I hold long colloquies with Your Majesty before going to sleep, and that gives me some very happy dreams.'

She waxed indignant over all the political troubles in Budapest, and declared that she would like 'to give a sound thrashing to all those disloyal Hungarians'. When Franz Josef repeated this to his wife, Elisabeth remarked with one of her rare flashes of humour that there was nothing the politicians would enjoy more than to be thrashed by such a pretty woman. Valerie, who disliked the way in which people were gossiping about her father and Frau Schratt, could not understand her mother's encouragement of this friendship, always bringing the actress into the conversation, and referring to her as 'the friend'. It saddened her to see how even a letter from the actress describing the carnival of Nice was welcomed by her parents as a diversion in the monotony of their lives.

Elisabeth was almost as pleased as Franz Josef when 'the friend' remembered them on 1 March, and masses of the traditional Viennese gift of mauve and purple violets arrived from the Riviera. Katharina had given them personally to the sleeping-car conductor of the Nice–Vienna Express, and they were still as fresh and scented as if they had just come in from the country. Franz Josef wrote:

> It was so kind and good of you to think of 1 March this year, and from so far away, and to take such care that we received the violets. I hope they bring us luck, if there is such a thing as luck for us any more. Nevertheless, they brought us genuine pleasure, and for the first time in a long while a cheerful atmosphere prevailed again at our dinner and lasted the whole evening. This is no mere phrase but pure truth, and perhaps it may give you satisfaction to know what a good deed you have done.

But Katharina's conscience, which for all her frivolity was very active, would not allow her to be satisfied by sending flowers. She had enjoyed herself on the Riviera, but was it right for her to be enjoying herself at a time when the Emperor and the whole court was still in mourning? And with a sudden and characteristic *volte face* she decided to make a pilgrimage to Lourdes. What may have appeared like an act deliberately planned to please the pious Emperor was in effect the completely spontaneous gesture of a highly emotional and religious woman. Franz Josef, who accepted it as a fresh proof of her affection, wrote, 'It touched me greatly to know that you specially wanted to receive a letter from me at Lourdes, and it does us good to know that you will be thinking of us there and praying to the Madonna for us all, and also for the dear departed one.' In praying for Rudolf Katharina Schratt would also have included Mary Vetséra in her prayers.

I I

Number Nine Gloriettegasse

At the beginning of March 1889 the Emperor wrote to Katharina Schratt from Budapest: 'I have been kept busy making a new will. When this is done I shall be more at ease, for one can certainly not know what may happen at any moment. I have provided for you and Toni, so that you can be free of worry after my death. The details I shall tell you in person.'

Among the unpublished Schratt papers is a copy of a codicil in which Franz Josef bequeathed after his death the sum of five hundred thousand gulden, an extremely large sum of money, 'to the court actress Katharina Kiss von Itebbe (born Schratt), to whom I am bound in the truest and purest friendship, and who has stood loyally and faithfully by me and the Empress in the hardest hours of our lives.' To protect Katharina from her own extravagance, the Emperor appointed her old friend Edward Palmer, President of the Alpine-Montan Company, to act as her trustee in administering the funds, the revenues of which during his lifetime were still however to be paid into his private account.

There is no mention of the actress in Franz Josef's last will and testament. But in November 1911, only five years before his death, the eighty-one-year-old Emperor instructed the director of his private family funds to hand over to Katharina Kiss von Itebbe the half million gulden, which were lying in her name in his private account. Three years earlier he had presented the actress with the magnificent Königswarter Palais on the fashionable Kärntner Ring, so that by the time of his death Katharina was an exceedingly rich woman, whose collection of jewels alone was said to be one of the finest in Europe.

But in 1889, apart from the Emperor's generous gifts to supplement her wardrobe and to pay off her debts, Katharina depended largely on her salary, eight thousand gulden a year. This was far from satisfying her needs, and she had many sleepless nights worrying over a destitute old age and the prospect of leaving Toni penniless. But she never made any attempt to economize, and Franz Josef, who was so frugal by nature that he even went to the lengths of writing his telegrams on old bits of paper, found that the tradesman's daughter from Baden had just as little idea of money as his wife.

One can picture with what joy Katharina received the news from Budapest. Her letter of thanks must have been overflowing with love and gratitude, for the Emperor wrote:

> I really should be cross with the way in which you overwhelm me with your thanks, but you do it so charmingly, in such touching words, that I cannot help being pleased, all the more so as it means my intentions have been fully understood. Yes! It was my heartfelt duty to provide for your and Toni's material future, and as you yourself speak of your death, and go so far as to express the wish that you should die before me, of which the very idea is a sacrilege, and an event which in all likelihood and by the grace of God will never take place, I nevertheless want to assure you that should such a terrible thing occur, then the bequest will immediately revert to Toni, whose future will therefore in all eventualities be secure.

Franz Josef might have been wiser not to inform the actress of the provisions he had made for her in his will, for now there was no longer any incentive to save, and the house in Hietzing she acquired in the spring of 1889 was beautifully furnished regardless of cost.

Number nine Gloriettegasse, a quiet little street adjacent to the gardens of Schönbrunn, is one of those yellow, green-shuttered houses built in the baroque style which are still to be found in Vienna's more elegant suburbs. Katharina must have added the decorated iron grille done in the art nouveau style which was just then coming into fashion, and the glassed-in veranda and conservatory giving out on to the garden, which made the Emperor refer to Gloriettegasse as her 'glass palace'. It was a very personal house, reflecting the owner's gaiety and warmth: pale-painted rooms always full of flowers and birds – her pet canaries, a presumptuous parrot, and several dogs, none of them handsome, for she collected strays. 'But dear to me because they belong to you,' wrote Franz Josef when he saw her once from out of his window in the Hofburg, walking across the square with two ugly little mongrels. Though the house must have been bought out of the Emperor's private account, there is no word of this in his letters where, with typical modesty, he writes: 'I do not want you to feel that you should move out to Hietzing on my account, and perhaps you do not wish to do so at all. I urgently beg of you to do what is most agreeable and convenient to you.'

It was certainly more 'agreeable and convenient' for Katharina Schratt to have her own luxurious villa in which she could entertain the Emperor, rather than to have their meetings confined to an hour in Ida von Ferenczy's drawing-room, or a mid-day walk in Schönbrunn. Also the Empress professed to be delighted that she was moving out to Hietzing, 'for in that way you will be nearer to us'. But though the actress was often a welcome guest, both at Schönbrunn and at the Hermes Villa at Lainz, and even on rare occasions at the Hofburg, Elisabeth up to the time of her death was never known to have crossed the threshold of number nine Gloriettegasse.

Though Katharina was delighted with her 'glass palace', where she spent the spring and autumn months, she realized that it meant she would have to be still more careful and circumspect in her behaviour, what in her Baden dialect she called '*Habt Acht*'. Anything which brought her relationship with the Emperor more into the public eye only made her more enemies at court, where a strictly aristocratic society could not forgive the fact that their proud and unassailable sovereign had chosen a woman of the bourgeoisie to be his confidante and friend.

Katharina was by now approaching middle age, and though the Emperor's early morning visits were immensely flattering they were nevertheless a strain on both her health and nerves. After late hours at the theatre it was not always easy to be coiffed and dressed at the breakfast table at seven-thirty in the morning, by which time Franz Josef had already been at work for a couple of hours and was ready to enjoy the fresh *Kipferls* and excellent coffee that she always provided. Fortunately she had the type of looks that were at their best in the morning, being bright-eyed and rosy-cheeked, even after what Franz Josef called 'one of her excesses at Sacher's'. Nor was she ever silent and morose. Her conversation flowed in a continual stream, politics mingling with theatre gossip, the latest jokes told in the Jockey Club and the latest news from Bulgaria where, in spite of the powers still refusing to recognize Prince Ferdinand, he had nevertheless managed to conclude some highly profitable trade agreements. Even Franz Josef had to admit that '*le petit Ferdinand*' was really doing very well, and was so much more intelligent than the rest of his Balkan neighbours. King Milan of Serbia, for instance, was causing considerable trouble at the time by insisting on abdicating in favour of his son who was still a minor, abdicating for no other reason than that he preferred his visits to Sacher's and his trips to Paris to the restricted pleasures of Belgrade.

After breakfast the Emperor and Frau Schratt would take a short walk in the gardens of Schönbrunn, which could be reached by crossing the Maxinggasse and entering a small door which gave straight on to the gardens. One of their favourite walks was to the private zoo, for Katharina, who loved all animals, had her favourites even among the bears, who were regularly fed with the remains of the Emperor's breakfast. During this time the royal coachmen would be waiting discreetly round the corner from the Gloriettegasse, but before long the carriage would be recognized, and a small crowd would gather, hoping to see their Emperor. When a zealous police officer gave orders for the crowd to be dispersed, Franz Josef countermanded the order, saying that there was no reason why the people should not greet their sovereign when he was paying a friendly visit in the neighbourhood.

But what was permitted to the citizens of Hietzing was avoided at Ischl, where the neighbours included too many aspiring courtiers. When Katharina Schratt, who was looking for a summer home, wrote that she had been offered a small house adjacent to the Kaiser Villa, which was prettier and more conveniently situated than the one she had already seen, the Emperor answered her by return, telling her, 'It would be better to take the villa that was not so near, for though the Villa Hanke would be very convenient for me, the less unnecessary gossip from our dear neighbours the better. Even if you live further away, I will always with your permission manage to reach you, and that is the main thing.'

No sooner was Katharina installed in the Villa Felicitas, which, though neither as attractive nor as romantic as Frauenstein, was to be her summer home for the next fifty years, than she was presented with a key which enabled her to take a short cut direct into the park of the Kaiser Villa. The key was given her by the Empress, who throughout the spring and summer made every effort to please her husband. Elisabeth's own unhappiness was so profound that for once she appears to have felt a certain relief in thinking of others rather than herself. And in her little attentions to Katharina Schratt she tried to make up to Franz Josef for having failed him in so many other ways.

But in 1889 the Emperor spent very little time either in Vienna or at Ischl. The stormy passage of the army Defence Bill kept him in Budapest negotiating with men he regarded as no better than traitors, and many of his Austrian subjects were beginning to complain that far too much time was devoted to Hungarian politics. Count Hübner wrote:

> When he comes to Vienna he only stays for a few days, and everything is done in a hurry. There is never sufficient time to examine a problem throughly, and the most urgent matters remain unsettled. The Emperor is no longer what he was before the catastrophe at Mayerling, he has become feebler and no longer takes the same interest in affairs. Up to the death of the Crown Prince he worked for the monarchy and for his beloved son; now that the son has gone there is a great void in the father's life. It is only a sense of duty which keeps him going, but his heart is no longer in his work.

Even Franz Josef's passion for hunting was no longer the same. 'Whenever I see a stag I keep thinking of Rudolf'; not of the Rudolf of the later years, but of the seventeen-year-old boy who had been so proud to accompany his father on his expeditions in the mountains. All that was left was little Erzi, Rudolf's seven-year-old daughter, who had all her father's charm and fascination. Franz Josef adored his grand-daughter and for her sake was ready to be pleasant to his daughter-in-law, whom he really disliked. Mother and child were living out at Laxenburg where Stephanie's situation in the family, to which she had always remained a stranger, was not a very enviable one. With her the humiliating circumstances of her husband's death outweighed the tragedy. She had suffered too much at Rudolf's hands to share in his parents' grief. What she minded most was the loss of her position as Crown Princess, having to take second place to Karl Ludwig's wife, the beautiful Marie Therese of Braganza. She hardly ever saw her mother-in-law, for in the first months the very sight of Rudolf's child reduced Elisabeth to tears, and later the tears turned into indifference.

A common interest in their little grand-daughter might have been a bond between husband and wife, for as Valerie noted in her diary with a depressing frankness,

> My parents have so little to say to one another; having to be with Papa is an added burden on Mama. The sacrifice she makes in order to stay with him becomes pointless, as he gets more and more taken up by his unfortunate relationship with the Schratt woman. The truth is that Mama and I are so much happier when we can be by ourselves. Papa has so few interests any more and has become so ponderous and narrow-minded that I can understand he gets very often on my mother's nerves, especially now that she has suffered so much. It is pathetic to see how my parents manage to get worked up over the smallest and most insignificant things. Papa gets more and more irritable, and she becomes more and more miserable.

The Empress's spirits showed no signs of improvement. Her only relaxation was to take interminable walks which exhausted both her daughter and her ladies-in-waiting, and in having lessons in modern Greek from a series of professors, each of whom her husband found more intolerable than the last. Small wonder if he missed the cheerful atmosphere of the Gloriettegasse and the easy laughter of Katharina Schratt, and wrote to her, 'I think of you often with the greatest longing, and in the last nights have dreamt of you so much.'

Franz Josef was incredibly naïve about women, and it never seems to have struck him that his daughter might regard his almost obsessional interest in the actress as an insult to her mother. Franz Salvator appears to have influenced Valerie in criticizing a friendship which, however harmless, nevertheless detracted from her father's mythical prestige. As her fiancé said, 'The Emperor should not be talked about.' Her mother's attitude was even more difficult for Valerie to understand. At one moment Elisabeth would be talking of Frau Schratt with the greatest affection, and at the next she would be complaining that her life was useless, 'I only come between your father and Frau Schratt. I am made to feel ridiculous, and then I envy Rudolf, and I wonder whether there is any point in living any more.' What her mother did not realize as yet, and what Valerie, who was herself in love, saw all too clearly, was that her father's feeling for Katharina Schratt was no longer an infatuation but that he was deeply and truly in love, and that all the difficulties in their way, the months of separation, the hidden aspects of her life – for Katharina was a woman who only told what she wanted to tell – all served to increase his attachment.

Lady Paget wrote in her journal:

> I hear the Emperor is just as devoted as ever to Madame Schratt. Every morning at six o'clock he can be seen going to breakfast with her. The Empress encourages it, and pays visits to her with Archduchess Valerie. Madame Schratt is a rather pretty woman, dark-complexioned with blue eyes and cendré hair which grows well on her forehead. Those who know her well say that she is rather stupid, but that she has a naïve way of blurting out the truth. Some people say she is the Emperor's daughter and nearly all agree in thinking the relation is a platonic one.

Lady Paget was repeating the exaggerated gossip of court circles. The Emperor did not visit the actress at six in the morning, nor did the Empress visit her at Hietzing or elsewhere. She can hardly have been stupid when the most brilliant men in Vienna praised her delightful conversation. She was, however, an accomplished actress, and knew that a calculated naïvety, a feigned stupidity, served to disarm those who would otherwise have been her enemies.

Where she was never modest or naïve, and where her naturally forceful character asserted itself, was in her dealings with the Burgtheater management, and it speaks for the integrity of Director Förster that he refused to give her any preferential treatment. In these years the Burgtheater was moving away from the contrived drawing-room comedy to the naturalistic drama of the great

northern playwrights. Katharina Schratt was essentially a comedienne with a limited range and her appearances in classical roles
such as the Queen in Schiller's *Don Carlos* met with respectful but
hardly enthusiastic notices. In moments of depression, perhaps
even of boredom, for Franz Josef was not always the most exhil-
arating of companions, Katharina may have thought back with
nostalgia to the old days of the Stadttheater, when Heinrich Laube
had called her 'a bird of paradise' and she had dreamt of becoming
a great actress.

The Emperor was always sympathetic to any setback in her
career:

> To act one day in eight is not very much. Also I am annoyed that you
> are so little occupied at present. I only hope that your frank talk with
> Förster may have had the desired effect. The straightforward line you
> intend to take is the best one, even if intrigues and flirtations with the
> secretary and stage management may achieve quicker results.

Katharina had evidently told the Emperor that these were the
tactics used by other actresses to further their careers.

In October 1889 Franz Josef had the satisfaction of hearing that
his beloved friend had scored a personal triumph in playing the
heroine in Ludwig Fulda's *Wilde Jagd* (*The Wild Chase*). Success
was all the more satisfying as the play had already been performed
by some of the leading actresses in the Burg, and the critics were
unanimous in their praise of Katharina Schratt's original interpretation. In a letter addressed from Meran, where he was visiting his
wife, Franz Josef wrote:

> You seem to have acted neither by the *die Gabillon*★ nor by the *die
> Lewinsky*★ recipe, but according to your own true interpretation. I
> read in the *Presse* a review which you probably have already seen
> which sounds extremely favourable and describes your entire manner,
> as well as your characterization, very sympathetically and accurately.
> I could not resist showing the paper to the Empress, whereupon
> Valerie read aloud the section mentioning you. . . . In your modesty
> you never told me how difficult the rôle is, and what a performance
> was again demanded of you.

Her success brought Katharina back into favour with the management. The Emperor wrote again:

★ Actresses of the Burgtheater.

I am so glad you found Dr Förster amiable. If he is halfway a clever man and knows anything of dramatic art, he must recognize the worth of your artistic performance, and at last appreciate and treat you accordingly.

But in the midst of her triumph, just as she had been promised new and exciting parts, Katharina fell ill with scarlet fever. For a woman who was fundamentally healthy she was always either catching an infectious illness or falling down and hurting some part of her anatomy, and the Emperor constantly exhorted her to be more careful, to look where she was going, and also not to be such a difficult and refractory patient. Now he was distraught on hearing that she had scarlet fever, for though the attack was a mild one the convalescence would be long and difficult,

> . . . and as I expected of Widerhofer there follows at once a ban on further visits. I am really an unlucky person, I had just been so happy at being able to call on you today and tomorrow, and now there will be such a long separation. In these moments I feel all the more how terribly fond I am of you, and I feel so cowardly at having to listen to doctor's orders, leaving you in the lurch and not being of any help just at a time when you have so much to cope with, what with Toni and running a double establishment. If it were not for Valerie and the Empress's anxiety, I would not let myself be deterred from visiting you.

No word of the actress's illness was allowed to reach Elisabeth, who by now was in Corfu, but the news spread like wildfire through Vienna, giving rise to many a ribald joke as to when the Emperor would be coming out in a rash. On her bed of sickness poor Katharina kept worrying whether she had given her beloved sovereign scarlet fever, only to be reassured when he told her, 'Widerhofer is not at all worried about me, for he had never heard of anyone of my advanced age catching the illness.'

Another of her younger admirers who was in Vienna at the time was very much concerned about his own health. Ferdinand of Bulgaria had been a constant visitor at the Gloriettegasse in the last days, and with a certain malicious pleasure Franz Josef informed her, 'Widerhofer tells me that the Bulgarian was at your house the day before yesterday and that he is so frightened that he has had the doctor come round at once and prescribe him a remedy.' The Coburg Prince had sufficient risks to run in his new country without catching scarlet fever while on holiday in Vienna. His popularity in Bulgaria was on the wane. The Orthodox Church, subsidized by Russia, was accusing him of making Catholic propaganda, while the severity with which his Prime Minister Stambouloff was suppressing brigandage in a country of which it was the principal occupation was making him enemies in every walk of life. There were constant rumours of plots of assassination, and the Emperor wrote to Katharina Schratt:

> In the final moments before his departure your 'brotherly friend' was still in a state of agitation and apprehension and could not decide as to what route he should take for his return and under what false name he should travel. He feared there might be attempts on his life in Serbia, that the train rails might be taken up, etc. Nevertheless he arrived safely by the route through Serbia, and on that same afternoon delivered a very good speech from the throne without any of the hoarseness he had feared. I am curious as to whether he will escape getting scarlet fever.

To spend a month isolated in Hietzing at the beginning of winter, without even feeling very ill, would have tried the patience of someone less capricious than Katharina, and the Emperor kept begging her to be good

> ...if only for my sake. Widerhofer complains a great deal that you are very thoughtless and, '*pardon de l'expression*', childish. Also the telegram you sent me saying you would not spend the prescribed weeks in bed is a bad sign. Scarlet fever is a disease treacherous in its consequences. Widerhofer even told me that it could very easily cause a complaint of the jugular gland. Imagine you with a goitre!

The fear of a goitre appears to have made Katharina more reasonable, and the Emperor's letters, which were those of a lovesick lieutenant, must have consoled her in her loneliness. 'If I were not so good and so submissive to doctor's orders, and so anxious for Valerie, I would break through your glass doors just to see you for a moment.' He even talked of taking a walk under her window 'to see your dear face if only from afar'. But the window promenade never materialized, for the Empress returned from Corfu and vetoed the idea – not, one feels, out of jealousy, but because she did not want her husband to appear ridiculous.

For all his frankness and incorrigible naïvety, there were certain incidents the Emperor did not confide to his wife. In a letter to Katharina Schratt, carefully omitted in the correspondence edited by Baron Bourgoing, we read: 'Yesterday it was exactly six weeks since I left you in your bed, hoping that in two days I should be sitting on it again, and look what has happened. But now at last the sad time is drawing to an end, and we will have a wonderful reunion.'

Evidently the actress did not always receive the Emperor coiffed and corseted in the breakfast-room at Hietzing. There were other, more intimate occasions, when the coffee and *kipferls* would be served on a table beside her bed, and Katharina, looking ravishing in a beribboned and ruffled negligée, would be lying back among lace pillows and satin quilts. But these occasions were never allowed to become a habit. In several of his letters Franz Josef wrote along these lines, 'Please do not bother to get up early tomorrow morning. Let me come and sit on your bed. You know there is nothing that gives me so much pleasure.' But Katharina was versed in the art of conducting an *amitié amoureuse*. Favours were dispensed but were never to be taken for granted.

12

The First Quarrel

A year had gone by since Rudolf's death and the shooting lodge at Mayerling had been turned into a cloister, dedicated by Franz Josef to the memory of his son. The room in which Rudolf and Mary Vetséra had died was now a chapel, where the Emperor attended mass on the day of consecration. In a letter to Katharina Schratt, written in the laconic style which was characteristic of him when deeply moved, he said:

> Yesterday I was out at Mayerling and came back sad and yet comforted. The cloister has turned out well and the chapel is really lovely. There is a feeling of serenity and peace over the whole region, which looked particularly beautiful in the fine weather. The nuns seem satisfied and their cells with their very scanty and simple furnishing have a pleasant view and good air. There are even some pretty young novices among them – what a decision – to bury themselves for their entire lives within those stern convent walls. Nevertheless they appear to be happy and will do a lot of praying, so that the purpose of my bequest will be fulfilled.

There is no hint of the inner torments he must have suffered on visiting for the first time the place where Rudolf had taken his life without leaving him a note of farewell, a word of explanation. Count Hübner, who was present on this occasion, noted in his journal: 'The Emperor was heard sobbing throughout the service, murmuring to himself "My poor dear Rudolf", so that even the nuns could not restrain their tears.'

What made life still harder for Franz Josef was the fact that he disliked his nephew Franz Ferdinand who, in view of his father's age, was now looked upon as the heir apparent. The twenty-seven-year-old Archduke was awkward, unattractive and morbidly sensitive, with none of Rudolf's charm or fascination. He was a mass of complexes, being at once arrogant and tactless, suspicious and morose, with a violent temper and a touch of brutality inherited from his maternal grandfather, the notorious King Bomba of Naples. But at the same time he had a certain grandeur in his character, a breadth of vision, a determination and above all a courage which poor Rudolf had never possessed. His first act of open opposition to the family was in refusing to marry Maria Josefa of Saxony, the niece of the Emperor's old friend King Albert, whom he dismissed as a bigoted German prude with whom he could never be happy. His stubbornness won the day and Maria Josefa was married off to his younger brother Otto, a handsome, weak young man who at twenty-two found himself saddled with a dull and unresponsive wife. This may have accounted for his subsequent life of debauchery, which ended in destroying his health.

Franz Ferdinand's refusal to comply with the family's wishes, his repeated assertion that he would never marry unless he was in love, was not calculated to endear him to his uncle, who was not used either to argument or to opposition, and the Emperor showed little sympathy when his nephew fell seriously ill with tuberculosis, which attacked his lungs so badly that the doctors held out little hope of his recovery. For several years Franz Ferdinand had to absent himself from Vienna, spending his winters in Egypt and going on long sea journeys, all the time conscious that in Vienna plans were already being made for the succession of his brother Otto, whom the Emperor had summoned to the capital and installed in the magnificent Augarten Palais. With a grim determination Franz Ferdinand fought his way back to health, never forgetting or forgiving the attitude taken by his uncle during his illness. Too proud to ingratiate himself with either Franz Josef or his entourage, he retreated in silent opposition, educating himself in the affairs of state and waiting as impatiently as Rudolf had waited for his turn to come.

There is very little mention of Franz Ferdinand in the Emperor's correspondence with Frau Schratt. For all his shortcomings Franz Josef's nephew was now the heir to the throne and her future sovereign, and no criticism either of him or of any other member of the imperial family transpires in these letters. Visiting royalties, however, were often described both with irony and humour, whether it was the Prince of Wales or his nephew the German Kaiser. Faithful to the German alliance, Franz Josef paid a state visit to Berlin in the very year of Rudolf's death, when the presence of his ebullient, overbearing host, who had been his son's exact contemporary, must have grated on every nerve. The wounds were still so raw and Rudolf's hatred of Germany still fresh in his mind, but he carried on with what he believed to be his duty. On his side, the Kaiser was inclined to be too frequent and too pressing in his visits, and on more than one occasion Franz Josef complained to Katharina Schratt: '*Aussi möcht I*', which in Austrian slang is equivalent to 'If only I could get out of it.'

There was a meeting in Innsbruck when the German Kaiser passed through on his return from his memorable visit to the Turkish Sultan. The two emperors travelled together as far as the German frontier and had what Franz Josef described as 'a very bad lunch, washed down by a keg of fresh Bavarian beer, which was brought on to the train and which gave me indigestion. But their German majesties were in a very good humour and told me a great deal about their eastern journey.'

We can picture Kaiser Wilhelm in the first flush of his enthusiasm for Sultan Abdul Hamid, full of visionary plans for a railway stretching across the Syrian desert, bringing German products to every khan and caravanserai in Asia, and the ageing Emperor, brought up in the school of Metternich, to whom the course of the Danube presented the limit of his eastern ambitions.

The year 1890 brought the fall of Bismarck. The great statesman who with a single-minded ruthlessness and at the price of two wars had obtained the unification of Germany under Prussian leadership, had now been brought down by the machinations and intrigues of little men who had encouraged the young Kaiser in the delusion that he could afford to shake off the tutelage of the man who had given his family an imperial crown. Franz Josef was shocked by the news, not so much by the fact as by the way in which it had been done. For the past decade Bismarck had been working in the cause of peace, but the Kaiser assured him that Germany would be a far better friend to Austria now that Bismarck had gone, and in a public declaration went so far as to commit his country to come to Austria's assistance in the

eventuality of a Russian attack in the Balkans. An invitation to
attend German military manoeuvres in Silesia was accepted, and
for the first time since Königgrätz Franz Josef sat down to dine in
a Prussian army mess and to the horror of his aides-de-camp
appeared to enjoy the coarse jokes of the German officers. Count
Hübner noted in his journal: 'The Emperor did well to attend the
Prussian manoeuvres. One always does right when one is doing
one's duty. But one must admit there's no form of unpleasantness
our Emperor has not had to swallow.'

Even Lady Paget, who was always ready to criticize, pays
tribute to Franz Josef's nobility of character, writing on the
anniversary of Mayerling:

> How well the Emperor stands out in this year of shame and sorrow.
> In the beginning he was overcome, but soon his piety and sense of
> duty showed him the right way and he not only worked as usual but
> he has constantly been seeing people, giving dinners and appearing to
> be interested and pleased with everything. The Empress on the con-
> trary bore up very well at first but she has been getting steadily worse.
> Having led a life of unalloyed selfishness, worshipping her own health
> and beauty as the sole objects in life, she has nothing to fall back on now.
> At new year she refused all congratulations. She will of course never
> show herself again and she will become a ghost in her own lifetime.

Walpurga Paget was being hard on Elisabeth, for events during
the year had given her little chance to recover. Only a few weeks
after the anniversary of Mayerling, Julius Andrássy, whom she
regarded 'as her last and only friend', died at the end of a long and
painful illness. His death brought back a flood of memories, all the
passionate emotions of the time of the Hungarian Compromise,
when in loving Andrássy she had learnt to love his country, and he
in turn had sacrificed their love to his patriotism. Or was it rather
his ambition? For the prize was high when Franz Josef made the
former rebel the first Foreign Minister for the dual monarchy.
For Elisabeth he always remained *le chevalier sans peur and sans
reproche*, and she did not hesitate to say in front of her husband and
her daughter that now for the first time she realized how much he
meant to her, that never until now had she felt so utterly deserted,
without a single counsellor or friend. Even Valerie, who had
always resented her mother's affection for the count, had to admit

that he had probably meant more to Elisabeth than anyone else in her life; and Franz Josef, who at the time had suffered so much from his wife's infatuation for the fascinating Andrássy, now mourned him as one of the only Hungarians who was in a position to impress his people and to tell them necessary truths. The Emperor wrote in a letter to Katharina Schratt: 'Andrássy's death is a great loss to me and has very much affected the Empress who was a true friend of his and in whom he inspired a special confidence.'

Yet curiously enough it was Count Andrássy's death that aroused Elisabeth from her state of apathy. For the first time she showed herself again in public. Her face regained its former sweet expression and she acknowledged the greetings of the people she met on her walks instead of passing them by with a wild, distraught look in her eyes.

In that summer of 1890 she had to face up to Valerie's wedding, an event she had been dreading for the past four years. Out of deference to her feelings it was to be a small family affair, held in the little church of Ischl, but 'only the family' meant hundreds of relatives, Habsburgs and Salvators of the Tuscan branch, Wittelsbachs and Bourbons, who all had to be housed in the hotels and villas of the little town, already crowded with summer visitors. Katharina Schratt would have been among the visitors, standing in the crowd or perhaps privileged by a seat on a flower-decked stand. The woman who had been closest to the imperial couple during the past year would today on this family occasion have been relegated to the background. But in the prettiest of her Spitzer gowns, and an elaborate flower-trimmed hat, she would hardly have passed unnoticed and there would have been many friendly greetings, many admiring glances for the popular actress, who, like Alexander Girardi and Johann Strauss, was considered an honorary citizen of Ischl.

The whole of the little town was *en fête*, with flags and banners waving from every house and a beribboned maypole in the square in front of the church. The Spanish etiquette of the Habsburg court played no part in what was essentially a country wedding, in which the Emperor's daughter and her mother drove through the streets, banked high with Alpen-rosen, and white-dressed girls directed the traffic in place of police.

For Elisabeth it must have been the most terrible of ordeals, but she played her part with dignity and grace, though it was obviously an effort for her to smile and her hands trembled so violently she could hardly hold her fan. It was only at the end of the ceremony that she broke down on seeing Valerie so radiantly happy, so utterly without regrets. In helpless grief she said to her daughter: 'What is to become of me now?' But the husband who would have been so willing to comfort her was never taken into account, and the day after the wedding she was already planning her departure. The Emperor raised no objection when she announced her intention of going on a long sea journey; he insisted only on including a doctor in her suite.

For Franz Josef Valerie's marriage meant the end of any form of family life. From now on he lived alone in his enormous palaces, peopled by silent servants and obsequious courtiers. His daughters came on visits. Elisabeth would appear occasionally, returning from one of her endless peregrinations which only left her more miserable and bored than before, until even the dream villa in Corfu could no longer give her peace or satisfaction.

Foreign ambassadors complained of the demoralization of the Austrian court, caused by the long period of mourning and the Empress's continual absences, coupled with the fact that she would never allow any of the archduchesses really to take her place. The great families stayed more and more on their country estates and the 'Second Society' took over the town. The finance barons had consolidated their position by their open-handed generosity to charities with aristocratic patronesses and the splendour of their entertainments. It was the era of the Rothschilds, of brilliant balls and cotillons with expensive party favours, and musical soirées of superlative quality, for talent was not lacking in a city in which Brahms and Bruckner, Hugo Wolf and Mahler were all living and working at the same time. It was a world in which the brothers Strauss were still conducting the orchestras at the court balls when Gustav Mahler was appointed director of the Opera House; in which Otto Wagner was planning the most modern housing estates in Europe, while Hasenauer was completing the baroque entrance to the Hofburg, designed by Fischer von Erlach two centuries before. It was a world reflected in the Ringstrasse which more than any other street in Europe conveyed the atmosphere of a hybrid affluence typical of the Vienna of the time. The Gothic Rathaus, the Renaissance museums, the classic Parliament house and the baroque theatre all had their place on the Ringstrasse, which a Viennese wit summed up as 'a menu of various dishes served up in stone'.

The Emperor who signed the decrees and presented the medals to the artists and architects who embellished his town would far rather have left it alone. He preferred the modest old Biedermeier houses, the cobbled streets of the inner city, and the open *glacis* where the soldiers paraded in his youth. But if anyone dared criticize the Ringstrasse to his face, and there were few who ventured to do so, he would reply: 'It has nothing to do with me. I leave such matters to the experts who are more competent to judge than I am.' Yet those who looked upon him as a philistine were mistaken. Young painters holding their first shows were often surprised by a visit from the Emperor, who on these occasions invariably bought a picture. He disliked sitting for his portrait, but he rarely refused if he thought it would help the artist, and in his letters to Katharina Schratt there are several references to visits to some artist's studio and his interest in his work, subjects he never seemed to mention when writing to his wife.

Legend presents Elisabeth as a poetical, sensitive soul who suffered from her husband's lack of artistic appreciation. But the villa in Corfu that she planned and designed and filled with marbles and bronzes bought at enormous prices in Naples and Rome is a monument of bad taste, while the verses she composed in painful imitation of Heine are little better than the jingling rhymes that one finds in Christmas crackers. Those who extolled the Empress were only too ready to decry Katharina Schratt as a simple, good-natured soul who supplied the Emperor with home cooking and cosy gossip, whereas in reality she was the more artistic of the two. Though her house in Hietzing (of which some rooms are reproduced in various books on interior decoration) reflected the florid, over-cluttered taste of the period, the pictures which crowded the walls and the objects which filled the cabinets were all chosen with discrimination and taste. Knowing of her love of beautiful things, the Emperor sometimes included a valuable picture or an antique bronze among his presents. At Christmas 1890 he wrote with characteristic modesty: 'Perhaps you will be able to use this Madonna and the little picture in your new house, although you already own so many beautiful objects that to increase them may be a burden to you.'

Katharina owed most of her artistic knowledge to her early association with Hans Wilczek. It was a friendship which had lasted through the years and on more than one occasion had aroused Franz Josef's jealousy. Count Wilczek was a man he both envied and admired, whose influence over Rudolf he had bitterly resented, and whose friendship with Katharina Schratt made him both unhappy and suspicious. Wilczek had all the qualities most likely to attract a woman of her character. She was equally fascinated by the adventurer who had accompanied the Austrian expedition to the South Pole and had planted the Habsburg eagles on Franz Josef Land and as by the romantic art lover who lavished a fortune on constructing a medieval castle. But there were many candidates for Wilczek's favours and Katharina resented rivals. They had many quarrels, and it was after one of them that she evidently decided to tell the Emperor of her past relations with the Count, for Franz Josef wrote to her from Budapest:

> The frankness with which you told me the whole of the story with Count Wilczek helps to put me in the right mood to bear the long weeks of separation which lie ahead. I have no doubt that in your angelic goodness the repentant sinner will soon be taken back into favour. But I am glad to know you do not have any secrets from me any more, though really it is none of my business and I have no right to mix in your affairs.

Poor Franz Josef, he asked for so little and was all too conscious that the bounds he had set on their relationship gave him no right to interfere in her life. He had only to be separated from her for a few weeks, either when he was in Hungary or during her long quarantine for scarlet fever, and he was already assailed by doubts, tortured by the idea 'that you are no longer in the least bit fond of me and that your friendship for me is no longer that of old'.

Katharina also went through periods of depression, frightened she might lose the friendship which had become so precious to her. This was usually at a time when Valerie and her husband were visiting Schönbrunn, for since her marriage the young Archduchess had grown noticeably cooler in her manner towards the actress. And on one of these occasions Katharina wrote to the Emperor: 'There are times when I feel I am becoming a burden to you and that is a terrible feeling.' These were the moments when she needed reassurance and craved for admiration and excitement. This need for excitement was something which Franz Josef could not begin to understand, and in the summer of 1890 led to their first serious quarrel.

Ballooning had recently become the fashion in Vienna, largely through the efforts of a well-known promoter of sporting events called Victor Silberer, who by financing the first balloon trips from the Prater laid the foundations of Austrian aeronautics. It was natural that such a new and exciting sport would appeal to Katharina Schratt, and Silberer had no difficulty in persuading the actress to make an ascent one fine afternoon in June. No word was said to the Emperor, who heard of it first from the newspapers. Fears for her safety, the thought that her enemies might accuse her of seeking cheap publicity, and above all the fact that she had kept it a secret from him combined to make Franz Josef angrier with her than he had ever been before. He made an effort to control himself in a letter which included a newspaper cutting from the *Presse*, but he made no secret of his annoyance on hearing that the companion she had chosen for the trip was none other than one of the notorious Baltazzi brothers. 'I cannot refrain from furnishing you proof in the enclosed clipping from the *Presse* to show that I am quite right about preserving silence to the newspapers.' The clipping to which the Emperor referred sounds very harmless by today's standards. It reads:

> Today on 6 June the court actress Frau Katharina Schratt undertook an ascent in the 'Father Radetzky'. Many people were present for this spectacle outside the aeronautical establishment and little boys climbed high trees in the vicinity to be witnesses of the ascent. According to the plans of Herr Silberer this was to take place at half past four in the afternoon ... but the time of ascent was delayed for about three hours as owing to a misunderstanding the worker needed to inflate the balloon did not appear until about four o'clock. At first Herr Silberer

wanted to postpone the ascent, but Frau Schratt wished to keep to the programme, even with the changed travel time, and he carried out her wishes. She waited patiently till the work was completed and at seven-fifteen in the evening climbed into the gondola together with the other guests. A shrill whistle gave the signal and the 'Father Radetzky' rose into the sky. After a calm one-hour trip it landed safe and sound with its occupants at Aspern, from where Frau Schratt, Herr Baltazzi and Herr Silberer went back to Vienna. Frau Schratt, who was making a balloon trip for the first time, seemed quite undaunted.

The Emperor, who had underlined certain passages in red, could not refrain from commenting: 'You ascended at nightfall at your request, an action against Silberer's wish. How indiscreet! And you gave no thought to all your friends left behind on solid ground. But I have no right to complain or to reproach you and so I shall not bore you any longer.'

But he could not refrain from harking back to the subject, and the next day he wrote again from Budapest:

> The balloon trip lingers in my mind. In the few years you have favoured me with your friendship, this is the first time I could really be angry with you. But as I am not and cannot be angry with you, I am only hurt, but not offended. I have already told you that the air trip was a great folly ... I said at once the papers would not be silent and sent you the first proof yesterday ... I know you too well not to realize that it was only done to satisfy your curiosity, but the way in which the newspapers seized on it, the telegram which so quickly acquainted the readers of the *Pester Lloyd* with the great event gives to what in your eyes is a harmless pleasure the appearance of a publicity stunt, a straining after fame which suits neither your character nor your simple manner which I esteem so highly.

It was very rare for Franz Josef to let himself go to this extent, for he knew how Katharina disliked any form of criticism, particularly when it was criticism of her friends:

> I have never objected to you associating with Alexander Baltazzi, because that would be ridiculous.... Upon my honour it is immaterial to me that you undertook the aerial trip under his auspices. But in the eyes of the malicious world it will harm you. The way in which the newspapers seized on his presence is a reminder that he and his family

are not welcome in all circles since our disaster. And in this whole affair it annoys me to think that your false friends and open enemies will attack you with the same weapons.

So now my scolding is at an end and you may lose your temper over the old busybody as much as you like. I can only plead that you are so very dear to me, that I thought that a fatherly friend (in contrast to a brotherly one) might dare to say this much.... Should you ever want to undertake such a foolish trip again, please mention it to me sooner and I will try to talk you out of it.

Her answer only reached him six days later, six days of apprehension for fear that this time she might be really angry with him, but the letter when it arrived was just as sweet and affectionate as always. Only there was very little contrition in it. Katharina was ready to admit that she had been wrong and deserved a scolding, but though she confessed that the stage setting for her excursion into space had not been entirely perfect, she nevertheless maintained that given the opportunity she would fly again, only this time she would take care to keep it a secret, 'so that your Majesty need not be worried on my account'.

13

A Campaign of Slander

Katharina Schratt's career at the Burgtheater underwent a radical change at the beginning of the 1890s when Dr Förster's death brought an able and intelligent civil servant to the directorship of the court theatre. The appointment of Max Burckhardt, a former under-secretary of the Treasury, caused a storm of protest among the higher ranks of the theatrical Olympus, who ever since Förster's death had been plotting and intriguing over the choice of his successor. Foremost in the fray was Katharina Schratt's rival, Stella Hohenfels, whose husband Baron Berger had all the qualities and experience to make a good director, had it not been that no one, least of all Katharina Schratt, wanted Stella Hohenfels for *Madame la Directrice*.

In Hugo Thimig's memoirs, under the date of 11 January 1890, he wrote:

> What I suspected has now been proved: *die Schratt*, who is the Emperor's closest friend, is the stumbling-block which is going to prevent Berger from ever becoming director. It is understandable that *die Schratt* does not fancy the idea of *die Hohenfels* as the boss's wife. By his marriage Berger has dished his chances of ever becoming director, for an actress as overbearing and as conceited as *die Hohenfels* would be quite impossible in that position.

Prince Hohenlohe, who was in charge of the court theatre, made a wise decision in appointing an administrator rather than an artist. Burckhardt's predecessors had all been playwrights or producers, personalities in their own right, but the new Director came to the job without prejudices or preconceived ideas. His enemies even went so far as to say that he had never been more than seven times to the Burgtheater in his life. But he had immense self-confidence and common sense, and gave short shrift to temperamental actors, ignoring resignations tendered in a fit of pique, till gradually the company began to settle down under his management. He was not an imaginative man, but he knew what appealed to the box office. Unlike his predecessor, he realized that Katharina Schratt, whom the whole of Vienna knew to be the Emperor's friend, was a bigger draw than the greatest of trage-diennes, and during the eight years he ruled at the Burg she never had any need to complain of lack of work. Not all her roles were suitable to her talents. Swathed in Grecian draperies, she made an unconvincing Niobe, nor was she at ease in a fifteenth-century comedy bt Hans Sachs. But the play was sufficiently popular for the artist Franz Matsch to paint her in this role, and later for the picture to be hung in the gallery of fame of the Burgtheater. In the early 1890s she appeared in a succession of historical dramas, till the Emperor, who preferred witty drawing-room comedies, questioned somewhat wistfully, 'Must you always play serious roles?' and some of his old favourites like Claude Ohnet's *The Iron Master* and Sardou's *Let's Get Divorced* were put back among the repertoire.

Under Burckhardt's management, Raimund's delightful play *Der Verschwender* (*The Spendthrift*), with Katharina Schratt in the part of Rosl, was given for the first time at the Burg. Ten years had gone by since she had played the part opposite Alexander Girardi in the summer theatre at Ischl, but Rosl was still the role in which, according to a fastidious critic such as Hugo Thimig, she gave of her very best. Thimig, whose family was later to be so closely associated with the work of Max Reinhardt, was an inti-mate friend of Katharina's. They shared a robust sense of humour and both indulged in practical jokes, though Thimig's jokes some-times went too far for Katharina's liking. She had a weakness for the extravagant hats, laden with birds and flowers, which were then the fashion. One morning during rehearsals Thimig got hold of one of her most beautiful creations, on which a brightly col-oured bird nestled among veiling, and, tearing the bird out of the hat, placed it in a cage and brought it on to the stage just as Katharina was about to make one of her most effective entrances. Tears of anger alternated with laughter; Thimig had his ears soundly boxed and was presented with a bill for a new hat. But for all their bickering and their teasing, their friendship flourished through the years, and Katharina associated herself with Thimig and her fellow actors in the bitter controversy over the costruction of the new Burgtheater, which so many saw as the grave of their talents.

Only two months had passed since Katharina Schratt had moved to Hietzing, when Thimig had the unprecedented honour of meeting the Emperor in her house for a frank, outspoken talk over a matter on which he felt so strongly that he was ready to jeopardize his whole career, knowing that not one of his colleagues would support him should the Emperor resent his going behind the back of the Lord High Chamberlain Prince Hohenlohe. But Thimig was a man who had the actors' interests really at heart. He cared for the theatre and the traditions of the Burg which, in his opinion, could only survive in a smaller and more intimate setting. Franz Josef appears to have appreciated his integrity, and Thimig's description in his journal shows the Emperor at his happiest and most informal in the congenial atmosphere of the Schratt drawing-room.

On a fine April morning I arrived at the Gloriettegasse, full of fears and trepidation as to how I was going to be received. I was ushered into the hall from where, through a glass door, I could see into the room where the Emperor and *die Schratt* were having their breakfast. I was invited in to join them, and His Majesty greeted me in such a frank and friendly way that I began to pluck up courage and feel more at ease. He offered me a large cigar wrapped up in silver paper and, seeing me hesitate, said 'Don't worry, if it does not lay me out, it certainly won't hurt you.' Then he came straight to the point: 'Well now, you have something you want to say to me?'

Nervously I began by expressing my gratitude for the great honour he was paying me, explaining that I had no official mandate, but was merely a self-appointed spokesman for my fellow actors, most of whom would never dare to speak for themselves. We all appreciated the fact that the new theatre was magnificent. Here the Emperor interrupted: 'Beautiful? Magnificent? This is all a preamble; now let us hear what is wrong.' Encouraged by his interest I began to enumerate the various defects of the new theatre. It was too big and too high. Many of the actors trained in the old school could not get their voices across the footlights. The heavy, domed ceiling, the wide corridors behind the boxes, affected the acoustics, and this could only be put right if the whole structure was changed. The best solution of all would be to build a small theatre as an annexe to the Burg.

The Emperor was sympathetic. He himself admitted that he was dissatisfied. There would have been no difficulty in building another theatre if the present one had not cost such enormous sums of money. Then he dismissed the subject, and Thimig had to console himself in the hope that he had at least planted a seed which might one day bear fruit.

What impressed the actor most of all was the interest the Emperor showed in the theatre, an interest entirely due to the influence of *die Schratt*. His Majesty enquired as to how they were getting on under the new management, and when Thimig replied that Burckhardt was proving to be a capable, energetic and hard-working Director who would be able to maintain the necessary discipline, the Emperor commented with a smile, 'So he has already managed to impose himself on the high and mighty lords and ladies of the Burg?' and the actor realized that *die Schratt* must have entertained the Emperor to all the gossip and quarrels of her colleagues.

Thimig was in two minds as to whether Katharina's influence was entirely beneficial. She was a *lieber Kerl*, but she was also a woman of strong likes and dislikes and apt to be carried away by her emotions. A sense of power might end in going to her head and be detrimental to the theatre. In the years to come the actor never allowed his friendship with Katharina Schratt to stand in the way of what he believed to be the interests of the Burg.

Hugo Thimig was not the only one of Katharina's friends privileged to meet the Emperor in the friendly atmosphere of the Gloriettegasse. Another was the loyal and devoted Edward Palmer, who had the invidious task of attempting to control her highly disorganized finances, and was often summoned by Franz Josef to discuss the situation. Katharina dreaded these meetings, which usually uncovered debts she had happily forgotten. In his letters the Emperor refers to Palmer as 'your father-confessor' or 'your yellow father-confessor' on account of his sallow skin, and he learned to appreciate Palmer's wisdom and discretion to the extent of employing him on certain delicate missions he did not wish to entrust to a court official. When the Empress's niece, Marie Larisch, whose ambiguous role in the tragedy of Mayerling had cost her banishment from court, sought to take revenge by writing a libellous and inaccurate account of her royal relatives, it was Palmer who was asked by the Emperor to go to Munich and stop the publication at all costs.

Franz Josef, who knew nothing about finance, enjoyed his business talks with the well-informed Jewish banker, and occasionally condescended to invite him to join him in a game of Tarock, a card game of which he was particularly fond. Number nine Gloriettegasse gradually became a home for the lonely Emperor who now for the first time, by coming into contact with Katharina's servants and familiars, saw how an ordinary household worked. There was the formidable housekeeper Netty, a superb cook, bossy, sharp-tongued and as temperamental as her mistress, but sufficiently discreet to be entrusted with personal messages for the palace. There was indispensable Anna Bauer, Katharina's old-time colleague from the theatre, reliable by nature and appreciated by the Emperor as a restraining influence on her volatile friend. Katharina was apt to resent what she called her unwarranted interference, her maddening habit of always seeing the other side, and there were angry scenes when poor Frau Bauer was accused of siding with Katharina's enemies. On one of these occasions the Emperor wrote, 'I hope the scene you intended to make turned out to be milder than anticipated, and that you did not get too excited, as that is so bad for you. Now that Frau Bauer has taken upon herself the role of mother or even grandmother, she deserves to be treated with a little more respect.'

In this household of women Toni Kiss was cherished and indulged. The little Theresianist was always coming home on holidays, bringing with him his friends so that the whole house echoed with their laughter. Katharina was a wonderful mother, constantly planning treats: fireworks and conjurors in the Christmas holidays; Easter trips to Italy, to Rome and Florence; and in summer visits to the Wurstelprater, Vienna's popular fairground where young and old, rich and poor flocked to the circus and crowded round

the booths of the Punch and Judy shows. The Emperor, who
paralysed the young archdukes into silence, and whom his own
daughters found so difficult to talk to, would listen with amusement to Toni Kiss telling of his adventures in the Wurstelprater,
with all the brio and gift of mimicry he had inherited from his
mother.

But Toni's first loyalty was to his father, whose rare appearances
in Vienna made him seem all the more romantic. Even the Emperor had to postpone his visits to the Gloriettegasse when Nicholas Kiss came home on leave. Katharina's estranged husband was
finding life as an Austrian vice-consul in Tunis a sad contrast to
the Vienna Jockey Club, and he was always complaining to the
Ministry of Foreign Affairs for not finding him a post more
worthy of his talents. Regarding himself as a martyr in the interests
of his family, he considered he had every right to profit by his
wife's good fortune, and the watchful Palmer noted the large sums
drawn by Katharina Schratt whenever Nicholas Kiss was passing
through Vienna. As a proud Hungarian, Katharina's husband
regarded it as his duty to protect her reputation, and on one
embarrassing occasion he challenged a fellow member of the
Jockey Club to a duel, accusing him of having cast aspersions on
his wife. The accusations were apparently unfounded and the affair
was settled with as little publicity as possible: 'I hope you are
relieved over the outcome of the duel,' wrote Franz Josef to his
friend.

Katharina was beginning to feel that Kiss had not enough to do
in Tunis, and she asked the Emperor whether it would not be
possible to find her husband a busier, as well as a more remuner-
ative post. The Foreign Minister Count Kálnoky, who does not
appear to have had a very high opinion of Kiss's diplomatic talents,
had nothing better to offer him than the post of Vice-Consul in
Barcelona, and in November 1892 Franz Josef wrote to her,

> At your wish I am reporting to you about my conversation with
> Kálnoky. He is again willing to appoint Kiss and give him the title of
> Vice-Consul, but maintains that it is not quite clear whether Kiss has
> either the interest or the application to accept the appointment. At any
> rate he said that Kiss should come to see him again or otherwise go
> and see Pasetti, the section head. I shall also have the latter informed

that I should like the matter to be settled soon. And so I hope I shall finally succeed in giving you some peace of mind.

A month later Katharina had the satisfaction of hearing that her inconvenient husband had been posted to the busy Mediterranean port of Barcelona, where his holidays would be much more limited. But for Toni's sake she never made any attempt to dissolve the marriage ties, and Nicholas Kiss could always rely on IOUs signed in Barcelona being settled in Vienna.

Given his father's example, it is strange that Katharina Schratt should have made no attempt to instil some sense of economy in her son, but Toni was brought up in the greatest luxury, consorting chiefly with the sons of the rich. The actress, who was without any snobbery in the choice of her own friends, was childishly pleased when Toni brought home the sons of aristocrats. But all her efforts to give him a suitable background could not protect him from the spite and malice of her enemies. She had only known the Emperor for a few years when she became the victim of scurrilous and anonymous letters, the contents of which were never divulged but which caused her considerable pain. Count Kielmannsegg referred in his memoirs to a conversation with Count Taaffe, who recounted with considerable amusement how he had been summoned by the Emperor, who told him in a shy, somewhat embarrassed fashion that the court actress Frau Katharina Schratt was being pestered with anonymous letters, and that he would like the matter taken up by the police and treated with the utmost discretion. But in spite of the efficiency of the secret police, the author of these poison pen letters was never discovered, either then or at a later date when a far more serious incident occurred.

It was towards the end of the school year in the summer of 1892 when Toni Kiss received an anonymous letter consisting of a vicious attack on his mother. Only someone consumed with hate and envy of Katharina Schratt could have been so despicable as to attack her through her twelve-year-old son. She was in Karlsbad at the time, and her first reaction was to interrupt the cure and to return to Vienna to be with Toni. But on this occasion, as so often in her life, both the Emperor and Edward Palmer, the two men who loved her most, got together to dissuade her from taking any action which would give too much importance to a matter which, for Toni's sake, it was better to ignore. The most touching of all was Franz Josef's concern over a matter for which he felt himself to be largely responsible. A hitherto unpublished letter, headed Schönbrunn, 24 June 1892, reads,

> Yesterday when I came back to my room I found a letter in your dear handwriting waiting for me on my writing desk. It was a joyful surprise as I had only received the last one the day before. But I was transfixed with horror when I read the contents and could think of nothing else all day. Also at night I could hardly sleep and kept worrying about you, for the beastliness of it over-reaches anything one could imagine and I can understand you being in despair. There is such a studied malice about the wickedness. What makes me profoundly unhappy is the thought that I am largely the cause of all the annoyance you have had to put up with in the last years, and also your present misery. If only I could help you. If only there was some way of exposing the author to prevent him from doing further damage. Worst of all is the impression which this horrible letter must have made on Toni, and one must think of some way to stop it from leaving any permanent mark, or in any way undermining the relationship between you. But this is difficult to judge before I have read the letter and its monstrous contents.
>
> I am waiting with impatience to hear all the news from Palmer, who I hope will be able to clear up the situation and, being a wise and practical man, find some solution. I thought it best to send for him direct and to have him come and see me in town as soon as he returns from Karlsbad. . . . Hawerda knows his address. . . . I am glad you have been dissuaded from coming to Vienna. The journey and the stay in town in the middle of your cure and in your present state of agitation would be very bad for your health. I worry about that a lot.

Both the Emperor and Katharina Schratt appear to have relied entirely on Palmer who, on his return to Vienna, went straight to the Director of the Theresianum School. The two men agreed that the matter should not be taken too seriously, for otherwise Toni might become frightened and suspicious. Acting on Franz Josef's instructions, Palmer then visited the police president who must have been somewhat surprised at finding the Jewish banker, whom he remembered from the days when he lent his apartment to the Crown Prince Rudolf and his friends, now bringing him instructions from the Emperor.

Meanwhile Franz Josef had read the infamous letter,

> ... which after all is only a collection of obscenities and therefore less dangerous than if it was a properly written pamphlet. Nor do I agree with you and Palmer in thinking that it is written by an educated person who has deliberately changed the style and handwriting. You should not take it so much to heart. I hope that Toni, for it is he whom one worries about chiefly, will, if properly handled, and given your loving care at Ischl, end up by looking upon it as nothing more than a jealous and spiteful attack against you. For this reason I think that Palmer has the right idea in wanting to show him some of those poison pen letters you have at the Gloriettegasse, for then he can compare the writing and see that they are all written by the same hand and only with the intention of hurting you as much as possible. In the end he will forget all about it. But what really upset me was to hear from Palmer how ill you are looking, and now that it is time for the 'Stille Woche' I worry even more.

Two days later came better news. Edward Palmer had invited Toni Kiss out on Sunday and found him his usual self, calm and very little interested in the letter, a large part of which he had not understood and of which he had not been able to read the hand-writing. Palmer had also had a second interview with the police president who had every hope of finding the culprit, and on his return to Karlsbad he was able to report to the Emperor that the '*gnädige Frau*' was beginning to recover her spirits. The banker had, however, incurred Franz Josef's displeasure by confiding the story to Count Wilczek, and there is a distinct note of asperity in an otherwise loving letter to his friend: 'I find it quite unnecessary that Palmer should have related everything to Count Wilczek, for the less people know about it the better.'

The first person whom Franz Josef confided in was his wife, who happened to be in Karlsbad at the time, taking one of her numerous cures, and who was nearly as indignant as her husband at the outrage committed against 'the friend'. All that was best in her came to the surface and she went out of her way to comfort Katharina Schratt, and to be seen with her in public. 'Now you realize again what an angel she is,' wrote Franz Josef, full of love and gratitude towards his wife. During the few summer weeks she spent in Ischl, visits which every year grew shorter, the Empress invited the actress and her son to tea at the Kaiser Villa, taking the little boy for a walk in the gardens and speaking to him of his mother with sweetness and affection, telling him what a wonderful person she was and what a help she had been to her in the most tragic months of her life.

Over half a century later, when Toni Kiss was an elderly retired diplomat, he could still remember that summer afternoon at Ischl, walking with the Empress through the park to the marble pavilion which she called her secret house, where she told him that only the most privileged were allowed to enter, and with her wonderful radiant smile made him feel that he himself was among the most privileged of all. In the following years he was the proud recipient of beautifully wrapped parcels from the court confectioners and of *glacé* fruits from the French Riviera, with little notes from 'your friend Elisabeth'.

That was what he remembered, or rather all that he wanted to remember, of an incident which had given his mother so much heartache at the time. Katharina Schratt always believed, and also led her son to believe, that the poison pen letters had been sent by a jealous colleague. This was partly the reason why Toni Kiss grew up disliking her contact with the theatre, so that he showed little sympathy when she was involuntarily retired. None of the mothers of his school friends was on the stage, nor had they ever received anonymous letters.

The Emperor's correspondence with Katharina Schratt, so carefully edited by Baron Bourgoing, a personal friend of Toni Kiss, hardly mentions the episode in which the Emperor's concern for the feelings of a twelve-year-old boy show us the most human and lovable side of his character. All one reads are a few lines under the date of 8 September 1892, when on the occasion of Katharina's name-day Franz Josef wrote, 'I hope that in the coming year you will be spared the grief which unfortunately you have had through my fault.' A brief footnote gives the explanation.

Both Toni Kiss, and his mother in her old age, were anxious to establish the fact that she had been the friend both of the Emperor and of the Empress. With all the appearance of truth, Katharina

Schratt once told Countess Wilczek, the daughter-in-law of her former lover, that if there had ever been as much as a *Pussl* (a kiss) between her and His Majesty he would never have allowed her to visit his wife. But it was the *pusseln* and the *streicheln* (the kissing and the stroking) to which Franz Josef keeps referring in his letters, and the happy intimacy of the Gloriettegasse, which helped to make life bearable for the tired, overburdened Emperor.

14

Balkan Machinations

The Emperor was growing old, and with age he became more demanding and exacting in his relations with the woman who was willing to sacrifice for him all except her independence. He was aware of how tiresome he could be, and would write, 'I know what a boring old fellow I am, and it is wonderful how you put up with me.' But the more he grew to love her, the more possessive he became, the more jealous of the life she enjoyed with all the zest of a woman who refused to accept middle age, and still wanted to share in all the pleasures of youth. What he resented most was the actress's natural craving for publicity. A charity performance at Ronacher's Variety Theatre, in which Katharina Schratt appeared with a well-known Hungarian actress in Nestroy's famous satire *Der Böse Geist, Lumpazivagabundus* (*The Evil Spirit, The Vagabond Rascal*) met with imperial disapproval. For Nestroy, one of the greatest of Austrian dramatists, had during his lifetime often been banned from the court theatre on account of his political satires, and the Emperor did not enjoy having his friend appear in the role of Nestroy's shoemaker in company with Ilka Palmay who, though married to a Count Kinsky, was a lady of very questionable morals. 'I cannot understand you playing Knieriem in the company of Palmay. I console myself in thinking that it is good for your profession, and that the purpose is a charitable one. Do not be offended at my writing this, and remember that it is only because I am so very fond of you.' The fact that she revelled in it only made it worse.

Tonight if I wake up I shall think of you at Ronacher's, where you will probably be till dawn. I am told that even the rehearsals took place at night instead of at a more healthy hour. Personally I shall be glad when all the commotion is over, though you seem to be loving it. Yesterday in *Floh* [a comic illustrated paper] I found a picture of you as Knieriem, arm in arm with Palmay. I am sure you must have already seen this work of art.

There were so many things the poor Emperor disapproved of. He was even jealous of the stage kisses given to any actor with whom he suspected she might be intimate, jealous of all the ministers and *Hofrats* who patronized the theatre and paid court to the leading ladies of the Burg. Nor were his dislikes confined to men. There was the fascinating Princess Metternich, who inspired the ballad

> *Es gibt nur eine Kaiserstadt*
> *Es gibt nur ein Wien*
> *Es gibt nur eine Fürstin*
> *Die Metternich Pauline.*
> (There is only one Imperial city
> There is only one Vienna
> There is only one Princess
> Who is Pauline Metternich.)

but whose very popularity made her *persona non grata* at court. Franz Josef had never forgiven her for having been more loudly cheered than the Empress on the occasion of the first May Day flower *corso* in the Prater. Katharina Schratt, however, was flattered when Princess Pauline enlisted her help in organizing *tableaux vivants* and amateur theatricals in aid of some of her numerous charities. 'I cannot see why you give yourself so much trouble, it will only tire you,' wrote the Emperor. But Katharina was never tired when she enjoyed herself. What really exhausted her was what he called a quiet day at Ischl, which she once described in detail to the German Ambassador, Count Eulenburg:

I get up at five in the morning and go and bathe in the Ischl [an ice-cold mountain stream said to have health-giving properties]. I then dress and at seven o'clock His Majesty comes for breakfast and stays till about ten, when I accompany him back to the imperial villa. After this I rest and dine, and at about three o'clock, whether it is rain or fine, I accompany both Their Majesties up the mountain for another three or four hours, after which you can imagine how glad I am to get to bed at eight o'clock.

It may have been considered a great honour to be invited to go walking with Their Majesties, but it must also have been a considerable strain, for the Empress never spoke above a whisper, and never stopped to rest. Yet Franz Josef could not understand why the actress should want to leave dear, cosy Ischl and go off on adventurous expeditions with her friends, crawling up glaciers and spending the night in mountain huts, with companions whose names she did not always tell him. Those wide blue eyes, that open smiling face, could be very evasive at times.

Katharina loved the Emperor, but she could not dedicate her whole life to a man who had so little time to spare for her. The delicious intimacy of Hietzing could not be recaptured in the stuffy atmosphere of Ida von Ferenczy's drawing-room which, throughout the winter months, was still their only meeting-place, except for an occasional walk in the freezing gardens of Schönbrunn, usually at a time when a busy actress would like to have had a rest. But she missed the Emperor when he was away. During those weeks in Budapest, which she called 'the weeks of fasting', daily letters would pass between the Gloriettegasse and the Castle of Buda, and the Emperor would write in a somewhat laboured attempt to be poetical that 'the *Streicherln* (little kisses) flew to and fro filling the air like so many bacilli'. In an excerpt from one of Katharina's letters we read, 'This evening I ensconced myself snug and warm in an armchair so that I could read your dear letter through in comfort, and then with the letter still in my hand I shut my eyes and dreamt for a little while, for after all it is not forbidden to dream and it sometimes makes one feel so much better.'

It was the poor Emperor who really suffered during those 'weeks of fasting', writing, 'You are the only ray of light in my drab life, my only consolation.' Even the presence of his wife and the inevitable Greek professor did little to raise his spirits. Elisabeth's willingness to come to Budapest and her refusal to stay in Vienna were estranging her more and more from her subjects and making life increasingly difficult for the Emperor. But by now she realized that all she had to do to placate her husband was to be friendly with Frau Schratt, and in the early spring of 1891 she invited the actress for the first time to visit them in Budapest. It was a gesture bitterly opposed by the whole entourage and enormously appreciated by Franz Josef, who was as excited as a schoolboy at the prospect, writing to Katharina 'Do not forget to obtain permission from Burckhardt for your excursion here, for otherwise there might be a conflicting repertoire and that would be too frightful.' But Katharina, who was never shy of asking for leave, had already obtained permission for a fortnight's holiday on the French Riviera, from where she travelled directly from Nice to Budapest. Unfortunately she was so unlucky at the casino at Monte Carlo that she had gambled away all her travel money and had to borrow for the journey. 'This time you seem to have played very heavily, and the passion seems to be growing worse,' wrote Franz Josef, but whatever scolding he intended vanished in the joy of seeing her.

> The news that you are to arrive at Budapest on the evening of the twenty-eighth has made me so happy, for then there will be a possibility of seeing you already on the morning of the first, and not having to wait till the dinner hour of five o'clock. As to the walk and the lunch on the second, that remains the same, for you must give us all the time you can. The Empress greets you most cordially and sends you the message not to breakfast too heartily on the first, so that you will have a good appetite at five o'clock. Like all good *Hausfrauen* she likes stuffing her guests full of food.

Whether *Blutwurst* (blood sausage) featured on the royal menu, or whether Katharina, who had a fondness for rich, indigestible food, indulged in it on her own, both Emperor and Empress were anxious to know after the visit whether the *Blutwurst* had had any adverse effects. But Katharina must have had not only an excellent digestion, but a tremendous resistance in order to stand up to the long journey from the Riviera to Budapest, where on arrival she was given no time to rest at her hotel before she was driven up to the Castle. After being shown the rooms she had so often envisaged in her thoughts, she was taken on what must have been a cold, wet walk in the gardens at the time of the first thaws, when the ice on the Danube was beginning to break up and great floes drifted down the river.

The whole of the two-day visit was entirely taken up by the Emperor and his endless questions as to what she had done and whom she had seen in the gay Riviera world so remote from his own. He had nothing but disagreeable news to report from home. The Hungarians were being more intransigent than ever. Count Taaffe was trying to introduce reforms for the benefit of the minorities, which were being bitterly opposed by both the Hungarians and the German liberals. Everyone was obsessed with their own interests, and he was tired and discouraged. Though he could still follow the hunt at Gödollo, as well as any of his younger officers, and go shooting wild boar in the worst of weathers, he now felt he was getting old. But Katharina encouraged him. 'Nonsense, Your Majesty, you should have heard the crowds on the Ring at the time of the German Kaiser's visit, all saying he could not hold a candle to Your Majesty who is so much more handsome.' And Franz Josef, who had been so irritable and disgruntled of late, beamed with pleasure and good humour. When it came to saying goodbye he could hardly bear to have her go. In the end she missed her train and arrived in Vienna late at night with a rehearsal early on the following morning. But the Emperor's letter of gratitude made the whole of the exhausting journey seem worthwhile:

> Thanks, thanks and thanks again for having come to visit us; for the exquisite violets which finally arrived yesterday evening, and above all for being so particularly kind to me in the two days of your stay here, and for having devoted so much time to me. Now I feast on the memory of those glorious days until I shall have the happiness of seeing you in Vienna. We talked a great deal about you after you had left, for the Empress also remembers your visit with pleasure.

The Emperor was continually assuring Katharina of Elisabeth's friendship and goodwill, so much so that one is inclined to question the sincerity of a friendship about which the actress herself sometimes had her doubts. The Empress might find her sympathetic and enjoy her company, and in her reasoning moments be grateful for her help. No one could have shown her gratitude in a more charming fashion than at the time of the anonymous letters. But Elisabeth did not always reason. There were moments when a black cloud passed over her brain, when she felt depressed and bored and haunted by the terror of growing old. Then a cruel, bitter streak would come out in her character, and it would amuse her to make mischief among her entourage, playing off one against the other, or to make unkind remarks to Valerie, reducing her to tears, or to accuse her long-suffering husband of indifference and neglect. At such times she would resent the Emperor's open admiration for the plump little actress whom she had never thought of as anything more than a cosy companion, and she would lash out against her with a mocking, wicked tongue. She, who was obsessed with her own weight and would complain she was 'becoming as fat as a tub' when the bathroom scales touched eight stone, hardly a normal weight for a woman of five foot seven, would take delight in making fun of poor Katharina's unsuccessful attempts to slim. Included amongst her papers is a cruel little rhyme which the Empress must have written in a particularly nasty mood:

> Imbued with aping mania
> Despite her pounds of fat
> She longs to play Titania
> Poor Katharina Schratt.

Elisabeth always saw herself in the role of Titania, but now Titania was in her middle fifties and excessive dieting had reduced her to what even her doting husband described as 'nothing but skin and bone'.

Lady Paget, who saw the Empress on one of her rare appearances, at a Hofburg reception to celebrate the engagement of her eldest grand-daughter, was shocked to see how much she had aged in the last years.

Nine and a half years ago when I saw her first she was still a beautiful and apparently young woman, in a white dress gleaming with embroidery of gold and silver with jewels in her hair standing in the blaze of hundreds of candles. Now she stood in a waning light, clad in transparent but deepest black, a crown of fluffy black feathers on her auburn hair, a ruche of black gauze disguising as much as possible the thinness of her throat. Her face looked like a mask, the lips and cheeks too red.

Yet still she persisted in her dieting, so that her devoted lady-in-waiting Marie Festetics wrote home from Corfu, 'I believe if I did not insist so much she would long since have died from starvation.' But the legend of her beauty survived, and even sensible, clear-eyed Katharina, who was alive to all her short-comings, still looked up to her as an ideal of loveliness, whom she vainly tried to emulate. Cure after cure was taken up – the milk diet, the fruit diet, the fashionable cold water Kneipp cure which only succeeded in giving her bronchitis. She even started on a hay cure, of which the Emperor wrote with a certain sarcasm that he was looking forward to seeing her immersed in a hayrick in a field at Ischl. There were also ordinary starvation cures which made Katharina feel so faint and bad-tempered that they were usually given up after a couple of days and ended in an orgy at Sacher's.

One of the chief links between the Empress and the actress was the interest they took in every new slimming cure. Elisabeth was always enquiring as to how many pounds 'the friend' had lost on the latest diet. But Katharina refused to divulge her weight, or to confess that she had already given up the cure, and Franz Josef would write, 'It is extraordinary how the two of you are always experimenting with the same slimming cures. Personally I disapprove of diets and I find scales a calamity.'

But there was one cure Katharina never failed to take. Year after year she returned to Karlsbad, spending the prescribed three weeks at the Schloss Hotel and regularly drinking the waters. Karlsbad was still among the most fashionable of spas, and Katharina enjoyed the smart international set, however much she might write to Franz Josef that she was counting the days till their reunion in dear, peaceful Ischl. Most of her friends and admirers were to be found at Karlsbad – the faithful Palmer; the 'fat Springer', one of the wealthiest of the *Finanz-Barons* of the 1890s; Nicholas Dumba, the Macedonian millionaire who had amassed a colossal fortune trading in the Balkans; the art Maecenas Baron Shey, who had kept Laube's Stadttheater going throughout the great crash of 1873; and, whether by accident or design, Prince Ferdinand of Bulgaria, who always managed to take his cure at the same time as 'Frau Kathi'.

During the first two years of his reign Ferdinand had not dared to leave Bulgaria for fear of revolution fomented by Russian agents. He had lived in continual fear of assassination, depending for distraction on the limited resources of a little Balkan town;

ruled and bullied by his Prime Minister Stefan Stambouloff, whose manners were far removed from those of the 'First Society' to which he was accustomed. But the Coburg Prince had shown himself to be of sterner stuff than anyone would have suspected, and the Emperor Franz Josef was the first to pay tribute to his unexpected courage and the ability with which he was bringing stability and progress to a backward country. Foreign governments had been persuaded to trade and invest in Bulgaria, and a loan from the City of London was transforming Sofia from an eastern village into a modern European capital. But the official recognition he craved for was still being withheld, for not one of his royal cousins dared to affront the Russian Tsar, who looked upon Ferdinand as a usurper. His subjects, above all his over-zealous Prime Minister, were pressing him to marry and produce an heir, and it must have been galling for someone as vain and proud as Ferdinand to find that not even the impoverished Grand Duke of Tuscany, living on Austrian bounty, was willing to give him his daughter in marriage as long as he was proscribed by Alexander III.

The Coburg Prince was to find in Katharina Schratt a more useful friend than all his royal cousins. There was the unfortunate occasion, on his first return to Vienna in the autumn of 1890, when she nearly gave him scarlet fever. But the tone of the letter written on his return to Sofia and addressed in the familiar 'thou' shows that their friendship had survived this contretemps and progressed to a degree of intimacy unsuspected by Franz Josef.

My dearest friend, my pen is broken so I have today a different handwriting. It seems to me that it rather resembles yours. I wouldn't be surprised, for you are constantly in my thoughts, so I may well have begun to copy your handwriting. How are you now, for you have been very, very ill? May God in His mercy watch over you, and protect you from any further mishaps. I enclose a photograph of my little study. . . . When am I going to have your portrait in oils to hang up on the wall? You promised it so please do not forget. I am well. Both here and in the country everyone seems to be content. We are being very industrious and with God's help hope to prove ourselves worthy of our task. Yesterday and today there was deep snow on the ground, but up to then everything was still green and in bloom. My gardener in Philippopolis sent me yesterday a box full of violets, Parma, Russian and white ones, and tall lilies whose scent fills the rooms and helps to counteract the stink of my ministers. Shall I send you some (I don't mean my ministers).

My cook is thoroughly bad and one has presented himself who says he was with you, so we shall see.

It was a brave letter to write for a man who had returned to his country to find half his army on the verge of revolt, and one of the most popular and legendary figures of the Serbo–Bulgarian War the ringleader of a vast conspiracy in which nearly the whole of the Sofia garrison was involved.

Major Panitza was not a Russian agent but a disaffected Macedonian, who had loved Alexander of Battenberg and had a personal grudge against Prince Ferdinand. The plot was betrayed to Stambouloff only a few days before the court ball at which the *coup d'état* was due to take place. It was a ball such as had never been seen in Bulgaria, organized by the Prince's mother with her memories of the Tuileries. Gastronomic delicacies had been brought in from Vienna by the Orient Express. The *cotillion* favours came from Paris. But it cannot have been a very pleasant evening for the guests, of whom over a hundred were said to have been involved in the conspiracy, and who must have been wondering when they were going to be arrested. Prince Ferdinand is said to have 'moved through the rooms with Princess Clémentine on his arm, his face a set mask of suppressed fury, pointing out to his mother each conspirator in turn'.

Commenting on the events ten days after the ball, Franz Josef wrote to Katharina Schratt:

> Yesterday I received a detailed report from Sofia. The conspiracy seems to have been rather serious, and your 'brotherly friend' appears to have shown great courage and calm. The Prince and his retinue carried loaded revolvers in their pockets at the court ball, at which the trouble was to have broken out. But it was frustrated by the arrest of Major Panitza immediately before.

The Emperor was so impressed by Prince Ferdinand's courage that he instructed his foreign minister to congratulate both him and Stambouloff on having foiled the conspiracy.

Arrests at a court ball, revolvers hidden in gala uniforms – the perfect setting for a Sardou play – Katharina Schratt was in her element, and full of admiration for her heroic Prince.

Your Royal Highness can imagine how eagerly I follow the news published in the press and everything that has been written about you. How happy I am to think that through your bravery, your intelligence and your true nobility of character, you are managing to overcome your difficulties to the general admiration of Europe. On all sides one hears nothing but praise.

Panitza was sentenced to death in the early summer of 1890. Ferdinand did his best to commute the death sentence to one of imprisonment, for fear that the execution of such a popular officer would only lead to further unrest. But Stambouloff was adamant that clemency would only be interpreted as weakness. Rather than assist at an execution of which he disapproved, the Prince boarded the Danube steamer for Vienna, and by the end of June 1890 was back in Karlsbad, 'strolling down the *"Alte Wiese"* with the charming Frau Käthi', pouring out his troubles into her sympathetic ears in the hopes that she might impart them to 'her illustrious friend'.

The 'illustrious friend' was more than a little jealous of this intimacy, and was not entirely convinced when Katharina assured him that she had kept the poor Prince waiting for weeks for a letter, and in order to avoid his attentions had registered at the hotel under the name of 'Frau Kiss'. 'I do not believe you will avoid the Bulgarian, for he is much too interesting and entertaining for you not to want his company, and he will surely not be irreconcilable because you have not answered his letters.... I am already curious about all you will have to tell me about him.'

Though the Emperor's relations with the Bulgarian Prince were to go through many vicissitudes, Franz Josef always retained a certain admiration for his talents, and in the summer of 1891 he allowed himself to be persuaded largely by Katharina Schratt to receive him in private audience at Gastein. It was a gesture calculated to infuriate the Russian Tsar, who sent his ambassador to complain at the Ballhausplatz that this act of recognition was in direct violation of the terms of the treaty of Berlin, to which

Count Kálnoky replied that his imperial master had received Prince Ferdinand not as the ruler of Bulgaria but as the Prince of Saxe-Coburg Gotha, who was related by marriage to the imperial family.

The Tsar would have been still more furious had he suspected that the little actress with whom he had flirted one summer's night at Kremsier so many years ago had been partly instrumental in bringing about this meeting. Preserved among the Schratt papers is a letter, almost fulsome in its gratitude, addressed by Prince Ferdinand to Katharina Schratt and dated 17 June 1891;

> I have been made so happy by this act of gracious condescension that I do not know whom I should thank the most, him or you – so much friendliness – so much sincerity, and above all so much wisdom, such as I will never forget. But I am so nervous about what will have been said about me. I will be accused of having talked too much, of having tried to show off. But I had to say everything that was on my mind. At the same time I was so shy and embarrassed that in spite of my huge nose I was hardly able to breathe.

Katharina would have smiled on getting this letter. The Prince was always so exaggerated, so dramatic in his language. She did not see herself in the least as a political Egeria, but she liked helping her friends, whether it was a Prince of Saxe-Coburg or a poor actor who had fallen on evil days.

15

A Faithful Minister Leaves

A private audience with the Emperor Franz Josef had not improved Prince Ferdinand's matrimonial prospects. Only a fortnight before he had written to Katharina Schratt from Karlsbad a letter full of bitterness over the failure of his courtship of Luisa of Tuscany.

> Shame and anger have made me feel quite ill. Oh these Italian highnesses! My poor mother has been so outraged by their falseness and their dishonourable behaviour that she has taken to her bed. It is all so humiliating and it is I who have been made to look like a fool. How could I have ever been so stupid.... Tomorrow afternoon at four o'clock I shall be arriving in Vienna and will be entirely at your disposal. I beg of you, Kathi, to be kind towards an unfortunate, broken individual. Let me take courage from your strength and spirit and let me pour out my heart to you. At ten-twenty I have to be at the Franz Josef Station to return to Karlsbad. But from five to nine o'clock I shall be entirely at your service, so if it is not too unpleasant in town can we meet at number nine [Gloriettegasse]. It would be terrible if you were acting that evening – couldn't you possibly put it off? For it is vital that I should see you. Your friend is so utterly devoted to you, and I like to think that also you, Kathi, have a certain affection for a faithful old fellow who kisses your hand with fondest love.

The 'faithful old fellow' was thirty-three at the time, seven years younger than the actress, and for all his anger at his matrimonial rebuffs does not appear to have been a very convincing suitor. Luisa of Tuscany evidently told him quite openly that he 'only wanted to marry her because she was an Austrian archduchess' and that the word 'archduchess' stood for 'love' in his vocabulary as he had promised his ministers to return to Bulgaria engaged to one. In Luisa's memoirs we read that the Prince was so dumbfounded that he made no attempt to contradict her, and after she had refused his proposal did nothing but 'wring his large white hands, repeating "*Mon Dieu, Mon Dieu*"'.

Katharina Schratt was more sympathetic to the vicissitudes of an unlucky suitor, for she knew how hard and domineering Stambouloff could be, and how lonely someone as highly civilized as the Coburg Prince must feel in his Balkan capital, where there was as yet not even the amenity of a court theatre. Preserved among her papers is the rough draft of a letter, so sympathetic and intimate in tone it could well have made Franz Josef jealous:

> My thoughts are often in Sofia and I would give anything to go there myself, either for Christmas or Easter leave, but as there are no magic cloaks to render one invisible how could I come without compromising us both? Perhaps when you have founded the court theatre you will invite me as a guest artist. Your protégé Gabillon★ could be the director, or would you, my dear friend, like me to come in disguise? Only let me know in time what role you would like me to assume. I am sending you the two pictures I promised you. Dr Schulz who is bringing them is travelling by the new train to Constantinople with a colleague from the Ministry of Commerce. I recommend him as my ambassador, for he will give Your Royal Highness the latest news of my insignificant self, apart from which he knows all that is going on in Vienna and is a friend of everyone so he will be able to tell you all that has been going on since you left, and on his return I look forward to having an eye-witness account of all that has been happening in Bulgaria.

Dr Schulz, who was a highly intelligent civil servant, would have been far too tactful to disillusion Frau Schratt over her 'sad and lonely friend' who was consoling himself quite happily with a charming Madame Petkoff, the wife of one of his aides-de-camp who was later promoted to the post of commander-in-chief of the Bulgarian army. Madame Petkoff shared the Prince's favours with a succession of handsome bodyguards ready to pander to his ambivalent tastes. But whatever might be those tastes, Stambouloff was determined he should marry. And at the beginning of February 1893 Franz Josef reported to Katharina Schratt, 'I have just received a telegram from the Bulgarian in Florence where he announces his engagement to the Duke of Parma's daughter....

★ A member of the Burgtheater.

So our friend is now happily settled and the rest is in the hands of God.'

The Emperor, who had taken a benevolent interest in the marriage and who had helped to bring it about, was particularly pleased over the discomfiture of Russia. A clause in the Bulgarian constitution stipulated that the heir to the throne should be baptized in the Orthodox faith. But the Duke of Parma had refused to give his consent to the marriage unless the children were brought up as Catholics, and it had required all Stambouloff's dynamic energy to persuade the Bulgarian National Assembly to alter the constitution and facilitate a marriage so vital to the country's interests. The patriotic statesman made himself fully responsible for a measure which would infuriate the Russians and could well cause further unrest in the country. Ferdinand, who by now had taken an intense dislike to his Prime Minister, was ready to let him take the blame for whatever troubles might occur. But contrary to expectations the marriage proved to be immensely popular with the Bulgarian people, and though both the Prince and his mother had hoped for a more spectacular match than the daughter of a dispossessed duke, they consoled themselves with the fact that the Bourbon-Parmas were descended from King Charles x of France, whereas King Louis Philippe had been only a usurper. The betrothal ceremonies were held in Vienna and a family dinner at the Hofburg held in honour of Prince Ferdinand and his father-in-law satisfied Coburg pride. But the marriage was strictly one of convenience and Ferdinand never made the slightest pretence of loving his bride. Franz Josef had no illusions on the subject, as is apparent in one of his letters to Katharina Schratt in which he asks her 'as to whether the Bulgarian has already adapted himself to his role as a future married man? . . . I have called on the bride and her mother at their hotel; unfortunately the Princess is not at all pretty.'

The actress's feelings towards her 'brotherly friend' appear to have cooled off after his marriage. Rumours of his ingratitude to Stambouloff, his absurd pretensions of playing the royal autocrat, the long letters in which he spoke only of himself and his grievances, made her feel that the witty and delightful companion with whom she had walked in the woods of Karlsbad was degenerating into an eastern tyrant. The Emperor agreed with her: 'He is a tyrant and a petty one at that.' From Gastein he wrote at the beginning of July to tell her that

> ... the Bulgarian Princess is already expecting a child.... Meanwhile our friend has again committed a folly. Two of his best and most loyal officers, who would not follow etiquette and the order of precedence set up in his famous levée, have not only been placed under arrest, which would not have done any harm, but have actually been dismissed from his service. He makes himself ridiculous with these pretensions.

Relations between the Prince and Stambouloff were rapidly becoming untenable, and the Emperor wrote to the actress: 'I hope *Le petit Ferdinand* will try and control his nerves and irritation and come to an understanding with his minister, who is certainly not always easy to get on with but nevertheless almost indispensable.' But after the marriage which Stambouloff had worked so hard to achieve, Ferdinand felt sufficiently strong to start undermining the position of the man who, having fought for the independence of Bulgaria and defeated Russian intrigues, now represented the chief stumbling block to a reconciliation with the Tsar and Ferdinand's recognition by the great powers.

Balkan politics were becoming too devious for Katharina Schratt, and since he was a married man Ferdinand no longer had the same claim on her affection. His letters remained unanswered, and by the Christmas of 1893 he was complaining of having received from her no more than a card, in spite of the card being attached to a very handsome present of a diamond and ruby tiepin which, even in the sumptuous days of the *belle époque*, could hardly be considered the gift of a casual acquaintance. Nevertheless it failed to console him for her neglect:

> So now we have reached the stage when I am sent a card like any stranger. *En vérité* that makes me very sad, for I would rather have a few lines from you than from anyone else. I know that for a long time I count as no more than third class in the scale of your affections. I have become an uninteresting, boring fellow who has nothing new to offer, and this is what I find so wounding, especially when you know what my feelings are towards you and that it is through no fault of my own that I receive such cruel treatment.

This letter, written while he was laid up with a bad attack of influenza, made no mention of the young wife who, two months later, was to present him with an heir. In February 1894 Katharina Schratt received a note from the Emperor giving her the news: 'So in spite of everything, an enormous strong child has been produced by that small, delicate woman. Our Bulgarian friend is lucky, for this event will help to consolidate his position in the country.'

But there were other, more serious matters to consider than the situation in Bulgaria. In the autumn and winter of 1893-4 the Emperor was fully occupied with the ministerial crisis at home which overthrew the Taaffe government after it had been in power for over fourteen years. Franz Josef lost in Taaffe the only minister he had ever liked since the days of Schwarzenberg. The two men had known one another since childhood, and though no two people could have been more dissimilar in character they understood one another perfectly. Both were essentially fair-minded, bent on obtaining justice and providing equal opportunities for all the various races of the Empire. Unfortunately in Hungary the terms of the Compromise were such that they were powerless to interfere; the chauvinistic Magyars blocked the way to essential reforms, and denied all rights to the Croat and Slav minorities unless they consented to become absorbed in the master race.

Edward Taaffe, whose Irish ancestors had fought in Wallenstein's army and settled in Bohemia where, over the centuries, they had acquired large properties, was a light-hearted, tolerant cynic who, while giving the impression of taking nothing seriously and of being bored by all ideologies, nevertheless worked harder than most of his contemporaries and achieved more during his tenure of office than most of his predecessors. He was a negotiator, above all a conciliator who modestly described his policy as 'muddling along' (*fortwursteln*), but his muddling along was remarkably successful and it was only after his departure that the Pandora's box of warring nationalities, which his deft and supple fingers had managed to keep shut, burst open and pan-Slavs, pan-Germans, Young Czechs and Italian *Irridentisti* came out to air their grievances and wave their banners, causing disruption in the Empire.

To curb the aggressive supremacy of the German liberals and

legislate in spite of Hungary, Taaffe formed what was known as his 'iron ring', government above party – a strange coalition made up of some very disparate elements: the clericals who represented the Catholic peasantry; the great landlords; and, strangest of all, the Czechs and the Poles, whom he had won over by his Language Ordinance Bill giving official status to the various minority languages. Civil servants operating in Poland and the crown lands of Bohemia now had to speak the language of the country, which paved the way for ambitious young men from the provinces, of whom the Czechs were the most numerous and the most intelligent, to become part of the state bureaucracy which until now had been almost entirely in the hands of German-speaking Austrians.

Taaffe, who was a true cosmopolitan, did more than anyone else to turn Vienna into a melting-pot of all the races, providing fertile soil for all the talents. But the German-speakers, and there were as many disparate elements among them as among the various minorities, were all bitterly hostile to Count Taaffe's championship of so-called subject races. It did not matter what political party they belonged to, whether they were the prosperous bourgeoisie of the old Liberal Party or Karl Lueger's Christian Socialists, the white-collar workers who crowded the gaunt, grey apartment blocks which fringed the inner city. It did not matter whether they were Schönerer's demagogues or Victor Adler's Social Democrats, the proletariat whom the Viennese saw for the first time in 1890 disrupting the May Day flower *corso* in the Prater, blocking the decorated carriages with their noisy demonstrations, calling for an eight-hour working day. Whatever party they adhered to, they all hated Count Taaffe. Yet curiously enough it was this suave Irish-Bohemian aristocrat, acting perhaps from expediency rather than conviction, who was ready to introduce reforms which till now no one had had the courage to contemplate. A bill in favour of universal suffrage and a limitation on working hours aroused such passionate opposition from all the vested interests in the country, ranging from the great landlords to the small shopkeepers, that the 'iron ring' disintegrated into an unworkable minority and Count Taaffe had to hand in his resignation. The Emperor saw his old friend depart with his customary phlegm. Years ago, when he was a young man fighting back his tears at the death-bed of Prince Schwarzenberg, his mother, the formidable Archduchess Sophie, had told him that no minister must ever be regarded as indispensable.

But Taaffe's departure left a void Franz Josef was never able to fill. His Irish charm and light-hearted attitude to life had alleviated the burden of government. Ministerial conferences had been prolonged by smoking a good cigar together and reminiscing on old times. Taaffe had refused to be harassed or upset by what he and his master called in private the *Schweinereien* (disgusting behaviour) of the Hungarians. His cynicism was always tempered with humanity and it was only after he had gone that Franz Josef realized how arid the business of government had become.

News of the ministerial crisis reached him in Budapest, from where he wrote to Katharina Schratt, in whom he was confiding more and more, though she was not really interested in politics and confessed that she rarely read the newspapers.

> I now have a crisis on my hands, so there is a touch of egotism in my longing for our meeting. Your dear company would comfort and cheer me in these difficult times. What could be better than to be sitting with you in your cosy room, reclining in your comfortable armchair and having a good chat?

Three days later he was back in Vienna.

> Here I am, and however disagreeable the complications that brought me back, at least it means that I will be able to see you sooner than I thought. It is the one ray of light in sight, but it is a very shining ray, for I long so terribly to see you and would like to rush round at once to the Gloriettegasse, but that will not be possible today owing to the ministerial conference.

A few days later the crisis was resolved, a new ministry had been formed, but the Emperor was far from optimistic:

> Up to now only this much is true. Prince Windischgrätz has undertaken to form a so-called coalition government after two interviews with me. He is selecting the ministers and then proposing them to me. The task will be harder because of a surplus of ministerial candidates rather than because of a lack of them, and one must seek out those who are the most able. I fear it will be some time before the government will be formed, and how it will then go remains to be seen.

Franz Josef's pessimism was justified. Three successive governments were brought down by obstructional tactics in Parliament and internecine fights which led to riots and demonstrations in the streets, till after several years the Emperor found in Ernst von Koerber a brilliant administrator who succeeded in breaking the power of Parliament by playing one party against the other, giving concessions to everyone in turn, making the one feel privileged at the other's expense, and meanwhile running the country above their heads and making it more prosperous than it had ever been before.

But that was in the future. For the last decade of the nineteenth century the Emperor concentrated all his forces on survival, using his ministers as instruments to make the Empire work, discarding them when they could no longer be of any use, placing his faith in the loyalty of his army and in the devotion of the ordinary people, to whom he was becoming more and more of a father figure whose mystical prestige prevented his heterogenous Empire from falling apart. His pessimism, combined with his dogged determination to survive, are reflected in his letters to Katharina Schratt, the one person on whose tact and discretion he could rely.

By the beginning of the 1890s his wife had withdrawn so completely from life that she was no longer interested even in Hungarian politics, and on her visits to Budapest rarely ventured out of the Castle grounds. A brooding melancholy had settled over her spirit and even the beauty of the Achilleon no longer gave her any satisfaction: first the Hermes Villa and now the Achilleon – fortunes spent in the vain hope that his wife might find a home or at least an anchorage for her unquiet spirit. Full of depression, Franz Josef wrote to Elisabeth, 'I had cherished the secret hope that after building your house with so much pleasure and enthusiasm you would be happy to remain in a place which is your own creation. Now alas that has come to nothing and you will go on roaming through the world.' But she had only to come home for a week and he was again under her spell. Even in her absence no one in the imperial entourage was ever entirely free from her presence. In the Hofburg, Ida von Ferenczy continued on the Empress's instructions to facilitate the meetings between the Emperor and Frau Schratt. But there must have been times when Ida, whose love for her mistress bordered on idolatry, resented her role as go-between. Or was she, as the German Ambassador suggests in a letter to the Kaiser, acting in her country's interests in trying to interest the Emperor's friend in Hungarian politics? It is doubtful whether she had any success, for Katharina had little sympathy for her husband's country, and from the little we know of her politics she was probably an old-fashioned German liberal.

Relations with Ida von Ferenczy can never have been easy. Both were temperamental and highly strung. There were trivial women's quarrels in which the poor Emperor sometimes became involved. Elisabeth suddenly became interested in home wine-making, with which Frau Schratt had been experimenting at Hietzing, and Ida von Ferenczy was charged to get into direct contact with the actress in order to procure the recipe. Unfortunately it was at a time when Katharina was not on speaking terms with Ida, and the Emperor wrote a pathetic letter, begging her

> ... quite humbly, and for my sake and to avoid a great deal of trouble which might disturb your friendly relationship with the Empress, to bring yourself to receive Frau von Ferenczy, as if you were not angry with her. Your honesty and frankness are two of your qualities which I admire the most, but sometimes in life one has to constrain one's feelings without falsehood, and know how to control oneself. I often have to do so, as witness my relationship with my Hungarian ministers.

It never seems to have struck Franz Josef that he may have been partly to blame for the fact that Katharina was no longer as sweet and even-tempered as when he first knew her. The very nature of their relationship, his demands and at the same time the limits he imposed, must have reacted on the nerves of a normal, healthy woman. References in his letters to scenes she had made, both in the theatre and with her friends, become more frequent. In October 1893, at the time of the ministerial crisis, he was writing:

> So also you are gloomy, despondent as I have never known you before. The violent scene you made at the rehearsal shows that your nerves are completely unstrung. It does not seem at all like you and is not right. Usually you are so calm, and if I tell you that I have been

violent or disagreeable you usually laugh at me, so please try and calm down and control yourself, for these outbursts of temper only end in making you ill.

Katharina had no real troubles, but a hundred petty worries; an old and exacting mother to whom she was a dutiful and loving daughter; a financially demanding husband; jealous colleagues; delays and arguments over the renewal of her contract; admirers she may have wanted to encourage more than she dared; and above all the constant battle against the encroachments of middle age – 'fat and forty' was a terrifying prospect for an actress who still aspired to play the juvenile lead, and the slimming cures which affected her nerves became ever more drastic, till even the Empress joined with her husband in expressing concern when the actress began taking thyroid pills without proper medical supervision.

But it was Elisabeth who, more than anyone else, was responsible for poor Katharina's efforts to slim. Perhaps it was an unconscious way of revenging herself on the woman who had captured her husband's heart when she had only intended to provide him with a comfortable armchair. One wonders if it was necessary for the Emperor to have been quite so honest in mentioning *die Freundin* in every letter to his wife, and his wife in every letter to *die Freundin*. On one occasion he went so far as to write to Elisabeth, '*Die Freundin* could not come and see me yesterday as she stayed in bed with bad cramps brought on by the *stille Woche*', a fact which one feels can hardly have been of interest to the Empress. It would have been as absurd for Elisabeth to be jealous of Katharina Schratt as it would have been absurd for Katharina to be jealous of the beautiful Empress. But how many times had a meeting with the Emperor been cancelled because Elisabeth had suddenly arrived at Lainz or Miramar and the dutiful husband had to be there to welcome her. 'We had a joyful reunion,' wrote Franz Josef to the actress when he went to join his wife in Switzerland. But only a few days later, writing from Territet, he told her, 'My longing for you grows every day and I do not think I have ever missed you so much before.'

16

Royalty on the Riviera

Though Elisabeth could travel through the world as the Countess of Hohenembs and people respected the anonymity of the tall, dark woman who glided past them in the streets, followed by a panting lady-in-waiting with a discreet detective in the offing, it was impossible for Franz Josef to preserve his incognito when he joined his wife for a short holiday on the French Riviera in the early months of 1894. Until now he had gone abroad only on state visits, since his days were taken up by military manoeuvres and official banquets. But apart from the red despatch boxes which followed him around, the fortnight he spent at Cap Martin was entirely given up to pleasure.

Cap Martin, the wooded promontory which lies between Mentone and Monte Carlo, was both the quietest and most exclusive of all the Riviera resorts. The hotel, with its olive groves going down to the sea, was adjacent to the villa of the ex-Empress Eugénie, and for those few days Franz Josef delighted in the sybaritic existence of a luxury hotel in beautiful surroundings. Even Elisabeth made an effort to lead a more normal life, planning little treats for her husband at the famous restaurants along the coast, and to his joy developing herself a hearty appetite in appreciation of the delicious food. In an impulsive moment she had suggested that Katharina Schratt might join them – a *Katzensprung* (flying visit) to the Riviera would do her good after her bad cold – but on second thoughts it was decided that the visit would be a mistake and would give rise to a lot of unnecessary talk. Half the royalty of Europe seemed to be visiting the Riviera that winter, all of them with their courtiers and dependants: a lot of curious people with nothing to do but gossip and only too ready to criticize the Emperor and Empress of Austria and their friendship with the Burgtheater actress.

'We talked it over,' wrote Franz Josef to Katharina Schratt, after sending her at the last moment a somewhat wounding telegram saying 'Not invited',

> ... and alas we came to the conclusion that, owing to the state of affairs here and the impossibility of preserving an incognito, it would be better to put off your visit. At home the people have on the whole learned to understand the nature of our friendship, but here in a foreign country, and in this unfortunately very crowded and fashionable place, it is somewhat different. The coast swarms with people who know us, and we are afraid that our relations with you would be subjected to malicious criticism. The Empress, who always has the most correct judgment, thinks that all this could not injure us old people, but that above all it would harm you and Toni. So now I've said it, and you are so kind and sensible that I hope you will not be offended. But I am very sad that I shall not see you for so long, and in spite of the pleasure of the reunion with the Empress, in spite of the beauty of the region and the magnificent air, I am sometimes quite melancholy and my thoughts are constantly with you.

The Emperor's embarrassment is evident in this letter. Elisabeth had obviously forgotten she had ever suggested a meeting with Katharina Schratt. Many of her relatives were on the Riviera, and even the most unconventional of Wittelsbachs might have questioned the actress's presence. Katharina, who by now was used to these last-minute decisions, was as 'kind and sensible' as the Emperor expected her to be, and on 1 March the imperial couple received the traditional basket of violets she had ordered through Edward Palmer, who was spending his annual holiday at Monte Carlo. She was sufficiently generous-minded to be pleased that for once the poor old Emperor was enjoying a holiday, and the very naïvety of his letters made them all the more touching. He enclosed some playing cards to show her he had visited her beloved casino,

> ... but I was chased away by the curiosity of the public.... I like Monte Carlo and Monaco very much, but found the gambling halls florid in architecture and not at all elegant. The gambling public too was quite vulgar, many old people, only a few pretty women and those mostly *cocottes*. It is said to be better in the evening. Accompanied by Liechtenstein (Lord High Chamberlain) and Paar (Chief Adjutant)

I succeeded in looking, still unrecognized, at the beautiful park grounds and terraces and going into the gambling hall. But after I had watched the roulette and *trente-et-quarante* at several tables, people began to be over-curious and it was high time to leave. Followed by a large crowd we succeeded in reaching our carriages.

He sent her the menu of a superb meal he had eaten at the famous restaurant called Noël et Patard.

We are trying all possible restaurants, one after the other, and eating really much too much of all the rich and varied food, so that even the Empress is developing an excellent appetite, though alas she will then fast all the more so as not to offend the scales. . . . Tomorrow I shall be dining with my gentlemen at the Hôtel de Paris at Monte Carlo where I am told there is a very mixed company of ladies. I am quite curious to see them.

Cannes, which was just becoming fashionable, was in the Emperor's opinion the most beautiful place on the Riviera. Some of the Empress's relatives, including the ex-King of Naples and his brother the Count of Caserta, had taken villas for the winter season, and in the harbour was the imperial yacht, the *Greif*, which had brought her from Corfu. Visiting royalty such as the Prince of Wales, who had his own boat at Monte Carlo, and the ex-Empress of the French, were entertained on board the *Greif*, and there was a family excursion to the Marghérite Islands where they were welcomed by fireworks and a gipsy band. That evening even Elisabeth came out of her melancholy; standing on deck wrapped in a white fur she looked so transcendently beautiful that everyone, from her husband to the youngest of deckhands, was completely subjugated.

Three days later Franz Josef was back in Vienna to find that Katharina Schratt had gone to Venice, where members of the Burgtheater were acting at La Fenice. 'All those colleagues, including the director, will hardly make for a rest cure,' wrote the Emperor, who was disappointed at not finding her at home. 'I have been very sad since my return and feeling very lonely, longing for your company and having had nothing but annoyances as you can imagine if by chance you ever happen to read the newspapers.'

Politics were now beginning to intrude even into Katharina's world. The growing strength of Lueger's Christian Socialists, allied to his own personal magnetism, was awakening a new political awareness in the most casual and carefree of Viennese. Karl Lueger spoke for the underdog, the waiter in the café, the office clerk, the small shopkeeper, the hundreds and thousands of little men clinging to their jobs, terrified of being ousted by the great tide of immigration from the provinces; resenting the foreigners and above all the Jews, whether they were the downtrodden Jews from the ghettoes of Galicia, whom they disliked having as neighbours, or the wealthy industrialists, the heads of the great combines who, rightly or wrongly, they accused of exploitation. It was so easy to fan the jealousy of these humble, defenceless people whom no one had ever cared for before. But Karl Lueger cared for them passionately. He really wanted them to have better and more prosperous lives, just as he wanted Vienna to be not only the most beautiful but the cleanest, the most modern and most progressive city in the world. Small wonder if this handsome, dedicated man, who had started life as a provincial lawyer, became the idol of the Viennese. People who would never have listened to Schönerer's tub-thumping demagogues were attracted by Lueger's far more insidious propaganda, and the Emperor wrote, 'It is terrible how anti-Semitism is spreading among all classes. There may be reasons for it, but the consequences are appalling.'

By 1894 Lueger had become a member of the city council and a year later was elected by a small majority as mayor. Franz Josef refused to accept the nomination but Lueger was again elected the following year, this time securing two-thirds of the votes. Many Jewish friends of Katharina Schratt were already talking of moving to Budapest, but the Emperor, who was not prepared to be dictated to by Lueger, again refused to ratify the appointment and dismissed the city council. It was not until two years later, in 1897, that Franz Josef finally had to give in to the force of public opinion and accept the nomination of a man who was destined to become the best mayor Vienna had ever known, whose term of office reflected the last golden rays of the *Franz Josef Zeit*.

The Emperor's hesitation to nominate a man whose administrative genius he was the first to recognize was partly on account of his anti-Semitism and partly on account of the opposition of the Hungarians. As a Member of Parliament, Lueger had campaigned against the unfairness of the trade and custom agreement which, being based on a ten-year term, entirely favoured the Hungarians, enabling them to blackmail the rest of the Empire whenever they did not get what they wanted. Lueger asserted that this agreement should be settled once and for all, something the Hungarians would never agree to, and which the Emperor was far too cautious to attempt to carry through. Franz Josef was determined to stand honestly by the terms of the *Ausgleich* of 1867, regardless as to how much it was being abused by the rapacious Magyar aristocracy, and this was the chief bone of contention between him and his heir.

As much as Rudolf had always favoured the Hungarians, so Franz Ferdinand loathed and despised them. This almost pathological hatred on the part of the heir apparent boded ill for the future of the dual monarchy. At the time of his illness the Hungarian press took an almost morbid pleasure in labelling him as incurable, and both he and his supporters criticized what they called the Emperor's kid-glove treatment of the Magyars, and accused the Empress of being responsible. But the Empress no longer played any part in politics, and it was poor Katharina Schratt who now had to listen for hours to the Emperor's complaints of the Hungarian ministers, and to take an interest in the intricacies of the *Ausgleich*, a subject which until now she had happily ignored. Well-known journalists and politicians began to be included among the dinner guests at Hietzing and the Gloriettegasse, where the banking world met with the élite of the Burgtheater and the leading artists and writers of the day. Though Katharina herself was curiously unmusical for a Viennese and could barely sing in tune, she was nevertheless on friendly terms with most of the great musicians, from Johann Strauss to Gustav Mahler. And in the last years of his life, on his summer holidays at Ischl, Johannes Brahms could often be seen walking across to Zauner's pastry shop to have tea with Kathi Schratt.

She had the gift of attracting men in every walk of life, whether they were sportsmen or intellectuals, artists or politicians. She moved in so many different circles that little went on in Vienna and little was said of which she was not informed, and her greatest talent lay in knowing just what to repeat and what to keep away from the harassed old Emperor, 'who had enough trouble on his hands without being unnecessarily worried [*sekiert*]'.

The death of the Hungarian patriot Louis Kossuth, in exile in Italy, gave rise to further anti-government demonstrations in the streets of Budapest. And after a short visit to Vienna Franz Josef wrote to Katharina,

> It is already three days since I have seen you and to me it seems an eternity, and a very sad eternity at that. Meanwhile I dream of you constantly, and though it sounds absurd at least it shows you that you are constantly in my thoughts. Here I am so lonely and so melancholy, and am kept busy with so many unpleasant things, that I have only one wish, [*aussi möcht I*] to get out of it all and be back in the lovely green Hermes Villa or the dear Gloriettegasse, or even in the stuffy rooms of the Vienna Burg. I am already becoming just like your friends, the Bulgarian and Count Wilczek, complaining all the time so as to arouse your sympathy.

Franz Josef admitted he was jealous, but his jealousy of the Bulgarian was partly assumed as a private joke between him and Katharina Schratt, whereas his jealousy of Count Wilczek was deep and persistent, lasting till the end of his life.

The Emperor's letters contain far more references to Prince Ferdinand than to Count Wilczek, for the distance between Sofia and Vienna was no deterrent to an indefatigable traveller like the Prince. The new Orient Express made the journey in under three days, and his private car attached to the train was the very quintessence of luxury. The drawing-room had pale green velvet walls and the bedrooms were lined with turquoise silk. A French journalist described it as '*un vrai bijou d'intimité voyageuse*', and guests who travelled with the Prince were treated to some of the best food in Europe. What a contrast to the Austrian Emperor who, when returning from the Riviera, complained to Frau Schratt that the Italian government 'has put a special train at my disposal which is sure to be very expensive'.

Prince Ferdinand made several trips to Vienna in the spring and summer of 1894, when all his Machiavellian talents were being deployed in getting rid of his uncomfortable Prime Minister and in deliberately encouraging a defamatory campaign to be carried out in his absence. Goaded by the injustice and scurrility of the accusations, Stambouloff went against the advice of his friends and launched a bitter personal attack against the man he had placed upon the throne. Balkan politics sunk to their lowest level, and, using the excuse of his wife's health, Ferdinand retreated to Karlsbad.

Franz Josef wrote to Katharina in Karlsbad:

> I read in the papers that the Bulgarian Princess is coming to Vienna on her way to take the cure at Franzensbad, so I am afraid it will not be long before you will be having the pleasure of the spiteful Bulgarian's company. Now that he has managed to rid himself of Stambouloff who, by all accounts, must have been a devil of a fellow, I fear he will be inclined to swim too deep in pro-Russian waters, and in this respect I do not trust him in the least.

Three weeks later the Emperor wrote again: 'To hear that the Bulgarian was together with you in Karlsbad annoys me and fills me with jealousy.'

Stambouloff's dismissal had been badly received in the European press, and the Bulgarian Prince was sorely in need of friends. One of the few he could rely on was Katharina Schratt who, however bored by his complaints, could never resist him when he set out to charm and to amuse. Discarding the trappings of a Balkan tyrant, he now behaved as if he had no other care in the world than to escort her to the theatre and the casino, and pick cyclamen with her in the woods. But in the following summer of 1895 it needed more than 'Frau Kathi's' loyalty to be seen on the '*Alte Wiese*' in the company of a man whom the international press branded as a murderer.

Though Ferdinand may not actually have connived at Stambouloff's assassination, he certainly made no effort to prevent it. The fact that he allowed his new government to have his ex-Prime Minister illegally put on trial, and at a time when his life was in danger refused him permission to leave the country, was equivalent to signing his death warrant, for he knew that the Macedonian conspirators who were arrested with Panitza had been released from prison and had sworn to avenge their leader's death. There

is no doubt that Ferdinand wanted Stambouloff silenced before he
could disrupt his new pro-Russian policy and make trouble with
the western powers. But with his innate fastidiousness and horror
of bloodshed, he would never have countenanced the brutality of
a murder which shocked the civilized world and reduced both
him and his Bulgarians to the level of barbarians. There were so
many ways of putting people quietly out of the way – a shot fired
at night in a deserted street, or a carriage accident with a runaway
horse – but to have Stambouloff literally hacked to pieces in one
of the main squares of his capital filled him with as great a horror
as any of his accusers. The wretched man, who knew he was
doomed, had sent Ferdinand a letter two days before he died,
giving him the names, addresses and occupations of the Macedonian killers who were threatening his life, and asking him as the
guardian of the law of the land to give him the protection which
was the right of every subject. Ferdinand never received this letter,
for by then he had fled to Karlsbad.

Stambouloff died in agony, butchered to death by his assailants,
and in the Bohemian spa where he was usually treated as the most
fêted and honoured of visitors Prince Ferdinand suddenly found
himself a pariah. Messages of condolence came to Stambouloff's
widow from all over Europe: the Emperor Franz Josef sent a
telegram; Queen Victoria sent two, and gave special instructions
to her envoy to place her wreath on the grave in person, a gesture
Prince Ferdinand found hard to forgive. His own wreath and
letter of condolence, delivered by one of his adjutants, was returned by the widow, who, pointing to her husband's severed
hands exposed in a glass bowl, said to the terrified young man,
'These are the hands that placed your master's crown upon his
head.'

One of the Prince's neighbours in Karlsbad, a daughter of
Princess Radziwill, wrote to her mother:

> Prince Ferdinand is here, inhabiting a villa next to my hotel. At
> the beginning of his stay one saw him frequently, but since this drama
> he avoids social life and goes around with two gentlemen and a detective
> who follows him everywhere. The Princess arrived here yesterday to
> see her husband. They say she wants him to abdicate. He is insulted in
> the streets and I believe he is terribly afraid to go back to his country.

Public opinion was against him, and Katharina Schratt kept away from Karlsbad. Ferdinand, who saw himself as the innocent victim of a campaign of slander, wrote to her in righteous indignation: 'I am miserable over the whole affair, and I have certainly done nothing to deserve the abominable treatment I have received. The *Freie Presse* has published the most infamous leading article against me, which should never have been allowed to pass the censor. I wonder what *Megalotis*★ will say about it when you see him.'

But *Megalotis* had nothing to say in the Prince's favour, for the Emperor knew that a Bulgarian delegation was already in St Petersburg, where the recent death of the Tsar Alexander III had paved the way for a reconciliation. When Ferdinand passed through Vienna on his way home from Karlsbad he found the portals of the Hofburg closed to him. Angry and frustrated, he wrote to 'Frau Kathi':

> I have tried to see the Emperor in order to talk over the recent tragic events and was told he was not at home. I tried three more times through his secretaries, and each time was told he could not be found, so there was nothing to do but leave. Here I am back in my beloved country, in the glaring heat of thirty-eight degrees, feeling ill, unhappy and abandoned.

For the next two years the Bulgarian Prince was *persona non grata* at the Austrian court. Franz Josef ended in accepting the fact that Ferdinand was not directly responsible for Stambouloff's murder, but he refused to condone the act of apostasy of which Ferdinand was guilty when he deliberately broke the pledges he had made to the Pope, his wife, and his father-in-law, and had his two-year-old son converted to the Orthodox faith. It was the price he had to pay for Russia's friendship, but political expediency was no excuse either in the eyes of that strict, ultra-montane Pope Leo XIII or his Catholic Apostolic Majesty of Austria, who abided by the decisions of Rome. The irony of the situation was that in incurring the anathema of the whole Catholic world, Ferdinand succeeded in obtaining the official recognition he had been waiting for during nine long years. Five days after the magnificent ceremony in which the infant Boris was received into the Greek

★ Megalotis: Greek for Ruler-King, the Empress's nickname for Franz Josef.

Orthodox Church, with a Russian representative standing in as proxy for his godfather the Tsar, Ferdinand was formally recognized as Prince of Bulgaria by all the former signatories of the treaty of Berlin, including Austria. After years of travelling incognito in Europe, of attending royal functions to which he was only admitted as a minor Prince of Saxe-Coburg Gotha, he was finally able to assert his royal prerogatives and take his place among his peers.

In Constantinople the wily old Sultan Abdul Hamid treated him not as a rebellious vassal but as an independent sovereign, and lodged him in one of the imperial palaces. St Petersburg, Paris and Berlin welcomed him with royal honours. But in Vienna the Emperor Franz Josef expressed no wish to see him, to the distress of his new Foreign Minister Count Goluchowski, who admitted to the German Chancellor Prince Hohenlohe that he was well aware of the political disadvantages of this decision but there was no way of persuading his master to go against his convictions. Kaiser Wilhelm was exasperated by the stubbornness of his old ally, forgetting that Franz Josef had been the first to press for Ferdinand's recognition when none of the other powers dared to act for fear of Russia. But now it was a matter of principle with the Emperor. As he wrote to Katharina Schratt, 'It is not so much a question of religion, only it shows that the man is completely without character. I hope you will not be seeing him. I shall be angry with you if you do.'

But Katharina had more sympathy and understanding of human frailties than the Emperor. In the theatrical Olympus of the Burgtheater, a world of fierce competition and conflicting ambitions, there was not one who would not have reacted as Ferdinand had done. He was himself an actor fighting for survival, striving for a place on the European stage where he felt called upon to play a leading role. Six months after the conversion of his son the Prince was back in Karlsbad with the Bulgarian standard flying from his hotel, and Franz Josef was writing to Katharina Schratt, 'Whatever you may say, I am afraid it will not be long before your reconciliation with the Bulgarian is completed.'

17

The Empress Relies on Katharina

'Now that Mamma is so much away there is no hope of Papa's unfortunate entanglement with *die Schratt* ever coming to an end.' This excerpt from Archduchess Valerie's journal was written in 1895 when she no longer made any secret of her antipathy towards her father's friend. The Emperor's youngest daughter, who had always been so close to her parents, could not but disapprove of his growing dependence on Katharina Schratt. And what annoyed her even more was to see this enthusiasm apparently shared by her mother who, on her rare visits to Lainz and Ischl, always made a point of inviting Frau Schratt and treating her as a family friend. To hear her mother calling the actress her adopted sister (*Wahlschwester*) must have been particularly irritating to Valerie, who remembered the time when she had sobbed on her shoulder, complaining of her father's infatuation for Frau Schratt. But by now the Empress had grown too remote and too indifferent to be jealous. All she felt was an immense relief that someone else was willing to cope with the sad old man she had loved so many years ago. There were even times when she felt sorry for the younger woman, when she would say to her husband, 'It may be a great honour to be your friend, but it must also be *assommant* with your continual questions, always wanting to know what one is doing and where one is going.' And with a flash of her old mischief she would add, 'I wonder if she always tells you.'

When the imperial couple returned to Cap Martin in February 1895 Frau Schratt was invited to join them, regardless of the fears for her reputation which Elisabeth had expressed the previous year. Baron Hawerda was even instructed by the Emperor to reserve rooms for the actress at Mentone. But Katharina showed her independence by going to Monte Carlo instead. 'I do not know why *die Freundin* has not taken the apartment which

Hawerda had reserved for her in Mentone,' wrote Franz Josef to his wife, 'but perhaps it is better she stays in Monte Carlo, near to "Notre Dame de Roulette", which saves having to travel to and fro.' This letter was written when poor Franz Josef, who had been so much looking forward to his meeting with the actress, had been called back to Vienna for the Archduke Albrecht's state funeral. Katharina, who had spent the first week of her holiday between Paris and a pilgrimage to Lourdes, arrived in the South of France two days after he had left.

Pilgrimages to Lourdes and to the Austrian sanctuary of Mariazell were very much a part of Katharina's life, the expression of a simple, childish faith allied to superstition, of prayers and candles for the Madonna and amulets and lucky charms. She saw nothing incongruous in making a pilgrimage to Lourdes in between buying clothes in Paris and gambling in Monte Carlo, for she was at once essentially frivolous and essentially good, and now she felt pity for the lonely Emperor and cut short her holiday to return to him in Vienna.

'That you should really want to come back earlier than expected makes my heart leap with joy, but what will the malicious world have to say that you return all at once so prematurely after having left for four weeks' holiday?' 'The malicious world' had plenty to say on the subject of Katharina Schratt. The German Ambassador, Count, later Prince, Eulenburg, who took up his post in 1894, wrote that 'during the whole of his fifteen years in Vienna, no one, of whatever rank or position, was so much talked about as *die Schratt*'. No one was so discussed, so envied or so admired. In the theatre she still had more friends than enemies, but in court circles there was a growing animosity against the woman whose influence was beginning to be feared. Not that there was anything to fear, for Katharina made no attempt to interfere in any affairs of state. She gave her opinion when asked, and her opinion was usually honest, clear-sighted and unbiased. But, as she said herself, her business was to entertain, and by now the Emperor had become so dependent on her company, so used to the pleasant little breakfasts and dinners in the Gloriettegasse, that when she moved for the winter into town he gradually fell into the habit of inviting her to dinner at the palace.

The first time he made this unprecedented gesture was in October of 1894 when he suggested she might like to dine with him in the Burg, following the Sunday afternoon performance at the theatre. This invitation must have been made shortly after the actress's quarrel with Ida von Ferenczy, at a time when she may have been unwilling to meet him in the apartment of a woman with whom she was not on speaking terms. But long after the quarrel had been made up, when Katharina and the Emperor were again meeting regularly in Ida's apartment, the dinners at the palace continued, gradually developing into a custom. It was typical of Franz Josef that every one of these occasions was faithfully reported to his wife, without whose sanction the invitations would never have been made.

The Emperor's valet relates that when the *gnädige Frau* was coming to dine, His Majesty was pleasurably excited all morning and carefully selected all her favourite dishes from the menu sent up from the imperial kitchens. Franz Josef made little use of the imperial kitchens when he was alone, and would often have a tray brought up to his study consisting of no more than a dish of goulash or of boiled beef and dumplings, washed down by a glass of beer. There was an occasion when he returned after a court ball feeling very hot and tired, longing for a cool drink, and on finding not even a bottle of mineral water in his room had to satisfy his thirst with a glass of tepid water out of a tap. When he told Katharina Schratt this she asked him why he had not rung for his valet to have a bottle of champagne brought across from the Redoutensaal where the ball was still in progress, and he replied that he had not wanted to disturb anyone at that time of night. Katharina lost no time in relating this story to Ida von Ferenczy, who was in constant touch with the Empress, and shortly afterwards Franz Josef wrote to Elisabeth: 'I ordered myself champagne before going to bed after the exertion of the court balls. *Die Freundin* reminded me about this, probably through your sweet thought.'

Katharina made a point of always referring to the Empress and fostering Franz Josef's illusions on his wife, for she felt so sorry for him in his vast, cheerless palace where, among the hundreds of liveried servants and titled officials, there was no one who gave a thought to his comfort. She was the only one who noted what he lacked. The presents she chose with such a loving care – a painted screen to protect him from the draught, a warm woollen smoking jacket, a plaid rug and the latest and most modern of electric fans – were the presents which any bourgeois wife might give her husband, rather than a successful actress to the richest monarch in Europe. She was an obsessive present-giver, never giving one singly but always seven at a time, which she believed to be her lucky number. And the Emperor, to whom hardly anyone dared give a present, treasured her gifts, from the electric hairbrush which delighted his grandchildren, to the music box she brought him back from Paris which gave a faithful reproduction of a nightingale's song. But the present he treasured most of all was a little hand-mirror on which was written, *'Portrait de celui que j'aime'*.

It was an exhausting life for a woman who still aspired to be a leading actress and was constantly either acting or rehearsing for new plays or giving poetry readings at the various literary societies which were then in fashion. The last was not a natural medium for her talents but it flattered her vanity to appear as the celebrated court actress reading from the classics in front of large audiences who came only to see Kathi Schratt. Apart from her professional work she was also eminently sociable, and the Emperor, who was always worrying about her health, wrote: 'Your constant activity these days goes beyond amusement and cannot be advisable for you.' At the same time he took pride in her success and was delighted when the great French actor Coquelin referred to her as *'une femme extraordinaire'*.

Foreign diplomats sought her company, knowing it would please the Emperor, and shortly after his arrival in Austria the German Ambassador, Count Eulenburg, wrote to Kaiser Wilhelm from Ischl, 'I went and visited the famous Frau "Kathi" Schratt, knowing it would be appreciated in certain quarters, and spent a very pleasant hour with that charming lady.'

What began as a courtesy visit developed into a real friendship, and in his memoirs Eulenburg devotes a whole chapter to Frau Schratt, whom he describes as being

> ... ravishingly pretty with extraordinary youthful looks, marvellous colouring, shining golden hair and great blue eyes with the sweetest

expression, a really good soul who never says an unkind word and is always pleasant and gay and ready to help whom she can. Apart from which she is delightful company and has a very original way of relating little anecdotes.

This is a glowing tribute from the cultured and talented Eulenburg, who was a musician, poet and diplomat, Kaiser Wilhelm's favourite, and on friendly terms with all the leading artists of Vienna and Berlin.

Before long Franz Josef was beginning to suspect that *die Freundin* was seeing too much of the fascinating ambassador.

> Your having seen Count Eulenburg three times is too often for my taste. The Empress observed at once that the Count would be a threat to me. I had already begun to fear that as you know, for the ambassador is very amiable and is much more witty and amusing than I am and will all too soon have displaced me in your heart. So I am full of gloomy thoughts and it is high time for me to reassure myself again by looking into your dear, clear eyes.

The Emperor may also have been nervous lest the subtle and accomplished diplomat might encourage the actress to be indiscreet. But from his memoirs it would appear as if Katharina had told Eulenburg no more than what she wanted him to hear, stressing her friendship with the Empress rather than with the Emperor.

> Her relationship with the Empress Elisabeth is a very close one. They often consult one another on matters concerning the Emperor, and the Empress relies on Frau Kathi to look after her husband and see that he gets sufficient fresh air and exercise. In return she is full of little attentions and is always giving her presents, and as Frau Kathi is very superstitious lucky charms and porcelain and metal pigs figure largely among the gifts. In certain ways the Empress is more intimate with the actress than with her own daughters, for even her love for Valerie is no longer the same.

Though Katharina's relations with the Empress were never quite as intimate as she led the ambassador to believe, she was nevertheless one of the chief links between Franz Josef and Elisabeth. All they had left to talk about was either her or the grandchildren, and there is hardly a letter between husband and wife in which there is not a reference to *die Freundin*. The chief interest in common between the Empress and the actress continued to be their respective slimming cures. At the height of a political crisis, Franz Josef reports that, '*Die Freundin* is desperate because she has gained six kilos in the last months. She has taken up bicycling in order to lose weight, but so far the only result has been a bad fall on the head.' From Karlsbad Katharina writes disconsolately: 'Other people suffer from galloping consumption, I seem to suffer from "galloping obesity"', a remark which amused the Empress, who from now on, whenever she gained a pound, would refer to her 'galloping obesity'.

Elisabeth's way of life was becoming ever more irrational with age. No cures or doctors could help a woman who starved for weeks on end, living on oranges and milk and occasionally indulging in a favourite violet-flavoured ice. Even the few months she spent in Austria were more often spent in places like Karlsbad and Gastein than in her own home. She would not visit Valerie for more than a few days, as she said the sight of other people's happiness always gave her pain, and she preferred the anonymity of large hotels to any of her palaces. Her reactions to people and to places depended entirely on her nerves, and she was now in almost constant pain from sciatica and neuritis. But as soon as she was better she would resume her marathon walks which exhausted the youngest and strongest of her ladies-in-waiting. Human contacts became ever more unreal to her, till in certain moods she was ready to enter into conversation with any passing stranger, confiding in them as if they were her closest friends. While staying on the Riviera it would amuse her to trespass into other people's gardens, causing intense embarrassment to her suite. She was usually recognized in spite of her incognito and the owners were flattered by her condescension. But on one occasion she was chased away by an indignant old lady and narrowly escaped having to be identified by the police.

Yet still Franz Josef continued to write to her every day as if she were an ordinary, rational human being, recording the birth of their first great-grandchild by Gisela's daughter Elisabeth, who had scandalized the Bavarian court by running away with a Baron Seefried. On this occasion Franz Josef, who was usually so severe and intolerant towards the peccadilloes of the younger archdukes, showed himself to be both human and compassionate in forgiving his wayward grand-daughter and accepting her husband as a member of the family. But as he remarked to his wife, 'It is strange to think that our eldest great-grandchild should be a Baron See-fried.' Elisabeth, however, was completely indifferent as to whether it was a Baron Seefried or a Royal Highness. In her letters she rarely mentioned any of her grandchildren, and of Erzi, Rudolf's daughter, whom the Emperor loved more than any of his other grandchildren, there was never a word, for Elisabeth still detested her daughter-in-law, the widowed Archduchess Stephanie.

Yet almost all of the Empress's letters to her husband contain some reference to *die Freundin*. She took an interest in her travels, recommended her some good restaurants in Florence and Rome, and told her to take Toni and his friends to eat a special kind of ice cream at the Café Gambrinus in Naples. She sent her a cake and flowers on her name-day, and was worried when she heard of her having resorted again to 'those dangerous thyroid pills'. As the Empress became ever more divorced from life, so she became ever more attached to her husband's friend. In the early spring of 1896, when the Emperor was holidaying with his wife at Cap Martin and Frau Schratt was kept in Vienna nursing her dying mother, he wrote to her,

> The day before yesterday, when we were enjoying a very good and much too copious breakfast at Perimont's, the Empress said suddenly, 'I miss something', and asked me if I also missed something, which I denied. When I questioned what it was she missed she replied, '*Die Freundin*, who should be sitting here as a third with us.' Such a thing had not occurred to me, and the Empress, who as you see is kinder than I am towards you, ordered me to repeat this to you.

Small wonder if the Archduchess Valerie, who felt that her parents' affection should be centred on her and her family, resented the large part the actress played in their lives.

In Vienna the Empress had become a legend rather than a living presence, and the court saw her preside for the last time at the gala dinner held in honour of the Russian sovereigns, Nicholas and

Alexandra, in August 1896. Eye witnesses recall that though Elisabeth still wore mourning, she not only gave the impression of belonging to the same generation as the Tsarina but looked so exquisitely lovely as to put the younger woman completely in the shade. Franz Josef reported to Frau Schratt, 'The Russian visit went off very well. Their Majesties were in excellent spirits and quite at their ease, especially at a flower-decorated, very cosy family dinner at Lainz.' But a rumour went round that on this occasion two men had lost their lives in securing the edelweiss, which were the Empress's favourite flower and which were only to be found on the highest and most inaccessible of mountain peaks.

In this same summer of 1896 the imperial couple attended the millennium festivities in Budapest. It was a particularly painful visit for Elisabeth, as the last time she had taken part in a public celebration in that town had been with Rudolf, who had been loved in Hungary not as a Habsburg but as her son. Even now her presence was sufficient to still the voice of opposition and arouse the enthusiasm of the Magyars when she sat enthroned beside the Emperor at the state reception of the Hungarian Parliament held in the Castle of Buda. The *Eljens* which resounded to the roof as soon as she appeared expressed all the gratitude and adoration of a nation.

It was a fitting occasion for the Hungarians to take leave of their Queen, whom they were never to see again. A few months later Elisabeth woke one morning to find her face covered with a horrible rash, and from that day she retreated into almost complete seclusion. The loyalty of her entourage was such that there are very few references to what, for a beautiful woman, must have been the most agonizing of all illnesses. The outside world now saw her either shrouded in veils or hidden under a large white parasol, with a fan always held in front of her face. The effect on her morale was appalling, and when the Emperor joined her in Cap Martin in the early spring of 1897 he found her in such a state of depression that it completely ruined his holiday. To Katharina Schratt, who was spending her vacation in Monte Carlo, he wrote:

> If you should be shocked at the Empress's unfortunately very bad appearance please do not show it. Also do not talk too much with

the Empress about health, but, if it cannot be avoided, encourage her and above all do not recommend a new cure or remedy. You will find the Empress quite exhausted, very much in pain, and in terribly low spirits. You can imagine how worried I am. This time it will be a very sad stay on the beautiful Riviera.

Elisabeth appears to have looked forward to the actress's visits almost as much as her husband. And Franz Josef wrote, 'She is only concerned about inviting you because she is always afraid of disturbing you in your amusements and much-needed relaxation.' Towards the end of her stay he asked:

> When are you leaving? I hinted gently to the Empress that you could probably visit us once more, to which she replied, 'The poor thing' [*die Arme*], for she always imagines it must be very boring for you to come and visit us two old people. I, however, have a feeling that you really do not mind it so much, and as I know it would give her so much pleasure, and a few hours with you would do her so much good, I ask you whether you would be so kind as to come again, but only if it would not be too much of an inconvenience to you.

But when the actress suggested his visiting her in Monte Carlo, Franz Josef replied, 'I discussed it with the Empress and she thought it better if I did not come. It would only do you harm and put too many people against you. It is hard for me to accept this. No doubt she is right, but knowing you to be so near makes me long for you all the more.' Nevertheless there were occasions when discretion went overboard, and the Emperor of Austria would be seen driving out in public with Frau Schratt, respectfully greeted by both the visitors and the local inhabitants. The more rigid members of the entourage whispered among themselves that His Majesty was growing old and such a thing would never have happened in the past. But those who were closest to him, like his adjutant Count Paar, and the Lord High Chamberlain Prince Rudolf Liechtenstein had nothing but praise for the actress whose cheerful nature alleviated some of the gloom in the Emperor's lonely life.

She was neither pushing nor interfering, confining her realm to the Burgtheater, her companions to her old friends. She might be seen in the afternoon driving in Mentone with the Emperor and that same evening be dining at the Hôtel de Paris in Monte Carlo in company of Edward Palmer, the Jewish banker who had been a faithful admirer from the days of her early struggles. Figures from the past were always reappearing in her life, and in the last month of 1896 she played a leading part in one of the *causes célèbres* of the time, when she saved her former fiancé and colleague Alexander Girardi from being committed to a mental asylum by a vindictive wife.

Girardi, who was the idol of the Viennese and had only to appear on the stage and wave a hand or raise an eyebrow for the audience to be convulsed in laughter, was like many comic actors shy and nervous by nature. His marriage to the German actress Helene Odilon, a woman who was as well known for her wanton promiscuity as for her talent, was miserably unhappy. His wife, who had only married him to further her career, flaunted her liaison with the wealthy Baron Rothschild and tortured him with jealousy. The scenes he made in public were so terrible that when she finally decided to be rid of him she had no difficulty in getting the theatre doctor to certify him as insane. Rothschild allowed himself to be drawn into the affair, using his connections and his wealth to procure the services of the celebrated psychiatrist Wagner-Jauregg who, tempted by an enormous fee, appears to have attached his signature to the certificate without having properly examined the patient. The unfortunate Girardi was ordered to be committed to a state asylum, but when the police and the doctors came to take him away the actor, who had been forewarned by a friend, had already fled.

On that same evening Katharina Schratt was at her Vienna apartment when the dishevelled, distraught Girardi arrived at her door begging her help. On hearing his story she immediately got in touch with a mutual friend, the Burgtheater actor Devrient, and persuaded him to accompany Girardi to Hietzing and to spend the night with him at her house where not even the police president would dare to break in without an order from the 'All Highest'. The following day she had her usual assignation with the Emperor and lost no time in telling him of poor Girardi's terrible plight, the wickedness of his wife, and the scandalous behaviour of Baron Rothschild. But Franz Josef listened coldly to her passionate defence of her friend; his legal and bureaucratic mind was profoundly shocked by this careless flouting of authority. Why had she not consulted him first? And had she never stopped to think of the scandal it would cause when it became known that the actor had been sheltering in her house? But Katharina dismissed his arguments. Had she waited to consult him, 'poor Xandl' (Girardi's nickname) would already be behind bars, and even with His Majesty's intercession it would take weeks, even months, to have him free. All she asked for was the cancellation of the warrant for arrest, and Girardi, who was suffering from a complete nervous breakdown, would go into a clinic of his own free will. She pleaded so eloquently and so convincingly that the Emperor ended in rescinding the warrant on condition that the actor, following Frau Schratt's advice, went into a sanatorium.

A few months later Alexander Girardi, completely restored to health and formally separated from his wife, was once more delighting his audiences as Frosch in a revival of Strauss's *Fledermaus*. But the 'Affaire Girardi' and the part played by Katharina Schratt was the talk of Vienna for many years to come. When she and Girardi appeared together in a special performance of Raimund's *The Spendthrift*, the Emperor, who disliked all forms of publicity, wrote: 'I see from the papers that you are appearing with Girardi at the Raimund Theatre. Is that really necessary?'

Franz Josef, who in the beginning had been so careful never to interfere in her theatrical commitments, was now, given his increasing years and growing dependency, becoming increasingly resentful of the claims made by her career. He particularly disliked her appearing as guest artist in foreign capitals, and the actress, who continued to cherish her independence, was apt to make arrangements without consulting him first. When she cut short her Karlsbad cure to appear with Hugo Thimig as guest artist in Munich, Franz Josef, who read of it first in the newspapers, was angry, hurt and disapproving:

> What you tell me of an engagement for you and Thimig to perform together in Munich just makes me very sad. I read in it a confirmation of what I had already seen to my alarm in the papers. So after such a long separation [one month] I shall not be seeing you in Ischl till five

or six days later than we arranged. Still I dare not complain for this once more is an unlucky year. And naturally the duties of your profession, your artistic reputation take precedence, which is quite proper, and if the projected guest performances please you I suppose I must also be content.

A few days later he wrote again:

I hope you will recover completely in Ischl, for the Munich guest performances so soon after the Karlsbad cure must be bad for the health and excite the nerves. I am very sad and anxious, also hurt that you said nothing at all to me about the guest starring plan, and arranged everything behind my back. Repeatedly I told you in the last days before our parting that I hoped to see you again in Ischl on 10 July. You did not contradict and agreed. That was really deceitful of you. I am always quite frank with you and you are not. That makes for very black thoughts.

By now Franz Josef was beginning to realize that *die Freundin* was neither as guileless nor as truthful as he had believed her to be. But her evasiveness, above all her sturdy independence, made him love her all the more, and he wrote, 'You may be frightful at times, but you are an adorable angel all the same.'

18

Assassination of the Empress

Under the heading December 1897 Count Eulenburg wrote in his journal: 'The only occasion on which Frau Kathi took an active part in politics was in influencing the Emperor to drop the unpopular Language Ordinance Bill and to get rid of Count Badeni.' Franz Josef had hoped to find in this Polish nobleman, who had gained fame in the army as an efficient governor of Galicia, a man who would be strong enough to implement Taaffe's Language Ordinance Bill and make it work in spite of obstruction. But the tactics which had been successful in feudal Galicia were disastrous in Parliament. To have a Slav Prime Minister from the forests of Poland trying to push through a bill which favoured the minorities infuriated the whole of the German-speaking population and led to such appalling scenes in Parliament that the police had to be called in to clear the House. A German-speaking Radical deputy publicly insulted the Prime Minister, calling him 'a Polish rascal', whereupon Badeni challenged him to a duel, of which Franz Josef wrote to Katharina Schratt, 'I think that the Count has done Herr Wolf too much honour in fighting with him; what he deserves is a caning.' But by now the whole situation had got out of hand. From Parliament the rioting spread into the streets – first the students, then the workers, encouraged by the Socialist politicians.

The Emperor, who had been in Budapest working out a new decennial settlement for Hungary, the second since the *Ausgleich* of 1867 and once more only achieved by granting further concessions to the Magyars, returned to his capital to find that a state of emergency had been proclaimed and the army had been called in to reinforce the police. In a note to Frau Schratt dated the day after his arrival he wrote:

> I had already looked forward so much to our meeting yesterday when, at four o'clock, I received a note from the police that they

were anticipating trouble from the students in the evening. Worry for fear that large crowds would gather and push towards the Burg, which might cause you annoyance on your drive here, and especially on your way from the Burg to the theatre, made me decide that it was better you did not come. But my longing to see you is so immeasurably great that I am bold enough to ask you to come and see me this afternoon between five and six o'clock, providing everything remains calm. It makes me so happy just to have you sitting by my desk during my meal.

Was it during this visit, as Count Eulenburg suggests, that Katharina advised the Emperor to get rid of Badeni? For the past few days she had watched from her windows the tumult growing in the streets, she had listened to rumours of threatened revolution and heard her friends like Edward Palmer, all solid German liberals who resented having their comfortable lives disrupted by the pretensions of the Slav minority, inveighing against the government. And with her vivid imagination she already envisaged a repetition of 1848, with a mob invading the Hofburg and the Emperor being forced to flee. A report from the suburb of Hernals of a drunken crowd having lampooned the Emperor as 'Herr Schrattenbach' was sufficient for her to see herself as another du Barry exposed to the fury of a mob. And one can scarcely blame her if she lost her nerve, and begged the Emperor to sacrifice Badeni.

Nor was she alone in urging his dismissal. The Foreign Minister Count Goluchowski, who was himself a Pole, and the Hungarian Minister President Count Bánffy, were both opposed to the ill-fated Language Ordinance Bill. But Eulenburg was probably right in affirming that neither of these two experienced politicians would have advised the Emperor to capitulate to mob rule. They would more likely have counselled the closure of Parliament and the opening of negotiations leading to the ultimate dismissal of the Prime Minister. The Franz Josef of earlier years would never have allowed himself to be intimidated by the rabble, but it had been an unhappy and frustrating year for the sixty-seven-year-old monarch. He had returned from Hungary after weeks of quarrelling and haggling over every clause in the settlement, and in a moment of discouragement may well have given in to the fears of a loving and anxious woman.

Foreign diplomats, and in particular Count Eulenburg, severely criticized the action of a ruler who was growing weak and old, and it made Kaiser Wilhelm more than ever convinced that it was up to Germany to take the lead in the running of the Triple Alliance. His visits to his ally became more and more frequent, and in one of his letters to Katharina Schratt Franz Josef complained, 'The Kaiser's approaching visit and the journey to St Petersburg are already giving me indigestion.' Though scrupulously loyal to the German alliance, he could not bring himself to like the impulsive, bombastic Wilhelm.

The new German Chancellor, Count Bülow, who accompanied his master to Budapest at the end of the millennium year, remarked on 'the complete contrast between the two Emperors', which may have been why Franz Josef was practically the only sovereign in Europe with whom Wilhelm never caused friction.

> Whereas Wilhelm was constantly and in everything personal, Franz Josef was as impersonal as a shadow. Wilhelm was vainglorious and boastful. The Emperor Franz Josef did not shine and, as far as his duties allowed him, kept in the background. He hated display and Wilhelm's court hunting dress, top boots, spurs and feathered hat filled him with horror. Wilhelm used the second person singular to all the German princes, not only to members of sovereign houses but also to those of non-sovereign houses; Franz Josef kept the second person strictly to his nearest relatives, and the idea of using the second person to a Lobkowicz or an Esterházy would have seemed a breach of etiquette for both parties.... Franz Josef did not understand the Kaiser's intimacies and regarded his jokes and puns as vulgar, his whole manner not quite that of a gentleman.

That he was never happy in the Kaiser's company is evident from a letter to Katharina Schratt written while on a shooting party at Prince Esterházy's: 'Today we are still just among ourselves, so everything is small and *gemütlich*. Tomorrow Kaiser Wilhelm is arriving with his large suite and then it will all be more awkward and strenuous. ... My frame of mind is grumpy and my mood is black.' The whole of the Hungarian visit was an ordeal, and Count Bülow noted how the Kaiser's eulogistic speech in favour of the Hungarians, delivered at the state banquet in the castle at Buda, got on the Emperor's nerves:

I was sitting opposite the two Emperors and could see from the face of Franz Josef that all the burning enthusiasm for the Magyars on the part of his guest went too far for his liking. The Kaiser ended his speech by eulogizing the Emperor for whom in Europe, and in particular in Germany, there was a glowing and boundless admiration which he, Wilhelm, shared in the manner of a son. This also was too emphatic. Fundamentally Franz Josef liked the new Germany as little as he liked the new Italy, perhaps even less.

Count Bülow was right, for the memory of the defeat at Königgrätz rankled more deeply than that at Solferino.

Franz Josef felt more at home in the cold, stiff atmosphere of the Russian court, exchanging civilities with the shy young Tsar. The visit to St Petersburg in 1897 resulted in the signing of a secret agreement between the two powers to maintain the status quo in the Balkans. It was an agreement dictated by expediency, for Russia at the time was heavily involved in the Far East and Austria-Hungary had too many internal troubles to allow it to engage in adventures on the Lower Danube. In the words of Count Goluchowski, 'The Balkans were put under a glass case', which was highly frustrating for the ambitious Prince of Bulgaria, whose future aggrandizement depended on his ability to exploit the rivalry between the two powers. Ferdinand wrote bitterly of being paralysed so long as Austria and Russia remained friends.

Franz Josef, who had not forgiven him the conversion of Prince Boris, told Katharina Schratt, 'I certainly hope that you will keep firmly to your intention of not seeing the Bulgarian, but I am not at all certain that you in your kindness might not in the end grow weak, which would be very disagreeable for me.' Whatever Katharina may have promised, she had never seriously quarrelled with Prince Ferdinand, who continually bombarded her with letters complaining of the unfairness with which he was being treated. The letters were often accompanied by gifts chosen with such exquisite taste that they were impossible to resist: a bunch of cyclamen in amethysts and diamonds, to remind her of those they had picked together in the woods of Karlsbad; a rare butterfly out of his collection, mounted in precious stones; a bird from the Rhodope mountains despatched in a golden cage; and orchids from his greenhouses which arrived packed in ice on the Orient

Express; all gifts of an infinite variety for a woman who always said there was nothing she liked so much as surprises.

Life in the theatre was composed of quarrels and reconciliations, and Katharina knew it would not be long before Count Goluchowski had persuaded the Emperor to receive Prince Ferdinand. Only two weeks after his admonishments, Franz Josef wrote to tell her,

> The Bulgarian is coming to see me tomorrow at two o'clock. He was with Goluchowski the day before yesterday for one and a half hours, speaking first with the utmost vehemence, quite domineering, then becoming servile, especially towards the end of a very animated conversation – in short the complete comedian. I am curious as to what attitude he will assume towards me.

Poor Franz Josef, who in order to steer his unwieldy ship had now to tack and trim. Gone were the days when Austria could dictate to her trembling satellites.

With Karl Lueger installed at the Rathaus, Franz Josef was no longer master even in his own house. When he and the new mayor arrived together at some public function such as the inauguration of the Great Wheel (*Riesenrad*) in the Prater amusement park, one of the great events of 1897, it was always Karl Lueger who received the louder cheers. The year 1897 had been in every way what the old Emperor called an unlucky year (*Pechjahr*), including a family tragedy when the Empress's younger sister, the Duchess of Alençon, died in a fire which broke out in a charity bazaar in Paris. Since then Elisabeth, haunted by death, had spoken and thought of nothing else, and would say quite openly that she longed to die and that she had nothing more to live for in this world.

The melancholy of the imperial couple affected their surroundings, and even the summer holiday in Ischl was no longer as peaceful as in the past. It was only in the company of Katharina Schratt that the Emperor found a little happiness and relaxation. But Katharina was beginning to feel the strain of always having to amuse and entertain, and there were times when she was tired and depressed. At forty-five she no longer had the stamina of a twenty-year-old, but she refused to renounce either her career or her social life. She lived in the grand manner, and with her extravagances and generosity was never free from money worries.

She was constantly entertaining and had one of the best cooks in Vienna. She travelled across Europe with her pet animals and a suite of attendants; on one occasion the Orient Express was held up for over an hour because Frau Schratt's pet monkey had escaped from her carriage, and guards and sleeping car attendants went searching up the line before it was discovered in a toilet happily pulling at the chain. Katharina's way of life far exceeded the salary of a Burgtheater actress, and Edward Palmer was often reduced to despair in trying to balance her accounts. Her debts caused her sleepless nights and brought on the fits of depression which worried the Emperor.

> I am really desperate. If only I knew what was really wrong with you and whether fourteen days on the Semmering will really restore you to health. It is certain that no one can endure the constant turmoil, agitation and commotion in which you live, added to which the lack of proper sleep. I have constant qualms that I am really to blame for it all, that it is your friendship for me which causes you all the bothers, importunities, and even a part of the continual callers. If you had not come to know me you would lead a peaceful life and probably be in better health.

Franz Josef blamed himself both for the anonymous letters, of which she was again a victim, and for the jealousy of her colleagues, a jealousy which was understandable in view of the privileged position she enjoyed under the Burckhardt regime. Even her friend Thimig was beginning to criticize the way in which *die Schratt* interfered in the management and tried to promote her protégées. 'In the theatre *die Schratt* reigns supreme,' wrote Count Eulenburg to the German Kaiser ...

> Everyone crawls on all fours before her, including the administrator, my old friend Berger. Unfortunately *die Schratt* has her knife into Berger's wife, the celebrated Hohenfels, and the poor man who suffers on this account talks of giving up his job and leaving Vienna.... The Burgtheater is now entirely run by Frau Kathi and two of her protégées, with the result that everything is going to pieces.

Even more serious was the fact that Katharina was sufficiently foolish to bring these two little protégées into contact with the Emperor. What was probably done out of pure good nature in an effort to amuse him was immediately interpreted as a proof of her demoralizing influence. Even someone as intelligent as Eulenburg exaggerated the importance that the hold of Frau Kathi's entourage might have on the ageing Emperor. The harmless game of Tarock played with Edward Palmer, the hours spent with two pretty little actresses, were bitterly resented at court and deplored by the Archduchess Valerie, who no longer made any secret of her antipathy towards her father's friend.

It was difficult for someone as natural and spontaneous as Katharina Schratt to keep her head among the intrigues and also the adulation which surrounded her. For the time being she was the undisputed queen of the Burgtheater. But in 1897 the theatre was closed for six months for extensive structural repairs; the seeds sown by Hugo Thimig in her breakfast-room at Hietzing had at last borne fruit. All the defects were rectified, and on its reopening it gave satisfaction both to the actors and to the public. But only a few months later Burckhardt resigned the directorship, worn out by the criticisms and dissensions of those whom Katharina called 'the gods', forgetting that she herself was as spoilt and difficult as any of the goddesses. They accused him of being an unimaginative civil servant, of engaging highly paid foreign stars at the expense of the regular members of the company. But he taught the Viennese to understand and appreciate Ibsen, and he brought to the Burg for the first time the works of a new dramatist called Arthur Schnitzler, whose plays are still included in the Burgtheater repertory today, evoking the Vienna of the *belle époque* in all its frivolity and charm, its underlying cynicism and disillusion.

That year was one of brilliant artistic achievement. While Schnitzler's *Liebelei* (*Light of Love*) was being performed at the Burg, Gustav Mahler was appointed Director of the Court Opera House, an appointment all the more surprising since his own compositions were not appreciated in Vienna at the time. At the Künstlerhaus a group of young artists led by Gustav Klimt broke away from academic traditions to found what became known as the Secession Movement. Names which were to be immortalized in the coming century contributed to the new periodical *Ver Sacrum*: architects like Olbrich and Loos, poets like Rilke and von

Hofmannsthal. But Klimt himself, who had evolved from the school of Makart to form his own highly stylized form of art, belonged to the *fin de siècle*. His figures which shock with the perverseness of their nakedness, his flowers which are already rank, reflect the sensuous decadence of a world which is growing tired. *Weltschmerz* was the fashionable illness in a city which, for all its outward gaiety, had the highest suicide rate in Europe. *Weltschmerz* expressed in Schnitzler's plays, in the sadness of Kasperl, the clown of the Punch and Judy shows in the Prater; and in the lyrics of the Strauss operettas sung by Girardi, '*Glücklich ist wer vergisst, was nicht mehr zu ändern ist*' (Happy he who can forget what can no more be changed).

Even someone as extrovert as Katharina Schratt was not immune from the prevailing atmosphere, an atmosphere as debilitating as the *Föhn*, the hot south wind so prevalent in summer. Moods of *Weltschmerz* intruded into her brilliant, hectic life, spent in the limelight whether she was on or off the stage. Gossip writers recorded her every movement, serious journalists dedicated long articles to her career as a woman and an artist, and curiously enough the Emperor appears to have approved of the glorification of his friend, which he really believed to be entirely due to her talent.

'Yesterday Counsellor Braun called my attention to the *feuilleton* in the *Tagblatt*, devoted to Frau Schratt, by Sigmund Schlesinger; with real pleasure I read his portrayal of your dear personality, so true and clearly written.' But there were times when criticism and adulation became equally enervating and Katharina had a longing to escape, which explains her passion for the mountains, for the pure air of the glaciers. Part of her summer holiday was always spent mountaineering, which the Emperor disapproved of so unreasonably that one suspects Count Wilczek may still have accompanied her on these expeditions. Franz Josef appears to have known of her visits to the Count's castle at Moosham, for a letter to the Empress dated 1895 reads, '*die Freundin* is back from her tour with Toni and his friends, ending up on a three-day visit to Hans Wilczek in an old castle south of Salzburg on the Carinthian border, which he owns and has restored in the medieval style. It is called Moosham.'

How much had he been told of Moosham and the months which Katharina Schratt, as a penniless young actress, spent there with her little boy? Katharina had continued to see Count Wilczek over the years, which led to many arguments and discussions with the Emperor, who made no secret of his jealousy. But in one letter, written in June 1898 and addressed to her at Bad Kissingen, Franz Josef, usually so careful and circumspect in his behaviour, gave full vent to his feelings:

> How can I thank you sufficiently for writing to me so openly, and at the same time so reassuringly, about your meeting with Count Wilczek. On this occasion I behaved again quite unpardonably and I should never have allowed myself to ask you not to receive Count Wilczek any more. My only excuse is my jealousy and the fact that I love you so very much.

In a postscript he added, 'Please tear this letter up at once.' But what woman would have had the heart to tear up such a letter, least of all someone as sentimental as Katharina Schratt. It is carefully omitted from the selection of letters edited by Baron Bourgoing under the supervision of Toni Kiss, but not even Katharina's son ever had the courage to destroy it. It is the last real love letter Franz Josef ever wrote, before the news of the Empress's assassination turned him overnight into an old man.

In this last year of 1898, the year which celebrated fifty years of Franz Josef's reign, it seemed as if the Empress was finally growing tired of her nomadic life. That summer in Ischl she seemed sad to leave her family, but by now she was in such a wretched state of health that there was no question of her being able to take part in the jubilee festivities, and the doctors ordered her to take the cure at Bad Nauheim, one of the most unattractive, but also one of the most efficacious, of German spas. From there she wrote loving letters to her husband, begging him to join her in Switzerland when she was finished with the 'tiresome cure'. But Franz Josef who was, as always, a slave to duty, replied that 'what with the political situation, the autumn manoeuvres and the jubilee festivities on top of everything else, it is quite impossible for me to get away'.

Bad Nauheim, however unpleasant, appears to have been beneficial, for the Empress arrived in Switzerland in better spirits than she had been for months. The rash had subsided and she was able to enjoy the lovely autumn weather. In a letter to Frau Schratt, who was again on what the Emperor called 'one of her breakneck mountaineering expeditions', he wrote, 'Thank God I have really good news from the Empress. She is enjoying the splendid situation of the Hôtel de Caux and the pure, invigorating mountain air. She is taking walks without over-exerting herself and is even planning further excursions.'

This was the last letter Franz Josef was ever to receive from his wife. Two days later Elisabeth was dead, stabbed to death on the quays of Geneva. The controller of her household had tried to stop her from visiting a city which was a hotbed of revolutionaries. But she had only laughed in replying, 'What should anyone want with an old woman like me?'

The Emperor's letter only reached Katharina Schratt at Mariazell, after she had already heard the terrible news and seen the black-edged notices in the village streets announcing the Empress's assassination. All round her people were asking the same question: 'Why should anyone want to kill her? What harm had she ever done?' But she was a predestined victim in the eyes of the young Italian vagrant hanging round the quays of Geneva. The boy whose mother had abandoned him on the streets of Paris, who had known no other home than the foundling hospital of Saint Antoine and the Italian army barracks, where he had spent his years of military service, had a grudge against society, the rich and the powerful in particular. Luccheni was in search of a crowned head at whom to strike a blow for his own self-justification, which would transform him from a penniless outcast into a notorious anarchist. How could he know that the proud, pale woman who walked so confidently towards him, was eager to die? His only triumph was in breaking an Emperor's heart, for Franz Josef never recovered from the impact of a blow which paralyzed the senses and made him in the harshness of his grief unable to respond to the sympathy of those who wanted to help him most. It was to affect even his relations with Katharina Schratt and lead to a misunderstanding which need never have been.

19

Sorrow and Estrangement

No sooner did she hear the news than Katharina Schratt cut short her holiday and returned to Vienna to find a city entirely given over to the dead. Black flags hung from every window. The Empress's portrait, wreathed in crape, was shown in every shop, and weeping crowds filled the churches. From the oldest to the youngest, from those who remembered her as a bride in the full glory of her beauty to those who had barely caught a glimpse of her, shrouded in veils driving past in a closed carriage, all were united in mourning the Mother Empress, the woman who had become a legend in her lifetime. In Schönbrunn the Emperor, impassive and atrophied in grief, was waiting to receive the royal guests who were arriving for the state funeral. His adjutant, Count Paar, had been the only one to hear the strangled sobs of a man questioning his God, 'Is nothing to be spared me in this life?'

Katharina Schratt was admitted at once. 'It is wonderful of you to have come, with whom can I talk better of the transfigured one (*Verklärte*) than with you. I shall await you from eleven o'clock onwards and please do not come through the garden, but straight through to my apartments. *Auf Wiedersehen*.' For all the ambiguity of their relationship, Katharina's grief for the Empress was deep and sincere, for she mourned her both as a protectress and as a friend. There may have been times when she had resented Elisabeth's egotism and heartlessness towards the Emperor, but like everyone else she had ended by falling under her spell, and a letter of condolence written to her by Ida von Ferenczy dwells on the closeness of the relationship between the actress and her imperial mistress:

My dear Frau von Kiss. As soon as I heard that you had arrived, I had a strange desire to come and see you and weep with you over the immeasurably great misfortune that has befallen us both. We can comfort one another in our grief, for in Her Most Gracious Majesty you have lost the best and the kindest friend, to use her own words 'your adopted sister' [*Wahlschwester*]. I unhappily have lost everything in Her Majesty. With a broken heart, I am your devoted Ida Ferenczy.

Elisabeth had recommended Katharina Schratt to her daughters, foreseeing the vulnerability of Katharina's position in the event of her death, when envy and jealousy would have free rein. Both Valerie and Gisela respected their mother's wishes, and in the first days treated Frau Schratt with kindness and consideration. But whereas Gisela always remained loyal to her father's friend, it was not long before Valerie's latent hostility began to show itself. Outside influences played a part. First of all there was her husband Franz Salvator, who had disapproved of the relationship from the very beginning; and second, and more important, there was her Jesuit chaplain Father Abel, who was closely associated with Karl Lueger's Christian Socialists and disapproved of Frau Schratt's predominantly Jewish entourage. The fact that the Empress had been given the sacraments when she was already unconscious and had virtually died unshriven was sufficient for the Jesuit to convince the impressionable and intensely religious Archduchess that her mother's immortal soul was in danger unless the Emperor dedicated himself to God.

Katharina complained to her friend Count Eulenburg,

They never stop worrying the poor old gentleman. All this talk of prayer and repentance gets on his nerves, but he lets himself be influenced and keeps going to confession when he has nothing to confess. When I tell His Majesty, 'What would a dear kind person like yourself have to confess?' he replies, 'Don't you want me to become better in my old age?' and I say, 'That is so. But there is no point in Your Majesty going to confess when you have no sins on your conscience to confess.'

Katharina's position in the imperial hierarchy was sufficiently important to warrant a visit of condolence from the German Ambassador, and the fact that he referred to it as a 'visit of condolence' when writing to Kaiser Wilhelm suggests that Count Eulenburg was already aware of the difficulties and unpleasantness the actress might have to face now that she had no longer the Empress's protection to rely on.

Yesterday I drove out to Hietzing to pay my respects to Frau Käthi Schratt, having announced my arrival by telephone. I found my charming hostess alone at home. From outside the house looks like any other. But once you have crossed the threshold you might be in a small manor house in the depths of the country. There are some magnificent old trees in the garden, which is separated from the house by a beautiful old iron fence, and the glassed-in courtyard is full of flowers.

Frau Käthi, who looked very attractive in mourning, had prepared for me a tea and made me sit on the chair where, she told me, 'His Majesty always sits'. I said I had come to commiserate on what I felt must be an irreparable loss for her, whereupon she burst into tears, and they were not just stage tears, but good, honest tears, saying, 'You cannot know what I have lost. She was my noblest and kindest friend. His Majesty even assures me that she has remembered me in her will.'

Katharina's famous discretion appears to have deserted her on this occasion, and she confided in Count Eulenburg as a friend rather than as an ambassador, forgetting that every word would be handed on to Kaiser Wilhelm. 'I can speak to you frankly, for I know you are well disposed towards me and are really devoted to the Emperor.' But was it necessary for her to discuss with a foreign ambassador the details of Franz Josef's private life and his relations with his daughter?

She tells me that the Archduchess wants her father to come and live with her at Wallsee and have the ministers travelling to and fro, but that the Emperor is quite firm in refusing, as Frau Kathi says, 'What should the poor old gentleman do with himself at Wallsee? But the arrangement would suit the Archduchess and her family and they never give a thought to His Majesty.'

The ambassador foresaw the growing tensions in the imperial family, with Valerie trading on her position as her mother's favourite daughter to try and loosen the ties between her father and his friend. From the German point of view, the influence of Frau Schratt was far less harmful than that of the bigoted Archduchess, who was completely given over to the Clerical Party to which the present Prime Minister, Count Thun, also belonged. Between them, minister and daughter would have the Emperor all day on his knees in the confessional, looking for guidance to Rome rather than to Protestant-dominated Germany.

Katharina's first disappointment was on finding that she had not been mentioned in the Empress's will, though Franz Josef made good the omission by giving her a golden talisman, a St George thaler, one of the few jewels which Elisabeth had always worn. But a far greater disappointment came towards the end of the year with the presentation of the jubilee awards. A special medal to be known as the Elisabeth Order had been struck to commemorate the fifty years of reign. Originally it was to have been presented by the Empress herself, who shortly before her death had assured Frau Schratt that she would be among the first to receive it. This order was now to be conferred personally by the Emperor in memory of his wife, and Katharina, who naturally thought that the Empress's wishes would be respected, was counting on receiving it. But as the day of presentation drew nearer and not a word was said by Franz Josef, she raised the matter herself, reminding him of his wife's promise, only to be told that what would have been natural in the Empress's lifetime would be quite impossible in the present circumstances and only lead to a lot of unpleasantness from which she would be the first to suffer. For once Katharina refused to be her 'dear sensible self'. She had counted on receiving this order and spoken of it to all her colleagues. It was to be the one proof of Elisabeth's friendship, more than ever necessary now that she had gone. Rightly or wrongly, she suspected Valerie of having influenced her father's decision, especially when the Emperor had the tactlessness to tell her that a former governess of Valerie's, whom the Empress had not even liked, was coming over from England to receive the order. Hurt and humiliated, she reacted by losing her temper and Franz Josef, who was not used to scenes, was shocked at her lack of control.

Fortunately her disappointment was mitigated by a week of theatrical triumph when Raimund's *The Spendthrift* was produced for the first time at the new Burgtheater with Katharina Schratt in her favourite role of Rosl, playing opposite Josef Kainz, the greatest living actor on the German-speaking stage, a star of international reputation who commanded a far higher salary than that of any other member of the Burg. Katharina, who was full of admiration for Kainz both as an artist and as a man, wrote of him enthusiastically to the Emperor, who replied with a certain irony, 'Yesterday must have been a very happy day for you, as you performed with the great artist and ideal man whom you seem to be so very delighted with.'

One can hardly blame Katharina for dwelling on her professional triumphs when she felt she had been deliberately slighted over the jubilee awards. The Emperor now needed her more than ever, but in these first months he was entirely obsessed by his memories of Elisabeth. From Budapest, where after two months the streets were still hung with mourning flags, he wrote, 'I am still best in your dear company, for with whom else can I speak so well of our *unforgettable one*, whom we both loved so much.' The tone was still as loving, but the letter lacked the ardour of the earlier years. He was too dedicated to his sorrow to respond to Katharina's warmth and, in spite of her wholehearted sympathy, there were times when she wished he could spare some thoughts for the living. Her nerves were in a bad way and the beginning of the menopause was manifesting itself in pains and headaches and above all in an exaggerated susceptibility. Franz Josef, who had not realized how much she minded not receiving the Elisabeth Order, wrote:

> I am afraid that I may be responsible for your depression, though I mean so well and am so inexpressibly fond of you. I only hope that your nerves will soon get better and that also the stomach pains will subside. . . . The time I spend in your company is the only thing which brightens my sad and melancholy existence and all I ask of you is for you to love me just a little bit and to try not to be angry with me.

Yet, all unknowingly, he hurt her time and again. A miserable letter, written from the castle of Gödöllo, which had been Elisabeth's favourite home, elicited a spontaneous if ill-judged offer to join him which met with a gentle rebuff.

> I am touched by your plan to visit me here, which is a proof that you are still fond of me, and had it been possible would have made me immensely happy. But though a visit to the Castle of Buda would have been comparatively easy, here it would be virtually impossible. I and my staff live in such close proximity, there are no women

servants except for one old maid, and every new arrival at the station is a major event. There would only be a lot of gossip, which would not be very pleasant for you and which it is better to avoid. Believe me, it would be wiser in our mutual interest if we denied ourselves the pleasure of meeting now and deferred it till after my return to Vienna.

Franz Josef was as usual thinking of the actress rather than of himself, but Katharina was only too ready to take offence and the Emperor, who was beginning to dread her growing propensity for making scenes, wrote two days later, 'I am a little afraid of our next meeting, as I do not know if you are angry that your wish to meet me at Gödöllo could not be fulfilled. Surely you will be as sweet and kind to me as ever and receive me as graciously as before.'

This was only one of a series of misunderstandings which gradually led to a temporary estrangement. Faithful to the promise made to her mother, the Archduchess Valerie invited the actress to visit her and her husband at Wallsee, an invitation which was accepted with pleasure and with pride, till the Emperor, who knew that his daughter's gesture was only dictated out of filial piety and feared that it might not be pleasant either for Valerie or for Frau Schratt, was sufficiently tactless to advise the latter to refuse. He had so little understanding of women, still less of a vain and temperamental actress at a critical time of life. In an angry scene, Katharina forgot herself to the extent of speaking openly against the Archduchess, a *lèse-majesté* Franz Josef refused to tolerate and to which he replied in harsher terms than he had ever used before. The result was that Katharina left suddenly for Monte Carlo without telling the Emperor of her plans, which he only heard of through Baron Hawerda. Grieved at her behaviour, he complained,

It was not very kind of you to conceal from me the fact that you intend to stay away for three weeks, and I was upset by the way in which you always only telegraphed your next overnight stop – Riva, Genoa, etc. – instead of telling me at once you were going to Monte Carlo, which was only natural and quite to be expected. At any rate, you are now in your favourite haunt and I only hope that the air of the gambling halls will agree with you better than the good mountain air which is what you need to calm your nerves.

Meanwhile the Archduchess Valerie and her family had moved to Schönbrunn, where their presence did little to alleviate the prevailing atmosphere of gloom. Count Eulenburg writes of how much he dreaded an invitation to dine at the palace,

> ... for the Emperor appears to have a stultifying effect on his daughter who, on her own, is rather an attractive woman but in front of her father is so overcome with shyness that she hardly opens her mouth. And as the old gentleman can hardly be described as amusing, the result is an evening of such excruciating boredom that both host and guests are glad when it is over. What a contrast to a dinner at Frau Kathi Schratt's. Whether at Hietzing or in town, the conversation is always sparkling and animated, the company varied and brilliant, and the hostess herself one of those life-enhancing people who always brings out the best in her guests.

In a private letter to Chancellor Bülow, the ambassador describes a dinner given by 'Frau Kathi' shortly before her departure for the Riviera. On this occasion his fellow guests included Prince Rudolf Liechtenstein; Marquis von Becquehem; the Director of the Royal Opera House, Herr Gustav Mahler; Herr Direktor Palmer; the Burgtheater actor Max Devrient and his wife; and 'Frau Kathi's newest friend, Countess Nora Fugger-Hohenlohe, one of the few women belonging to the *Erste Gesellschaft* to ignore the virtually Indian caste system which dominates Vienna society. Frau Kathi, who was wearing the most beautiful pearls, was as always the perfect hostess.' But beneath her smiling amiability, Katharina was a worried woman, who after dinner took the ambassador aside to pour out all her grievances. The ambassador's letter goes on:

> Till now she had refused to become involved in politics. But from all sides she was hearing nothing but complaints of how the Emperor was falling completely into the hands of his Prime Minister Count Thun and his Foreign Minister Count Goluchowski, both of whom were Slavs and therefore determined to keep all right-thinking Germans out of the administration.

But when Eulenburg suggested that it was up to her, who had so many opportunities of seeing the Emperor, to inform him of what was being said in the town, she only replied that he had quite enough to worry him without having his few moments of relaxation spoilt by those tiresome politics. There was never any good news and the poor old man worked so hard and gave himself so much trouble. But no one was ever satisfied, and there were times when he became so discouraged that he felt he could not go on any more and that he was so unlucky, the country might be better off without him. Then Kathi's blue eyes would flash in anger and she would say, 'I keep telling His Majesty it is mad to talk like that, for without him everything would fall to pieces at once.'

Politics were not Katharina's only worry. Edward Palmer, who always heard the latest gossip, told her there was a strong cabal forming against her which included the Emperor's son-in-law and the Foreign Minister Count Goluchowski. She immediately repeated this to Franz Josef, who appears to have taken it sufficiently seriously to discuss it with one of the highest of his court officials. On 24 February 1899, he wrote to the actress,

> Yesterday Prince Liechtenstein came again to see me regarding the intrigues repeated to you by Palmer. His news on the whole was reassuring. There is no question of Goluchowski being involved in the plot, and also my son-in-law appears to be innocent in the matter, so there does not seem to be much truth in Palmer's assertions. But whatever may have been said, no plots or intrigues can in any way affect my friendship and undying gratitude towards you.

But though Franz Josef might convince her of his friendship, even of his love, Katharina complained to Count Eulenburg that he did nothing to protect her against the malice of his entourage. In her inimitable Baden dialect, half in laughter, half in tears, she would say, 'Every child who has a favourite toy makes a fuss when someone tries to take it away and refuses to let it go. But His Majesty does nothing and allows me to be destroyed.'

Valerie's presence at Schönbrunn only made matters worse, for whether by accident or design, she arranged for the children to visit their grandfather at the time when he usually took his afternoon walk with Frau Schratt, and however much the Emperor might grumble, he always ended by giving way, till in connivance with the actress Dr Widerhofer insisted that fresh air and exercise were essential for his health.

Monte Carlo and the excitement of the gambling tables was a

welcome change to the petty intrigues and constant pinpricks to which Katharina was being subjected in Vienna. But the arrival of Edward Palmer, who was taking his usual Riviera holiday, brought more unpleasant news. According to Palmer, there was talk of the Emperor's remarriage as soon as the period of court mourning was over. The idea was said to have originated with the Foreign Minister, the object being to provide the country with an Empress who would fulfil her representational duties and make the court again the central pivot of society. The natural choice appeared to be the Archduchess Marie Therese, the forty-two-year-old widow of the Emperor's brother Karl Ludwig, who had died two years before. But the Archduchess Valerie, who detested the heir apparent, was said to favour a younger candidate – a pretty Orléans princess who might still bear the seventy-year-old Emperor a son.

At first Katharina refused to believe what she scornfully dismissed as stock exchange gossip. But on her return to Vienna she was concerned to find that no less a person than Count Eulenburg gave credence to the rumour, for though the Emperor's present state of mind appeared to preclude the possibility of remarriage, his sense of duty might in the end persuade him to act in the interests of his country. Katharina, however, still refused to believe what would be disastrous not only for her own future but also for Toni's, who was now eighteen and about to finish his military service and take his diplomatic exams.

Franz Josef's letters to the Riviera were still those of a sorrowing widower. He wrote, 'How I envy you seeing all those beautiful places we visited together with our beloved one.' But he was gradually beginning to be bored with family life and being nothing but a grandfather, and the letter with which he welcomed her return recaptured some of his former ardour:

> These lines will be here to greet you on your arrival in the dear Gloriettegasse before we meet again after what seems to me an endless separation. I need not tell you how I look forward to tomorrow, for I still hope you realize how much you mean to me.... If you allow me to, I will come and see you at the usual hour of seven-thirty. Should that be too early for you, I could come at eight or even later.... As you will be very tired after your journey and I also hear

that you have not been well lately, I beg of you not to get up, but to stay quietly in bed, which will be very good for you and will give me the greatest pleasure, for there is nothing I find so cosy as to sit by your bed and have a good chat. We will have so much to talk about.

Here he alluded to their recent arguments, by adding, 'Let us talk quietly and without getting excited', and he signed himself 'your infinitely loving Franz Josef'.

Katharina must have been at her most beguiling when she received the Emperor on that early spring morning of 1899 in her pretty, flower-filled bedroom with its tempting breakfast table laid with gleaming silver, the hot rolls and steaming coffee drawn up beside the bed, and she herself ensconced among her lace-encrusted cushions, wearing the most feminine and extravagant of negligées, her famous *café au lait* complexion still as smooth and unwrinkled as that of a young girl, her golden hair with hardly a streak of grey. However much she might complain about her health – and she was a great complainer – however much she might worry about her figure, which was now certainly middle-aged, to her elderly admirer she still appeared the epitome of youth and beauty.

Edward Palmer's gossip would not have been referred to on this occasion, when nothing was allowed to disturb the harmony of their reunion. But a few days later on one of their early morning walks, when Katharina was regaling the Emperor with some of the latest gossip, she informed him that the most persistent of all the rumours circulating in his capital was that of his remarriage. Franz Josef greeted this news in genuine astonishment and laughingly said, 'You are joking.' But she assured him she was being serious, the rumour was widespread, and Count Eulenburg had told her it was even being discussed in diplomatic circles. Whereupon the Emperor looked at her with his tired, kind, blue eyes and said, 'You can tell Count Eulenburg from me that I have no intention of remarrying, whatever people may say.' Katharina's mind was at rest. But she may have wished he had said a little more. The Emperor never gave her any of those surprises she longed for, or uttered the words she imagined in her daydreams. As she told Count Eulenburg, she was no more than a favourite toy, and toys can be very breakable.

20

An Ageing Actress

For eight years, from 1890 up to the time of Burckhardt's retirement, Katharina Schratt ruled as undisputed queen at the Burgtheater, promoting her favourites, continually exceeding the regular amount of leave, expecting and receiving leading roles at the expense of younger and more highly qualified actresses. Forceful by nature, she had grown more domineering with age, and old and devoted friends like Hugo Thimig deplored the way in which she was exploiting her position. Matters came to a head with the appointment of a new director. Paul Schlenther was an East Prussian who, as dramatic critic of the powerful *Vossiche Zeitung*, had been one of the most important figures in the theatrical world of Berlin, where he had earned the respect both of actors and of playwrights. Thimig was among those who had obtained his nomination to the Burg and unfortunately he had done so without consulting Katharina Schratt, who immediately took a dislike 'to the unprepossessing Prussian journalist and his shrew of a wife' and voiced her disapproval to the Emperor. Fearing her opposition, the management told Thimig that Schlenther could only survive by paying court to *die Schratt*. But the new director was of a strong, uncompromising nature and far too sure of himself to kowtow to a wilful actress. He could also rely on the support of Prince Montenuovo who, since the recent death of the Lord High Chamberlain, Prince Hohenlohe, had been in charge of the court theatres.

Hohenlohe had had a genuine love for the theatre, whereas his successor, Prince Rudolf of Liechtenstein, who was a personal friend of both the Emperor and Empress and incidentally also of Katharina Schratt, was interested in horses rather than in art, and the jurisdiction of the court theatres had passed into the hands of the Second Chamberlain. Prince Alfred Montenuovo could claim royal descent through his grandmother the Empress Marie Louise of France, who after Napoleon's death had contracted a morganatic marriage with Count Neipperg, and he was more obsessed by the mystique of royalty than any of the archdukes. To please his beloved daughter Marie Louise, the Emperor Franz had elevated her descendants to the rank of princes of Montenuovo, and Franz Josef's morganatic cousin was now among the most trusted and influential of all the court officials. He was fanatically devoted to his master, and, being jealous of his prestige, was the first to disapprove of his intimacy with Frau Schratt and the people with whom he associated in her house. It offended his sense of propriety to have His Catholic and Apostolic Majesty sitting down to a game of cards with Jewish bankers. And no sooner was he in charge at the theatre than he decided to put an end to the privileges and abuses of an actress whose talent was equalled if not surpassed by half a dozen of her colleagues. Paul Schlenther had a powerful backer in Prince Montenuovo and Katharina discovered, much to her indignation, that her complaints about the new Director made no impression on the Emperor.

At first she had little cause to complain. Old favourites like Ohnet's *The Iron Master*, Raimund's *Verschwender* (*The Spendthrift*) and Sardou's *Divorçons* (*Let's Get Divorced*), in all of which she starred, were revived with considerable success. There was even a new performance of *The Taming of the Shrew*, with Katharina Schratt playing her favourite Shakespearean role. But among the laurel wreaths of praise were a few insidious thorns, suggesting that a forty-six-year-old actress was a bit too mature to play Kate. And in the new naturalistic theatre which was now the vogue, comprising the plays of Sudermann and Gerhart Hauptmann and the psychological dramas of the great Scandinavians Ibsen and Strindberg, there were no *Glanzrollen* (star parts) for Katharina Schratt. The years of Schlenther's directorship saw Arthur Schnitzler's greatest triumphs, *Reigen* (*La Ronde*), *Liebelei* (*Light o' Love*) and *Die Grüne Kakadu* (*The Green Cockatoo*), in all of which Katharina could have starred ten years before but which were hardly suitable for a solid though still fascinating matron, who every year was becoming more difficult to cast and more demanding in her claims.

Ill health, stomach cramps, headaches and dizziness brought on by the menopause contributed to the periods of depression, the bouts of nerves to which Franz Josef was always referring in his letters. But the weeks they spent that summer at Ischl were happy and serene. And on 29 August 1899 Franz Josef thanked his friend 'for the great kindness and forbearance with which you have blessed me during the last almost two months'. His gratitude appears to have expressed itself in a particularly generous cheque to help in settling the ever-present problem of her debts, to which she replied with hyperbolic praise: he was a 'super-angel', 'an archangel', and she herself 'the most ungrateful of creatures'. 'How you exaggerate in your glorification of my decrepit old person,' wrote Franz Josef. But not a penny went to pay her debts. It was promptly spent on a new and expensive journey.

In September she was taking sea baths at Biarritz, staying at the fashionable Victoria Hotel, and October found her at the Grand Hotel in Paris, where she appears to have bought, on her own responsibility, the rights to a play which she considered to be a perfect vehicle for her talent. It centred round the early amours of the Emperor Napoleon III and the Englishwoman, Miss Howard, whose money helped to stage the *coup d'état* which put him on the throne. In spite of Katharina's enthusiasm, it was a shallow, insipid little piece which Schlenther had every right to refuse as being below the standards of the Burg. Indignant at his refusal, she demanded the dismissal of 'this Prussian who has no idea of the taste of the Viennese public'. But Montenuovo upheld the Director's decision and again the Emperor refused to become involved.

From now it was open warfare between Schlenther and Frau Schratt, and Hugo Thimig noted in his journal under the heading of 7 January 1900:

> The quarrel between Schlenther and *die Schratt* appears to have come to a head. The director is determined not to produce the silly little play which *die Schratt* brought back with her from Paris. She on her side is determined to get rid of him at all costs. Her ill temper is now vented on the Emperor, who for once has refused to comply with her demands. The other evening he went to the theatre for the first time since the Empress's death. It was to accompany the King of Serbia to the last performance of *The Spendthrift* in which Käthi Schratt was

performing, but this time the actress did not give her usual friendly glance towards the Royal Box. His Majesty was so upset by this behaviour that he sent for her faithful old housekeeper, Netty, to ask her for an explanation.

It seems as if *die Schratt* has been contemplating for some time the possibility of loosening her ties with the Emperor. She is said to be sick of the everlasting restrictions and longs for her freedom. So now we will see who wins in the end – the theatre, that is Schlenther, or *die Schratt*. Should Käthi's power over our old Emperor be so strong that he cannot do without her cherished company, then our poor old Burgtheater will suffer a blow which will completely destroy it. On the other hand, should our Emperor, who is usually so correct and so sensitive to public opinion, refuse to give way, then *die Schratt* will lose, which for our theatre will be the best thing that can happen.

Katharina Schratt had powerful friends inside and outside the theatre. Rudolf Liechtenstein, who was devoted to the Emperor and knew how much he depended on the actress's friendship, would willingly have sacrificed Schlenther for the sake of her good will. But he was tired and old and most of the court business was now being carried out by Montenuovo. In the spring of 1900 Schlenther was still Director, and all Katharina's efforts to dislodge him had so far proved unsuccessful.

There was further dissension when it came to the renewal of the contract, and the actress found herself treated with no more regard than any other member of the company. What particularly enraged her was a clause to the effect that any leave which was exceeded by as much as a week would be subject to heavy penalties. In the past years she had taken her holidays when and how she wanted, many a time at the Emperor's express desire. Now she found herself being dictated to as if she were a novice at the Burg.

But in those spring months of 1900 the Emperor was faced with far greater problems than the matter of Katharina's contract. The line of the House of Habsburg was put in danger, and the future of the succession at stake, when the heir apparent, now completely restored to health, fell irrevocably in love and insisted on marrying a woman who, though of noble birth, did not belong to one of the few mediatized families within the sacred circle of eligible royal brides. However hard and pugnacious he might appear in everyday life, no one was more romantic or more faithful as a lover than Franz Ferdinand from the evening he first caught sight of Sophie Chotek at a court ball in Prague. She was a penniless girl on the verge of spinsterhood, neither young nor particularly beautiful, but even her enemies, who later included most of the Austrian court, had to admit that she possessed enormous intelligence and charm.

The Archduke loved Sophie Chotek in secret for five years, and to facilitate their meetings she had taken a post as lady-in-waiting to the Archduchess Frederick who, with five marriageable daughters, hoped to see one of them as a future empress and did all she could to encourage Franz Ferdinand's visits to her castle in Pressburg. One day, after a tennis party, he left behind his gold watch, to which was attached a medallion. The curious Archduchess made the fatal mistake of opening it, only to find instead of the plump, smiling face of her eldest daughter, that of her lady-in-waiting. Frustrated and enraged, she went to complain to the Emperor, and Franz Josef, who was just beginning to tolerate his heir and admire his military efficiency, found to his horror that what he was about to reprimand as an indiscreet flirtation was now openly admitted to be a passionate love affair, with the Archduke demanding the right to marry Sophie Chotek. For the Emperor there was only one solution – marriage meant the renunciation of all rights to the throne, whereas Franz Ferdinand was determined to have both Sophie and the throne. And Franz Josef's first serious quarrel with his hitherto favoured Prime Minister, Count Thun, was brought on by this very issue. Sophie Chotek came of an old Bohemian family that traced its line back to the medieval feudal lords. Most of her ancestors had been exterminated in the religious wars of the sixteenth and seventeenth centuries and Thun saw no objection to a marriage that would be enormously popular in a country where the Czechs were always chafing under a sense of inferiority to the Hungarians. But when the minister suggested that the Choteks might be included in the list of eligible families, the Emperor's reply was a curt refusal, and a few weeks later Thun handed in his resignation.

Franz Ferdinand and his uncle, with the whole court hierarchy solidly behind the Emperor, were now in open conflict, and not even the Archduke's brothers dared to support him in what they believed to be a hopeless cause. Only his stepmother, the frail, gentle Archduchess Marie Therese, who ever since his childhood had given a difficult boy a love and understanding rare even in a mother, now took upon herself to plead on his behalf. Marie Therese was one of the only members of his family whom Franz Josef really admired and respected, and it was she who finally persuaded her brother-in-law to consent to a morganatic marriage, a phrase which to Franz Josef had a shameful stigma. The future Emperor would have a wife who could not even bear his name, and children who could never inherit the throne. But perhaps this was preferable to what might happen after he died – and at seventy one had to envisage the possibility of death – when Franz Ferdinand might violate the laws and traditions of his house and raise Sophie Chotek to the rank of Empress. The Emperor finally gave his consent and the ubiquitous Montenuovo drafted the solemn act of renunciation by which Franz Ferdinand swore in the presence of the Papal Nuncio, the princes of the Church and the assembled Archdukes to deny his children their rightful heritage.

That Montenuovo could have played a leading part in a matter which earned him the undying hatred of a man as hard and unforgiving as Franz Ferdinand shows him to have been not so much of a careerist – for who could have foreseen that the Emperor would live for another sixteen years – as a fanatical upholder of what he believed to be the sacred laws governing the House of Habsburg.

The estrangement between the Emperor and the heir apparent was now complete, with disastrous results for the future of the monarchy. There were now two courts, the Hofburg and the Belvedere, the beautiful palace on the hill dominating the city, built by Hildebrandt for Prince Eugène of Savoy and now embellished by Franz Ferdinand with all the treasures inherited from the Estes.★ Gathered at the Belvedere were the discontented elements in the capital, the administrators, scientists and technicians cold-

★ The Este treasures came into the possession of the younger branch of the House of Habsburg when the last Duchess of Modena married a younger son of the Empress Marie Therese.

An Ageing Actress

shouldered by the aristocratic Hofburg *camarilla*. Franz Josef never forgave his nephew for his misalliance, and state secrets were never entrusted to a man who might be tempted to confide in his wife. The Emperor's relations with Sophie Chotek were courteous but distant. On her marriage she was created princess and later raised to the rank of Duchess of Hohenberg. But at court the youngest of the archduchesses took precedence before her, and she was neither allowed to drive out in a court carriage nor given a seat in a court box at the theatre. There are only brief references to her in Franz Josef's correspondence with Katharina Schratt. Three months after her marriage he mentioned her for the first time in a letter dated 9 September 1900: 'Yesterday my nephew Franz presented his wife to me at my invitation. It went off very well. She was natural and modest, but appears to be no longer young.'

Franz Ferdinand's morganatic marriage and the future of the succession obsessed the Emperor to the exclusion of almost everything else. But it was not the only matrimonial crisis he had to deal with in the spring of 1900. His daughter-in-law, the widowed Stephanie, Crown Princess of Austria, had fallen in love and wanted to marry a Hungarian gentleman of her entourage, and on this occasion Franz Josef showed a far greater tolerance and kindness than Stephanie's father, King Leopold of Belgium, who not only disinherited his daughter but forebade her sisters to have any further communication with her. The Emperor, on the contrary, continued to remit his daughter-in-law's allowance and permitted her to marry Count Lónyay, but he stipulated that, as an imperial archduchess, her seventeen-year-old daughter Erzi could no longer remain under her mother's roof.

These family troubles left the Emperor with little time to sympathize or listen to Katharina Schratt's comparatively trivial worries. The fact that his rigid sense of honour forbade him to criticize the behaviour of his heir apparent, even to his dearest friend, contributed to the actress's sense of neglect and the feeling that she was in a false position, one which had been progressively more onerous ever since the Empress's death. The antagonism of the Archduchess Valerie and the Emperor's growing dependence on his daughter, with whom he discussed all the family problems; the closeness of his relations with the Archduchess Marie Therese – all contributed to make Katharina feel that it was high time for her to get away from the machinations of an envious court. By now her nerves were in such a bad state that the slightest grievance was exaggerated a hundredfold, and at the beginning of March she and the Emperor had an argument in which the tired and irritated monarch tried in vain to persuade the unreasonable Katharina to accept her Burgtheater contract and not to make an enemy of Montenuovo. Her reaction appears to have been so violent that he finally lost his temper and on the following day wrote her a letter of apology, which shows the depths of his affection for her and the power she had to hurt:

My dear good friend. Actually I do not know if I may still use those words, or if I should not write '*Gnädige Frau*'. But I cannot give up the hope that yesterday's black thunderclouds will disappear and the old happy relationship be re-established. You rejected so obstinately and passionately my earnest, well-meant remonstrances and pleas made in our mutual interest, that I let myself be overcome by a vehemence that I regret and on account of which I ask your forgiveness with all my heart. I mean also to forget the hasty, insulting and to me deeply painful manner of your departure yesterday. But let the voice of your kind heart speak, think over the situation quietly and you will find that we can by no means part, that we must find each other again. Think of the long years of our serene friendship, of the joys and sorrows, unfortunately more sorrows, that we shared and which you helped me to bear. Think of our dear unforgettable (*unvergessliche*) one whom we both loved so much and who hovers over us as guardian angel, and then I hope you will be disposed to reconciliation. ... In the morning on arising you were always my first thought; the prospect of being able to see you gave me the courage to get through the day. Surely your kind heart will not allow all that to change, and for me to live on lonely in my old age without your dear company to cheer and strengthen me. The way you left me yesterday, I regret to say, awakened in me the doubt whether you are still fond of me. But if you still feel something of the old friendship for me, think of how terrible the uncertainty is for me and give me some sign that will let me hope that all can be well again.

Katharina replied by telegram, pleading a headache which prevented her from writing at length, but promising a meeting at some early date. Ill health, however, did not prevent her from acting, and Franz Josef wrote on the following day, 8 March:

> I should not have thought that you could have acted yesterday after a wretched night with a bad headache. It is a proof of your strength of will and sense of duty. But much as I had long looked forward to seeing you as Cyprienne, I could not make up my mind to go to the theatre after what had happened. To see you like that from afar would have been too painful for me.

Katharina did not miss a single performance throughout the spring, for she was determined to show the management that she had lost none of her popularity with the public and could still command as large an audience as any of the great stars. But her health could not stand the strain and the doctors ordered a complete rest. The nerves from which she suffered at the time, and which finally led to a complete breakdown, were due not so much to her quarrels in the theatre and to her difficulties with the Emperor, as to the appalling state of her finances for which she was not always responsible. Bills of change and IOUs signed by Nicholas Kiss kept arriving from his various posts abroad, obligations which he knew would always be honoured by a wife who wanted no scandal attached to Toni's father. Also Toni, encouraged by his mother, was living at a standard far beyond his means and already showing the family talent for getting into debt to an extent which could not be confessed even to Edward Palmer.

Katharina's relations with Franz Josef continued to be tenuous throughout the spring, ready to break at the slightest offence. When she was on holiday in the Dolomites at Easter, he wrote to her from Vienna of the greatest theatrical event of the season, the performance of the Italian actress Eleonora Duse in Gabriele D'Annunzio's *La Gioconda*.

> The day before yesterday [8 April] I sat through the whole of La Duse's performance of *La Gioconda*. The theatre was sold out, the public very elegant. The performance was really very good, if one gets accustomed to much that is strange to us, for La Duse, rather old, without make-up, with greying hair and without a corset, acts remarkably well and perhaps in an exaggeratedly natural style.

In ordinary times Katharina was the most generous and enthusiastic admirer of her theatrical colleagues: when in Paris she never
missed a performance of Sarah Bernhardt and was proud of the
friendship of Coquelin, and on her travels in Italy she had been
the first to write to the Emperor of La Duse's extraordinary genius.
But now La Duse's triumph meant the triumph of Schlenther for
having brought her to the Burg, and her dislike of the new
Director and the fact that she had been unable to dislodge him had
become almost pathological.

A cure at Karlsbad, where she was pestered by the attentions of
an unbalanced young man who in the past year had been pursuing
her from place to place, in no way improved her health. The
correspondence over her contract became ever more acrimonious
till, in a fit of temper, she finally tendered her resignation – a
gesture intended to set the Burgtheater management by the ears,
rouse the compliant Liechtenstein to action, and force Montenuovo to get rid of Schlenther rather than have the Burgtheater
lose the most popular of its actresses. But nothing happened
as Katharina had expected. A polite note from Schlenther
merely expressed the hope that she would reconsider her decision,
and on Montenuovo's advice the official acknowledgment of
her resignation was postponed till the beginning of the autumn
season.

Meanwhile the court had moved to Ischl, and Katharina Schratt
was as usual in residence at the Villa Felicitas. Here she was visited
by Prince Liechtenstein, charming and compromising as always,
ready to humour her to the best of his abilities. To Liechtenstein
she confessed that her quarrel was not only with the theatre, that
everything had changed since the Empress's death and her position
had become a false one. She had become a burden to the Emperor
and she had decided to go away, which would make certain
people very happy. Later the Prince described her as a sick woman
whose nerves had completely gone to pieces. But for the moment
nothing had changed. The Emperor still breakfasted every
morning with Frau Schratt, taking the short cut across the park
to the bath-house, where the actress bathed every morning in an
icy mountain stream. On fine days breakfast would be served
out on the verandah and passers-by would see their Emperor

drinking his coffee and having his first morning cigar in the company of Katharina Schratt. Katharina was immensely popular in Ischl, and no one resented the friendship of their Emperor with a woman so kind, so generous and so ready to help her neighbours.

Franz Josef's seventieth birthday, 18 August 1900, brought a great wave of loyalty to the whole of the Salzkammergut. Bonfires blazed from every mountain-top and every village street was hung with black and yellow flags. Deputations came from far and wide to offer their congratulations, and presents poured into the Kaiser Villa from every part of the Empire. Among the family gifts were those of Katharina Schratt, for which the Emperor thanked her, 'How you spoil me with your charming, useful but much too expensive presents.' But it was only ten days later, as the holidays were drawing to a close, that the Archduchess Valerie, noting that her father was looking particularly depressed, asked him if he would like to go out that afternoon with the children, only to be told that he had to go and visit Frau Schratt for the last time, as she had made up her mind to leave him, perhaps for ever. Valerie was stunned by the news. It was all she had worked and hoped for in the past years, but the sight of her father's stricken face, those sad, tired eyes so near to tears, prevented her from rejoicing. Now for the first time she felt the burden of her responsibility in having deprived him of the only company which brought him a little gaiety and happiness.

All that is known of that last meeting is from a letter of Franz Josef written to his friend barely twenty-four hours after their parting, a letter so heartrending in tone that it is hard to understand how Katharina could have persisted in her decision. She appeared to have written him a few lines which afforded some measure of comfort, for he said,

> I can imagine you would have liked to add much more. It is the same with me. Perhaps you will tell me everything some time when your nerves are better, which with God's help will happen in not too long a time, and I will again be receiving your dear, *dear* letters. Thank you for looking back at me so long yesterday after our parting, which was one of the most painful moments of my life. The clock tower is just striking six o'clock. I left my room twenty-four hours ago for our

last walk, my passionately beloved angel (*heiss geliebte Engel*). Yesterday, after you had disappeared from my sight, I met a chimney sweep – you consider such things a sign of luck. Perhaps this meeting will bring me luck and, for me, luck means seeing you again.

21

A European Celebrity

The news of Frau Schratt's departure spread like wildfire through Ischl. In the Kurhaus and casino and at Zauner's pastry shop they talked of nothing else. There was jubilation in court circles, and particularly in the Archduchess Valerie's household, but those who were close to the Emperor, like Dr Widerhofer and his adjutant Count Paar, viewed the future with fear and apprehension. Ida von Ferenczy, who had been living in Hungary since the Empress's death, arrived in Ischl to find a wasps' nest of gossip and intrigue, and wrote immediately to Prince Liechtenstein to find out the truth.

> Forgive me if I allow myself to bother you with a letter, but I have heard the news which, though it makes the ladies very happy, fills me with anxiety and foreboding. Please write me what the truth is. If the break comes from His Majesty, then there is nothing to worry about. But if the daisy (*Gänseblumchen*) has broken off the relationship, then it would be a tragedy. To change your life at seventy and renounce a pleasant distraction is dangerous, and our dear Emperor does not deserve it. But there is no form of suffering he is being spared.

The somewhat contemptuous reference to Katharina Schratt as the daisy, which in German has the more humble name of goose flower, shows that, after all these years, the Empress's adoring friend refused to admit that the actress was ever more than a distraction in the Emperor's life. Liechtenstein, who really loved his master and knew how much he depended on the actress, wrote in reply:

> It is difficult to explain a situation which arises not out of one but out of several reasons. It appears that since Her Majesty's death Frau Schratt has been feeling the lack of her protection. Actually there has been nothing definite. But she has come to the conclusion that she is

in a false position, that she is being accused of something which never happened. She has nothing to blame herself for, as her relationship with His Majesty was entirely platonic. This feeling has been growing on her for some time, fed by imaginary and at times justifiable grievances, till she has come to the decision to retire from Vienna, to get out of everybody's way and to have some peace. The crisis came during the summer holidays at Ischl. She has promised not to sell her house at Hietzing, and also the villa at Ischl remains furnished, so there is still the faint hope that she may consent to return in the spring, though when she left she refused to commit herself in any way. Her nerves are quite *kaputt*, and some peace may do her good. His Majesty is desperate and will find it hard to exist without her cheering company. He now feels he has lost the distraction Her Majesty wanted him to have. Frau Schratt is at the moment a sick person ... her position from the very beginning was equivocal and she has only realized it since Her Majesty's death. In the last two years the wish to get out of it all has gradually become an obsession and there was nothing to do but to let her go. Once she has had her rest, perhaps even to the point of boredom, it may be that her old feelings for His Majesty will come back, and she will remember the debt of gratitude she owes him. The parting appears to have been very loving and devoid of any bitterness, only she would make no promises about returning. To those who reproach her that in her behaviour she has shown herself ungrateful to the Empress, she replies that the situation has changed. And it is true that she has certainly become more vulnerable. I am so sad to think of the dreary winter which lies ahead for our poor old Emperor. It is not fair that he should have lost his only distraction. But when one looks at it from her point of view, then one cannot fully blame her, and the people who are pleased about it are empty-headed fools.

Liechtenstein was fair and generous-minded and a personal friend of Katharina Schratt's. But he also refers to her as the Emperor's 'distraction', and by now she may have grown tired of being no more than a distraction. After the Empress's death she may have hoped to be given some measure of the love and protection he had given to Elisabeth in always shielding her from the harsh realities of life. But he could not even protect her from the malice of his family or defend her position in the theatre. Above all, she was tired of always being discreet and of never being able to break through the nimbus of majesty with which

Franz Josef was surrounded even in the moments of their greatest intimacy. By nature she was a chatterbox. Her flow of *Tratsch* (gossip) was what rendered her so irresistible to a man as reserved and as laconic as the Emperor, but there were others who profited by her love of *Tratsch*, which sometimes over-rode discretion. Like many a pretty woman she was susceptible to flattery, and no one was more versed in the art of flattery than the German Ambassador, now raised to the rank of prince by his grateful sovereign. In spite of Franz Josef's reluctance to discuss the matrimonial affairs of the heir apparent, 'Frau Kathi' was sufficiently well-informed on the situation to give Prince Eulenburg some highly useful information. And there were times when the Austrian Foreign Minister, who was no friend of Katharina's, would warn his sovereign that Frau Schratt was talking too much to the German Ambassador. Criticisms of this kind were bitterly resented by the actress and only strengthened her determination to get away.

Her colleague Hugo Thimig noted in his journal:

> There are many versions of why *die Schratt* has left. I think I can explain it quite simply. She is probably filled with an insane or perhaps very sane longing to get away. Being enslaved in golden chains appears to have brought her to the verge of a breakdown. After a few months of freedom she may return. She now talks of leaving Austria for ever. I must confess it would be a blessing for our theatre to be rid of such a glaring example of protection in high places.

Katharina had never expected the Emperor to accept her resignation or to sign without a protest the decree which authorized her retirement and placed her on the pensioned list. Up to the very last moment she had hoped for Schlenther's dismissal. But however miserable he might be, however anxious to do all in his power to facilitate her return, Franz Josef feared that any intervention on his part would only serve to damage her reputation and add to the flood of gossip already caused by her departure. In the same impassive manner in which he had accepted the resignation of Count Taaffe, one of the only ministers he had ever trusted, he now signed the decree depriving his beloved Burgtheater of the only actress whose performances he had never tired of, whom he could watch day after day and always find a new delight in every little gesture and every fleeting expression. His unhappiness showed itself in a nervous irritation towards his ministers and an increasing grumpiness in the family circle, where all the Archduchess Valerie's efforts to entertain him with her children failed to rouse him from his misanthropic gloom. The only grandchild in whom he took any pleasure was the seventeen-year-old Erzi, who since her mother's remarriage had been living with him at Schönbrunn. For Erzi's sake he made an effort to appear at balls and *thés dansants*, but even the most charming of seventeen-year-olds could not compensate for what Eulenburg describes as the 'warm, womanly beauty' of Frau Schratt, and the gay, effortless chatter over the breakfast table at the Gloriettegasse. He still wrote to her, 'though I do not know if it is agreeable to you for me to write to you. But so long as it does not annoy you and you do not say anything to the contrary, I shall keep to the dear old custom and imagine that I am gossiping with you as in the good old days.'

Occasionally he received a letter in return, but more often it was a telegram, keeping him informed of her latest address: Gastein – Paris – Munich. She complained of sleepless nights and blinding headaches, but those who met her on her travels reported that she appeared to be in the best of spirits. Ill health did not prevent her from mountaineering in Gastein or from visiting all the pavilions of the Great Exhibition in Paris – an exhibition which stretched along the Seine from the Place de la Concorde as far as the Champs de Mars and displayed all the latest wonders of modern technology. Katharina was an indefatigable sightseer, delighting in all that was new, whether it was the latest automobile of De Dion Bouton or the model of the Trans-Siberian Railway, where visitors could sit in a luxurious dining car while painted landscapes of the Russian and Chinese countryside revolved outside the windows and local dishes were served partly by Russian *moujiks*, partly by Chinese boys. She ate ices in a reconstructed Piazza San Marco and drank tea in the fashionable Ceylon Pavilion. Everything was of interest to her, whether it was the pavilion devoted to the study of the occult or the one devoted to sport, where she was proud to find a lifesize photograph of her Emperor dressed in his hunting clothes, and the record of his prowess as a sportsman – 48,345 head of wild game shot in the fifty-two years of his reign.

Everyone of note was in Paris that autumn, and Katharina was not lacking in escorts, whether it was the faithful Palmer or Ferdinand of Bulgaria, a recent but by no means inconsolable widower on an incognito visit to Paris and only too ready to accompany his dearest 'Frau Kathi' to theatres and art galleries, where Monet's *Water Lilies* were on view for the first time, and Rodin's *The Kiss* was shocking even the most sophisticated of Parisians. On the boulevards, Réjane was delighting her public in the role of Madame Sans Gène, and Sarah Bernhardt was having her greatest triumph as the young Duke of Reichstadt in Rostand's *L'Aiglon*. Katharina could imagine the horror of Prince Montenuovo if a Jewish actress dared to appear at the Burgtheater wearing the white uniform of an Austrian marshal, impersonating an Emperor's grandson. It was only recently that Arthur Schnitzler had had his name removed from the list of reserve officers for having depicted on the stage the peccadilloes of a 'Lieutenant Gustl' and thereby casting a slur on the honour of an officer of the Royal and Imperial Army.

The continual round of gaieties, the lunches at Doyen and the suppers at Maxim's, had a disastrous effect on Katharina's already debilitated health, and the last weeks in Paris were spent in bed under the orders of Dr Staniek, who had been specially summoned from Vienna. She had been prone to excess all her life and moderation had not come with age: cream pastries and rich pâtés continued to be her undoing and contributed to her increasing *embonpoint*. She was excessive even in her generosity, for it was slightly absurd of her to buy the most expensive of Louis-Seize dressing-tables as a present for one of the richest monarchs in Europe, who had palaces crowded with priceless furniture, yet preferred to sleep on a truckle bed and wash at an iron washstand. If Franz Josef appreciated the gift it was an account of the 'dearly beloved giver', and he used the exquisite dressing-table, which looked so incongruous among the spartan furnishings of his room, up to the day of his death. Baskets of roses, boxes of the mildest cigars, and the finest of cognacs arrived as usual for his name-day. But presents came more frequently than letters, and the poor old Emperor tried to glean what news he could from Katharina's old housekeeper, who had remained behind at Hietzing; from Edward Palmer when he returned from Paris; and even from young Toni Kiss, whom he invited to Schönbrunn 'in the hopes of hearing all your latest movements'.

According to Hugo Thimig, Toni had been the first to encourage his mother to leave the theatre, in the belief that a mother on the stage would be damaging to his career. But he thoroughly disapproved of her behaviour towards the Emperor, behaviour which if carried to extremes might be disastrous for the future. Whether it was Toni Kiss for the sake of his career, or Prince Ferdinand for the sake of Bulgaria, or Prince Eulenburg for the sake of the Austro-German alliance, almost all of Katharina's friends and intimates were beginning to feel that it was time for her to forget her grievances and remember her debt of gratitude towards the Emperor.

Eulenburg wrote in his journal of 13 October:

> I hear that Princess Gisela and Rudolf Liechtenstein and all those who are closest to the Emperor are doing everything they can to try and get Frau Kathi to return, as it is the only means of cheering the poor old gentleman. The Archduchess Valerie may disapprove of these attempts, but she no longer tries to influence her father into definitely breaking off the relationship. It is difficult to foretell as to what psychological effect a prolonged separation might have on the ageing Emperor. But I don't think Frau Kathi will let matters come to such a pass.

Eulenburg was wrong, for the actress continued to sulk. The official news of her retirement from the stage, which contrary to her expectations had not raised the storms of protest she had hoped for, contributed to her ill humour. A deferential letter from Director Schlenther, written at Prince Liechtenstein's instigation and expressing his deep regret at the untimely resignation at the very height of her career of an actress who, by her beauty and her talent, had contributed so much to the glory of the Burg, received only the briefest of acknowledgements. It was too late for Schlenther to write, 'In the past year and under my directorship your performance in certain plays opened out the prospect of a long and eventful career in front of you.' He should have shown his appreciation before, not now when she was receiving tempting offers from nearly every theatre in Germany. No sooner had she recovered from her illness than she began appearing as a guest artist, first at Stuttgart and then at Munich, where Princess Gisela gave her the most friendly of welcomes. Even more flattering were the attentions of Gisela's aunt, the Countess Trani, whom Katharina had met with the Empress on the Riviera, and who now invited her to accompany her to Rome for the closing celebrations of the Holy Year. In a letter to her father, Princess Gisela wrote: 'Aunt Spatz shares our sorrow at Frau Schratt's decision and hopes it will not be irrevocable.'

The projected trip to Rome was sufficient to make the scandal-loving Viennese go so far as to assert that Frau Schratt was going to Rome to seek a dissolution of her marriage ties to Herr Kiss in order to marry the Emperor. These rumours were even said to have penetrated the Vatican and to have reduced the old Pope to such a state of excitement that he tried to postpone the audience accorded to Countess Trani and her suite. But when the day came and he discovered that Frau Schratt wanted no more than a blessing, his relief was such that he received her particularly graciously, which in no way pleased her enemies among the Clerical Party at home.

No one who really knew Katharina Schratt ever gave credence to this talk. Basically she was far too intelligent and sensible to harbour such illusions. She had witnessed the insults which even a Countess Chotek had to put up with, and the fury Franz Josef felt towards his heir for having by his marriage threatened the inviolability of the House of Habsburg. It is doubtful whether she would ever have wanted to be the morganatic wife of a grumpy, irritable old man too worn down by care, too burdened by his duties to spare her even an hour of happiness.

For a woman who lived in a crowd, Katharina's private life remained curiously secretive. If her relations with the Emperor were as platonic as both would have us believe, but which given their two characters seems hardly credible, then Katharina must have had more than her share of suffering. And now all the memories of these sufferings and humiliations had accumulated in the mind of an ill and hysterical woman at the beginning of the menopause, a woman who, if she had still been in love with Franz Josef, could never have inflicted the pain which is reflected in his letters.

On the first day of the new year he wrote,

> Let us hope that when you return to Vienna we can again re-establish our former happy relationship. I will gladly forget the pain you caused me and how hard and unjustly you treated me, and I hope that after this long separation you will have regained sufficient control over your nerves to forgive me, If I have in any way offended you, then we will not speak any more of what had happened and regain our old and cherished friendship.

Another time he wrote,

> It is sad to hear from Netty that your spirits are still so low and that you constantly have anguish and worry. . . . If it would only be possible to help you and to bring an end to your nomadic life. If only some way would present itself which would be feasible for fulfilling your unfortunately unknown wishes and putting your mind at ease. Prince Liechtenstein will rack his brains over it and I shall even consult the ingenious Hawerda in this direction.

On succeeding to the post of Lord High Chamberlain, Rudolf Liechtenstein had never thought he would have to play the role of Mercury in persuading the offended Frau Schratt to return to her royal master. Against the advice of Montenuovo he forced the reluctant Schlenther to write a second letter to Frau Schratt saying that, owing to the misunderstandings, exaggerations and deliberate falsehoods which had got about, it would be in both their interests if they could meet during her stay in Vienna. But again the Director received the curtest of replies, this time by telegram from Rome: 'Had you really wanted to meet me the time would have been three months ago. Now you are only acting on orders from above, and in this case there is no point in our meeting.'

Having failed in this direction, Liechtenstein now approached the Archduchess Valerie as to whether she would be willing to send a friendly message to Frau Schratt urging her to return. It was a difficult thing to ask of anyone as proud and as reserved as the Archduchess, who confided in her journal, 'Liechtenstein has asked of me something I cannot bring myself to do.' And she confined herself to telling her father to send her kindest greetings to Frau Schratt.

Among the most active in trying to heal the breach between the actress and the Emperor was Prince Philip Eulenburg, who, on hearing that Frau Schratt was in Munich, went there in the hope of persuading her to come back for Christmas, only to find that she had already left for Rome. When she returned to Vienna it was only for the briefest of visits, and in a private letter to Kaiser Wilhelm dated 18 January 1901 Eulenburg wrote of the difficulties he had in dealing with a spoilt and temperamental actress:

> Frau Kathi returned a few days ago to the great joy of the Emperor, and I went and paid her a visit, which alternated between laughter and tears. The lady is still highly offended and it is difficult to make her see reason, for she invariably ends in saying 'But after all I am right!' Her chief grievance is against the Emperor, who according to her does not lift a hand to protect her. In the old days the Empress would intervene on her behalf, now she has no one, for the Emperor cannot bring himself to say one energetic word in her defence.
>
> I told her I understood her feelings, that a temperamental woman who loves – and I presumed she loved the Emperor – expected the object of her affection to be as passionate as herself. But she could hardly expect the Emperor to behave like a fiery, full-blooded young man, any more than she could expect the cupboard in her room to walk. It was after all only a cupboard and the Emperor could only act according to his character. He obviously wanted to help her in every way, but what could he do when she herself did not know what she wanted! Frau Kathi admitted that this was true, all she wanted was for the Emperor to be different. I told her that she could only expect to be protected if she specified who or what she wished to be protected from. For how was His Majesty and his entourage to know if she continued to sulk in silence. I assured her that, to the best of my knowledge, those who had been opposed to her in the beginning were now all in favour of her return. People were terrified as to what might happen after the Emperor's death and would do anything to preserve his precious life and assure him a contented old age.

Eulenburg had no illusions over '*die liebe Frau Kathi*'. She was a selfish and capricious woman who thought of herself more than of her sovereign. 'She tells me she has no desire to go back to the theatre where she has been so badly treated, that in fact she wants nothing for herself.' Once more we hear her favourite phrase, 'what she really likes are surprises', and the ambassador was sufficiently cynical to suspect that Frau Kathi's surprises could be very expensive.

His letter to Kaiser Wilhelm went on:

> Having listened to the lady's grievances, I then began to upbraid her for her ingratitude and lack of consideration for her sovereign, whereupon she burst into tears, asking me whether I expected her to submit in silence while the Emperor allowed his courtiers, his daughter and even some of the clergy to abuse her in the vilest manner. Frau Kathi went on to say, 'I told His Majesty how hurt and unhappy I was, but though he was as sweet and kind as usual, he kept on repeating, "Don't be so angry. Don't let us talk about it any more." I insisted, for what is the point of being friends if one cannot speak frankly and openly with one another.'

This was hardly the kind of language to be appreciated by a diplomat, and Eulenburg told the Kaiser:

> I warned her that if she went on in this way she would end by irritating the Emperor. She could count on me as a friend, in so far as I had the Emperor's interests really at heart and my gracious sovereign, who had always admired her as an artist, was in favour of my intervening on behalf of his friend and ally. At this I was treated to a fresh outburst of tears with many devoted messages and hand kissings for Your Majesty.

But neither Eulenburg nor Liechtenstein nor even the ingenious Hawerda could persuade a nervous, restless woman to give up her nomadic life. Having retired from the Burgtheater with an annual pension of twelve thousand kronen she was ready to give her services to whatever theatre paid the highest price. But what she wanted even more than money was public recognition: a benefit gala performance at the Burg, her portrait to hang in the theatre's gallery of fame, the official title of Reader to His Royal and Imperial Majesty the Emperor Franz Josef – a title which, as Eulenburg commented, was equivalent to that of *Maîtresse en Titre*. Wherever she went the press was at her heels, and she gave interviews freely and not always as discreetly as in the past. An interview with the German press while she was acting in Berlin provided another source of discord between her and the Emperor, who disliked any form of publicity. 'In searching through the papers for some news of you, I found an interview with a Berlin journalist in which you told him more than was good and useful for him to know.' A few years earlier he could have made the same remark and Katharina would have replied in her charming, artless fashion apologizing for her indiscretion. But now she immediately took umbrage. She was a famous actress and the press had the right to report her movements and to satisfy her public. She was no longer a member of the court theatre, bound by the antiquated laws and regulations of the Burg. If her utterance and actions gave offence, then it was better to cease all communication and she would no longer trouble His Majesty with letters, which in her present state of health were tiring for her to write. Poor Franz Josef could only reply, 'I am immensely sorry that my remark in my last letter has troubled you, and once more I ask your forgiveness. I hope you will not bear me a grudge over my careless remark.' He did not know what proportions a harmless if somewhat tactless remark could assume in the mind of a hysterical woman.

That year there were no violets sent on 1 March – no loving greetings. The death of a little great-grandchild went unnoticed, and Franz Josef wrote, 'I was so naïve as to hope that you would give an indication of sympathy upon the death of my poor little great-granddaughter in memory of fifteen years of faithful friendship. Even in that I was disappointed and it hurt me very much.' But the worst of all was for him to hear that she had passed through Vienna without sending him a line or expressing a wish to see him.

The months went by and all that he heard was an occasional message through her housekeeper. In the papers there was talk of the actress acquiring a castle in the vicinity of Salzburg, and the seventy-year-old Emperor still felt a twinge of jealousy when he heard of her staying at Moosham with Count Wilzcek. But perhaps Moosham had lost its charm and a plump, middle-aged Kathi may no longer have had the power to fascinate the ever romantic

Wilczek, for no more was heard of the castle in Upper Austria, and on the evening of 19 June 1901 Baron Hawerda appeared at Schönbrunn to say that the *gnädige Frau* had returned to the Gloriettegasse.

22

A Tired Old Man

From the letter she wrote to him on her arrival, it would seem as if she had never been away.

> I am really very happy to be back at the Gloriettegasse, and I admit there were times when I was very homesick for my glass house. My nerves are still in a bad way and I am often overcome with melancholy. But to find Your Majesty's dear sweet letter waiting for me at home worked like a ray of sunshine on my spirits.

Nothing appeared to have changed, only the tempo had grown slower. The two lonely years had left their mark on the ageing Emperor. He still had the figure of a young man, the erect carriage and the springy walk. He could still spend all day on horseback during the military manoeuvres and get up at dawn to work with the same precise attention to detail. But he nevertheless seemed to have lost the initiative, the will to command. And in Vienna it was said that the brilliant *Franz Josefzeit* had died at the end of the century with the death of the waltz king Johann Strauss, and that the Emperor reigned but no longer ruled.

Nevertheless he reigned with all the consummate experience gathered over the years, using men for his own purposes, selecting his ministers not only from among the aristocracy but from among the lawyers and civil servants, able administrators like Ernst Koerber and Max Vladimir Beck who pushed through social reforms and economic measures regardless of the various pressure groups in Parliament at loggerheads with one another. People would say that the old Emperor was becoming fossilized, but it was not Franz Josef who was fossilized, it was his court. In a violent outburst of temper when Franz Josef had refused to give him the coveted order of the Golden Fleece, Ferdinand of Bulgaria wrote to the French Ambassador Paléologue:

In Vienna one breathes the atmosphere of death and decrepitude. When the old Emperor Franz Josef deigns to receive me at the Hofburg, he always appears to me surrounded by his tragic legend, his sinister ghosts. I know of nothing more lugubrious than dining at the Emperor's table; there one only comes across archaic countenances, shrivelled intellects, trembling heads and worn-out bladders. It is an exact image of Austria-Hungary today.

But the court played little part in Franz Josef's life; with advancing years he became ever more adverse to ceremony and reduced the time for the serving of a state dinner to the minimum, so that a young man sitting at the end of the table had barely partaken of his first mouthful before his plate was removed and the next course was served. The family dinners, which took place on the first Sunday of every month when the Emperor was in residence at the Hofburg, and where every member of the Imperial House who happened to be in Vienna at the time was due to appear, but where no one was able to utter unless they were directly addressed by the sovereign, were events which every young archduke had learnt to dread. After his seventieth year, when the Emperor lived almost entirely at Schönbrunn and his relations with the heir apparent became always colder and more distant, these family dinners were gradually dispensed with.

But from his correspondence with Katharina Schratt one sees that Franz Josef was interested in all the new discoveries of the age. Time and again he told her, after an audience given to some scientist or explorer, that 'he had so much to tell me that was new and interesting'. After visiting an exhibition held at the Museum of Applied Art on the Stubenring, he wrote, 'I stayed an hour and a half as there was so much to see. It was very full and was a great success, though for my taste it was a little too much tinged with the Secession. You would have enjoyed it as there were a lot of modern interiors.' He liked to hear of the latest cults and fashions of the day. Spiritualistic seances were then the rage, and as always Katharina followed the latest trend. 'I hear that you are again occupying yourself with spiritualism and hypnotism. That can only injure you and exhaust your nerves still more. However it would be interesting to hear something about it.' During the absence of Katharina Schratt he had missed the stimulation of her company as much as he had missed the warmth and charm of her presence. 'You will have so much to tell me of your travels and the time will be all too short,' he wrote before their summer reunion in Ischl, where the inhabitants were pleased to see that the *gnädige Frau* was again at home and that the Emperor was going to have breakfast at the Villa Felicitas on his birthday.

At the end of the month he was back in his lonely palace of Schönbrunn, and wrote:

> It occurred to me too late and only after our parting that I did not thank you for coming to Ischl and by your kindness giving me such lovely and happy hours in your company. I look forward immensely to our meeting in Hietzing at the end of September. . . . I think a great deal of dear Ischl where it is so beautiful and green, whereas here it is quite autumnal, the trees yellow, the lawns burnt, and I think of our ascent of the Jainzen, and above all I think of you my dearest friend, and I worry about your mountain tours.

But Katharina herself was still restless and unsatisfied. Her debts had not been settled and her problems remained unsolved. She would brood over her future and her health, seeing herself as a penniless old woman, and yet the very next day launch out on some fresh extravagance.

In the autumn of 1901 she had the satisfaction of appearing again on the Vienna stage, both as Cyprienne at the Deutsches Volkstheater and as Vroni in a special performance of Anzengruber's *Der Meineidbauer* (*The Perjured Peasant*) held at the Theater an der Wien on behalf of the Anzengruber monument fund. On both occasions she received a public ovation, and soon the news was going round that she had accepted a dazzling offer from America, news which horrified both the Emperor and his entourage and also some of her personal friends.

On 5 November 1901 Prince Eulenburg informed Kaiser Wilhelm,

> It is being said that Frau Kathi Schratt has taken on an engagement to appear in New York. She says it is on account of her career. But evidently it is going to bring her in a lot of money, and she has no idea of what she is letting herself in for. I can just see the enormous posters all over New York, displaying her picture next to that of the Emperor.

Let us hope that here they will have sufficient sense to realize the
danger of such a journey, and will prevent her from going by charging
the expenses on to the promenades in Schönbrunn, which incidentally
have been resumed. But things are not quite the same. Frau Kathi is
still being difficult and playing the offended one. Still it cannot be too
bad, for the Emperor is always in a better mood when she is about.
One thing has changed: there are no more seven o'clock breakfasts at
the Gloriettegasse, as Frau Kathi has given His Majesty to understand
that she cannot be amiable before nine o'clock in the morning, with
which I fully sympathize.

Whether it was Liechtenstein or Hawerda, or the ever tactful
Palmer, someone in the end made the Emperor understand that
most of Frau Schratt's 'nerves and anguish' were due to financial
troubles, and he wrote to her in a tone of relief, 'Everything can
be settled quite easily through Palmer. Please understand that I
always want to do what is best for you, even if you do not always
make it easy for me. There is nothing I would not do to content
you and put your mind at rest.' It was shortly after this that
Katharina Schratt became the owner of a handsome apartment
house at the beginning of the Mariahilferstrasse, which Eulenburg
estimated to have been 'in the million krone bracket', news which
can hardly have endeared her to the Archduchess Valerie, who
was always concerned for the future of her large and ever-increas-
ing family. But in the eyes of the Viennese nothing was too good
for Kathi Schratt, who had lost none of her popularity when she
left the Burg.

In October 1903 she appeared in the title role of *Maria Theresa*,
a comedy by Franz Schönthan. The event brought large crowds to
the Deutsches Volkstheater and filled columns in the newspapers.
Admittedly, the publicity given to the fact that she would be
wearing her own jewels, and that these were generally known to
have been given her by the Emperor, considerably added to the
interest. Franz Josef's reaction can only be guessed at, from a curt
reference in one of his letters addressed to her from Budapest: 'I
have read in the newspapers that you will be playing the role of
the Empress Maria Theresa at the Deutsches Volkstheater in
October. Is this true?' Court circles were appalled at the actress's
incredible tactlessness, and in spite of the laurel wreaths presented

by her fans and the fulsome praise of some of the hired critics, the performance does not appear to have been an unqualified success. The actress's natural exuberance appears to have been crushed by the august significance of the role.

In the meantime Katharina had celebrated her fiftieth birthday, on which occasion she wrote to the Emperor that 'with Palmer's help, I am resolved to put my financial affairs in order'. But she had barely written these lines so full of good intentions before she was off on another of her journeys, which every year took her further and further afield. One year she was in the Canary Islands, the next she was off on a cruise in the Mediterranean, stopping off at Messina, Malta, Tunis and finally Algiers, where she found her husband, recently installed as a full-fledged Consul General and dispensing hospitality on an ambassadorial scale which was well beyond his means.

In the early spring of 1904 she was in Egypt, where a photograph taken by the pyramids shows her riding a camel with a group of friends, including one of the Baltazzi brothers. But judging by her letter to the Emperor, Egypt under the tutelage of England does not appear to have appealed to her:

> What started as my 'flight into Egypt' has turned into a chase in search of mosques, temples and graves which end in lying on the stomach and giving one acute indigestion. Unfortunately the English civilization has managed to transform the inhabitants so completely that they are now only recognizable by the colour of their skin. Even their native costume has suffered, for there is nothing so hideous as to see one of the local blue and white shifts worn under a modern frock coat. And this is called progress! But why should I bore your majesty with descriptions of a country and a people which you yourself have visited under far more interesting conditions.*

From her letters it would appear as if Katharina was still harbouring a grievance. On her cruise she complained that the Emperor had not spoilt her with his letters. 'If it were not for that dear good Palmer, I would not have an idea of what is going on in Vienna.' From Egypt she wrote, 'Here is the letter already announced by telegram. I apologize to Your Majesty for the delay,

---

*The Emperor had visited Egypt on the occasion of the inauguration of the Suez Canal.

but I feel there is no great longing to receive it.' But perhaps the most significant of all was a letter addressed to Budapest in which she questioned 'Why did it all have to turn out to be so?' What had Katharina Schratt expected after Elisabeth's death? In what way had Franz Josef failed her? She herself would have been at a loss to answer, other than by repeating what she had already told Prince Eulenburg – she only wished the Emperor had been different. She had wanted with all her heart to help and comfort him after the Empress's death, but had found the barriers were more rigid, the distance between them greater than they had ever been before. Her sacrifices (for in her mind it was she who had made the sacrifices, both in her personal life and in her career) had been for nothing. She was too vain to accept the fact that her talent as an actress was of a kind which had flourished on vitality and youth, that if at fifty she was still courted and admired it was largely on account of her romantic friendship with the Emperor – a friendship which gave rise to so much speculation and surmise. She had come back to Franz Josef on her own terms, hurt, disappointed but finally appeased. The violets came as usual on 1 March to cheer the poor old Emperor in his solitude at Schönbrunn, from where he wrote, 'Though much unfortunately has changed, I still hope that our good true friendship will continue and that I shall find in your dear company one of the few rays of light in my dreary existence.' His life was drearier than ever now that he had stopped going to the Burgtheater – a silent gesture of resentment at the way in which the management had treated his friend. It was not in his nature to interfere. But he was no longer to be seen in the Royal Box since Katharina Schratt had left the theatre.

From Budapest, where the Hungarian Nationalists were fighting like wild cats to disrupt the unity of the army and establish Magyar as the language of command, he wrote to her in a mood of the deepest depression, 'You will find me greatly aged and mentally enfeebled. I think a great deal about the past and a great deal of the sad and hopeless future and also about death.'

One by one he had seen the familiar landmarks disappear – friends and enemies whose ways he had learnt to understand, and even to respect – Bismarck and old Kaiser Wilhelm, Victoria of England and the Tsar Alexander. Albert of Saxony, who had been his only friend, was no longer there to go hunting with him in the mountains, his favourite nephew Otto was dying a slow and lingering death from a shameful disease, and at the Belvedere Franz Ferdinand and his intriguing, ambitious wife were only waiting on his death. There were times when the poor old Emperor would confess to Katharina Schratt, 'I am so tired, I cannot go on. But how can I leave things in the hands of that madman?' All those years of patience and manipulating in trying to make the dual monarchy work would founder in the clumsy hands of Franz Ferdinand, with his psychopathic hatred of the Hungarians. The Archduke might be right in asserting that Hungary's treatment of her minorities was causing unrest among the hitherto loyal Croats, the Romanians of Transylvania and the Serbs in the Vojvodina. But Franz Josef was still trying to abide honourably by the terms of the *Ausgleich*. And it was not until 1906 that the intransigence of the Magyars forced him to resort to extreme measures by dissolving the Hungarian Parliament and introducing universal suffrage, which broke once and for all the powers of the Hungarian nobles.

Serbia, too, was no longer the compliant ally, or rather vassal, it had been in King Milan's day; in the last years he had made his home in Vienna and in his will had expressed the wish to be buried on Austrian soil. His son Alexander had never known how to win the affection of his people and, after a disastrous marriage to a woman of notorious reputation whom he insisted on crowning as queen, he had ended in losing even the loyalty of his army.

The first warnings of the troubles which ten years later were to plunge the world into war came to Vienna on the feast of Corpus Christi in May 1903, while the Emperor was taking part in the great procession which carries the Blessed Sacrament through the centre of the town. He was walking beside the Cardinal Archbishop when Count Goluchowski suddenly appeared at his side and whispered, 'There is grave news from Serbia, Your Majesty – a group of rebel officers have brutally murdered King Alexander and the Queen.' Franz Josef listened attentively before saying in a firm voice, 'Is there anything we can do?' to which the minister replied, 'Nothing, Your Majesty.' And the Emperor walked on in the procession.

European reaction to the Serbian atrocities was even more violent than at the time of Stambouloff's murder. Several countries recalled their ministers and consuls. And the accession to the throne of Peter Karageorgevich, who belonged to the rival dynasty to the Obrenoviches and was known to be both a Russophile and a pan-Slav, promised little hope of peace in the Balkans. The only person who took a certain cynical pleasure in these events was Ferdinand of Bulgaria, not only because the mutilated body of Draga Mashin provided the world press with better copy than a butchered prime minister, but chiefly because a Russophile Serbia would force the Austrians to court his favours and break the uneasy status quo in the Balkans which Russia and Austria had maintained during the past years.

Ferdinand was a frequent visitor to Vienna in these days, his eighty-three-year-old mother providing him with an excellent excuse for appearing at the Palais Coburg on the Seilerstätte, where the old lady was still busily intriguing in the interests of the son she hoped to see a king before she died. On these occasions he never failed to call at the Gloriettegasse to see if '*die hohe Frau*' (her ladyship), as he called Katharina, happened to be at home. She was still his principal link with Schönbrunn and he had been seriously worried during her absence, doing all in his power to persuade her to return, advising her to count her blessings rather than to dwell on her grievances. Karlsbad was still their favourite meeting place, though Ferdinand was also an assiduous visitor to the Riviera. Here his interests lay in plants and gardens rather than in the casino, where Katharina Schratt appears to have been dogged by an almost constant ill luck.

Not even Franz Josef was able to exercise a restraining influence, and in letter after letter he implored her to desist and to refrain from reckless gambling. 'You are still so very happy-go-lucky and all my good advice is of no use. Please gamble prudently in the future and don't try to recover what is lost by playing high.' In the spring of 1903, the Emperor heard that Toni had accompanied his mother to the Riviera, and he wrote on a note of irony, 'So you have settled in the vicinity of your beloved gambling halls, where you are now probably initiating Toni in the pleasures of the '*rouge-et-noir*'. What a successful method of education!'

There was one disastrous occasion when Katharina gambled away her entire travel money – no less than two hundred thousand francs – and was stranded ill and penniless on the Riviera, suffering from a nervous rash brought on by anxiety and worry. It was in the spring of 1906, at the height of the Hungarian crisis, when Franz Josef had grown tired of making concessions, and the Imperial Chief of Staff had already alerted the army to be prepared for war. Harassed and unhappy, the Emperor, who had graver matters to think about than the debts of Katharina Schratt, kept her waiting for an answer. And to his belated letter full of admonitions and advice she replied,

> A thousand thanks for your dear kind letter. The doctor, who at first thought I had chickenpox, is now of the opinion that Monte Carlo is responsible for my rash. My heavy losses appear to have upset my stomach, then my nerves and finally affected my skin. If only Your Majesty had inherited the gambling instincts of some of your ancestors, then you would be able to sympathize and understand, and I would not have to go through the world disfigured and misunderstood.

It was a letter calculated to soften the Emperor's heart; having little idea of money, he was probably less shocked by the enormous size of her debts than was Baron Hawerda, the meticulous civil servant who had to travel down to Monte Carlo to settle her accounts. Katharina was forgiven and Franz Josef, amused by her self-dramatization, wrote, 'I am glad you are happy again and so hope that by now you are fully recovered. Medical science has obviously made a new discovery through your illness, for I have never before heard of a rash brought on by bad luck at gambling.'

But Katharina's passion for gambling did not confine itself to the casinos. The adventurous nature which in her youth had taken her to Russia and across the Atlantic now tempted her to indulge in the wildest speculations. In the autumn of 1904 Franz Josef heard to his horror that she was seriously considering investing in tobacco plantations in the West Indies.

> When you spoke of it first, I did not think you were in earnest and our conversation included nothing at all about a trip to the West Indies. Reading the news in the *Fremdenblatt* gave me a nervous shock, as I could not have imagined you could have mixed yourself

up in such a gigantic swindle, for the business in which you want to be involved is just the sort of swindle in which you could risk your future and would experience nothing but annoyances and disappointments.

The Emperor went on to praise the twenty-four-year-old Toni Kiss for disapproving of his mother's speculations:

> Your prudent son, who is always right in his opinions and takes the most reasonable and accurate view, is opposed to the whole affair and is very sensibly keeping aloof. The journey to the West Indies is complete nonsense and would only injure your health, and I really do not know what you want to do there as you would be a very bad businesswoman.

Katharina never went to the West Indies, but her restless temperament was always providing the poor old Emperor with some fresh cause for worry, whether it was a new slimming cure or a new automobile, which opened out vistas of dangerous driving and likely accidents. But however capricious and self-willed, Katharina was still as compassionate and kind as ever, ready to travel down to Budapest just to spend a few hours in his company – and to make the long and tiring journey to and from the Riviera to be in Vienna during a Cabinet crisis. After twenty years Franz Josef still wrote with love and gratitude, 'If you really undertook the strenuous and tiring trip here and back merely to see me again, then it shows that you are still a little bit fond of me and I am deeply touched. I think constantly of those happy days in which I was able to see you here, and I long for your return.'

23

The Diamond Jubilee

In 1908, the year of his diamond jubilee, Franz Josef reached the zenith of his popularity. He was the father figure, loved and revered by all, placed above faction, untouched by politics, so that even the most chauvinist of Hungarians felt himself bound by a personal union to his King-Emperor, and the rawest of recruits from the forests of the Bukovina still felt a surge of loyalty on hearing the strains of '*Gott Erhalte Unseren Kaiser*'.

Vienna was a city given over to festivities and a continual influx of foreign visitors. First to arrive was Kaiser Wilhelm, heading a deputation of German princes to pay homage to the old Emperor who, in his youth, had presided over the Frankfurt Diet, and now felt a certain satisfaction in seeing the sons and the grandsons of those who had robbed him of his leadership come to pay tribute to one who in the words of Kaiser Wilhelm 'was a model for them all'. Just as impressive was the family gathering at Schönbrunn, when all Franz Josef's relations and descendants from the oldest of his cousins to the youngest of his great-grandchildren gathered round his throne, the only notable exception being the children of the heir apparent, who were not even allowed to bear the name of Habsburg.

But the most popular of all the festivities, and the one which drew the largest crowds, was the great historical pageant representing six centuries of Habsburg rule, when twelve thousand men drawn from the various races of the Empire, with the exception of the Czechs who had refused to participate, paraded down the Ringstrasse. Marching to the sound of clarions and drums, the procession, which ranged from the armoured knights of the first Rudolf of Habsburg to the veterans of Radetzky's armies, passed in front of the Emperor, who stood for three hours firm and erect on a dais. But he who was usually so calm and impassive was seen to have tears in his eyes when the soldiers with whom he had served in Italy in his youth passed by, leading his pet pony. There may have been another cause for tears – memories of another pageant, designed by Makart to celebrate his silver wedding, in which the eighteen-year-old Rudolf had taken part, riding down the Ringstrasse to the delirious cheering of the crowds. All this pageantry and glory, which had been part of Rudolf's heritage, was now nothing but a burden to an old man who had grown tired of living, but did not dare to die for fear of what might happen after him.

The mastermind who had organized the pageant, commissioned the artists and historians and supervised every detail down to the authenticity of the earliest flintlock, was none other than Hans Wilczek. It was a noble gesture on the part of a man on whom the Emperor had only grudgingly bestowed the honours due to a lifetime devoted to his service. Jealousy had always marred the relations between Franz Josef and one of the most outstanding of his subjects: jealousy first on account of Wilczek's influence on Rudolf and, what was perhaps more human and understandable, jealousy of his relationship with Katharina Schratt. Even now that age had blunted his emotions, he could still feel a twinge of jealousy on hearing that Count Wilczek had called at the Gloriettegasse, even though he was assured by *die Freundin* that it was only in order to discuss some theatrical details for the procession.

By now Katharina Schratt had settled down to comfortable middle age. As she told a friend, 'I have outlived the unpleasantness of my equivocable position, and can now aspire to be left in peace to enjoy the rewards of years of labour and minister in my own way to the needs of my beloved sovereign.' Even the imperial entourage, from the Archduchess Valerie to the haughty Prince Montenuovo, were forced to admit that life at Schönbrunn was far easier when the *gnädige Frau* was around. The *gnädige Frau* was the only title she had ever sought, and the one by which she was always known.

The royal servants adored her. In his memoirs the Emperor's valet, Eugène Ketterl, gives many examples of her kindness and solicitude – how, on hearing that the household staff at Schönbrunn had received neither presents nor bonuses at Christmas, she immediately took the matter up with the Emperor and from then on there was a Christmas tree with presents under it for all. The valet relates how she would consult with him as to what the Emperor might be in need of, and how it was always she who provided him with the various amenities and comforts of old age, a warm dressing gown, a bedside carpet, the mild cigars to replace his favourite Virginians no longer allowed by his physician. Ketterl gives a touching picture of the Emperor's growing dependence on his friend, the delight he took in the little dinners at the Gloriet-tegasse, dinners which in summer would be enlivened by music on the terrace with a Schrammel★ quartet from one of the *Heurige* at Grinzing playing arias from Lehar's latest operetta. Franz Josef regarded it as a special occasion when the *gnädige Frau* came to dine at Schönbrunn, and the valet recalls 'the pleasurable excitement with which he awaited her arrival, continually jumping up from his chair to go to his bedroom to brush his hair or comb his beard'.

The world had grown to accept Katharina Schratt on her own terms as a woman who never intrigued or interfered and whose favourite rôle, for she was still an actress at heart, was that of fairy godmother. She loved to please and with her soft, sympathetic ways was always ready to listen to the troubles of others – the young officer seeking permission to marry; the old actor who had fallen on evil days; the girl with a fiancé disapproved of by her parents were always sure of finding a champion in Katharina Schratt. When the only daughter of the wealthy Baron Springer wanted to marry a Frenchman against her father's wishes, she immediately sought the intercession of the *gnädige Frau*. Eugène Fould, a native of Lorraine, never forgot his first meeting with the Emperor in Frau Schratt's drawing-room at Hietzing, when the august head of the House of Habsburg-Lorraine greeted him with a smile and said: 'I hear we are compatriots as we both come from Lorraine.' Baron Springer could hardly dismiss his daughter's fiancé as a foreigner when the Emperor called him a compatriot and later created him a baron.

At fifty-five and retired from the fierce, competitive world of the theatre, Katharina Schratt renounced the last illusions of youth.

★ A quartet of popular music, which took its name from the musician Schram-mel who brought it into fashion.

Princess Radziwill, who knew her in these later years, describes her as 'a stout, middle-aged woman with no pretensions to a figure and a fat face which occasionally turned red at the end of a meal. But she was a delightful companion and a very amusing one.' The Princess, who had a high opinion of the actress's intelligence, regretted that 'she does not use her influence more often in politics and never allows her mind to stray further and higher than on matters of local interest'. The ageing Emperor, who stayed always longer in Schönbrunn and became ever more isolated from the ordinary life of the capital, now confided in Katharina Schratt on matters he would never have begun to discuss with her before and which, for all her intelligence, she was not capable of understanding. She herself would say, 'I am an entertainer, not a politician.' How could she be expected to grasp the political implications behind the Austrian annexation of Bosnia-Herzegovina which disturbed the peace of Europe in the year of the diamond jubilee? The 'Young Turk' revolution in Constantinople, forcing the Sultan to accept the Constitution; a future in which Turkish deputies might attempt to interfere in the internal affairs of a province which was legally still a part of the Ottoman Empire, but which since the days of the Congress of Berlin had been administered by Austria; and the growing unrest among the south Slavs deliberately fomented by Belgrade were all valid reasons for the annexation. But they were hardly likely to be grasped by a woman who looked upon the Balkans as a subject for operetta rather than for serious politics.

At the height of the Bosnian crisis Katharina Schratt was more concerned with her own personal problems, expecting the new Foreign Minister Count Aehrenthal to interest himself on behalf of her ailing husband, whose health could no longer stand the climate of Algiers. The dynamic and ambitious Aehrenthal, who saw himself as another Metternich and believed that Austria-Hungary could still play a decisive and independent role in the concert of Europe, was not a man to concern himself with the health of an elderly consul in Algiers. When Frau Schratt complained of him to the Emperor, Franz Josef ventured to remind her that there were more important matters to be considered than her own family affairs. Irritated but still polite, he wrote:

My dear good friend, unfortunately I must ask your indulgence as I am absolutely not in a position to ask you to visit me either today or tomorrow. In the rush and excitement of these days, when the most important matters are to be discussed and perhaps decided, I could not designate a moment when I could talk to you quietly. As soon as there is some peace for me I will ask you to visit me. Very earnestly I beg of you not to get too excited and to consider how very busy Aehrenthal is in these days with the weighty and urgent matters to which I have already called your attention.

Small wonder if Franz Josef was nervous. After keeping the peace for over forty years, his Foreign Minister had tempted him to embark on a Balkan adventure which could have dangerous consequences.

But all that Katharina Schratt replied was, 'I am sorry to have bothered Your Majesty but I know that if it were in my power to help a friend I would not hesitate for a moment.' This time the Emperor remained unmoved. Nicholas Kiss stayed on in Algiers until the following year of 1909, when he returned to Vienna and died shortly afterwards. In a condolence message sent on 20 May 1909, Franz Josef expressed his warmest sympathy at 'the death of poor Kiss', and went on to say, 'in spite of everything it will surely grieve you and in any case will tax your strength. The event which must have happened sooner than expected made me feel quite sad yesterday.' Katharina appears to have genuinely grieved over her husband's death. The man who had left her after two years of marriage, penniless and crippled with debts, had nevertheless been the one great love of her life and given her the son whom she adored. With Kiss dead and Toni posted abroad in the foreign service, she suddenly felt lonely and forlorn and more than ever dependent on her friends, first and foremost the old Emperor.

The fact that both of them were free gave rise to fresh speculation and surmise. There was talk of a secret marriage, and though none of these rumours was substantiated they persist to the present day, and every now and then one of the more sensational of the Austrian weeklies appears with an article on the subject. At the age of eighty Franz Josef's thoughts were concentrated on death rather than on marriage, and one of his principal concerns was to ensure the future of his dear and faithful friend. When in 1908 the

Königswarter Palais on the Kärntner Ring came up for sale, it was secretly acquired out of money paid from the Habsburg family funds and shortly afterwards became the property of Katharina Schratt. Three years later the capital of the two and a half million kronen (approximately half a million pounds by today's rates) which since 1889 had been lying in a special account administered by Baron Hawerda, and of which up to now Frau Schratt had only enjoyed a part of the revenues, was transferred directly into her bank, the Emperor's only stipulation being that Baron Hawerda should continue to act as her trustee.

Till then Katharina appeared to have been in continual financial difficulties, and a letter written from Monte Carlo in the spring of 1909 and addressed to a friend, the singer Katharina Rosen, harked back to the familiar theme of her uncontrolled passion for gambling.

> When I telegraphed you that day I was in a terrible state of excitement and in the blackest of moods. Then that same morning I won in ten minutes over ten thousand francs and another two thousand besides, but after that it has been one long chapter of disaster; day after day of losses. Yesterday was a bit better, but nothing like the first day. I am feeling very low but intend to stay here for another nine or ten days. I must thank you for having gone to the Escompte Bank on my behalf. Unfortunately one has to think of paying back. You can imagine how I dread returning to Vienna when there is so much to pay and nothing to pay it with.

But the letter ended on a note of optimism, typical of a woman who, for all her worldliness, had still something of a child: 'When you receive this letter think of me and keep your fingers crossed. Perhaps a little magic might help for I can still win it all back.'

But from the time when Katharina Schratt became a rich woman in her own right, she appears to have lost her enthusiasm for gambling. In later years Toni Kiss would complain to his friends of his mother's close-fistedness with money. But that was after the great financial crash of the post-war years, when Katharina had seen all her securities and bonds so carefully invested by Baron Hawerda become as worthless as the paper they were printed on, and such money as she had left came from the sale of some precious object, some treasured jewel.

In the last years of Franz Josef's reign Katharina Schratt could sit back and enjoy what she called the fruits of her labours. Since she was a realist at heart a solvent bank account meant more than the dubious honour of a morganatic marriage. The only honour or title she ever asked of her sovereign was for Toni to be made a baron – the vanity of a fond mother, envisaging a future when Baron Kiss Von Itebbe would represent his country as ambassador in Paris or in London.

Meanwhile the ill effects of the annexation of Bosnia-Herzegovina and of Aehrenthal's inept diplomacy were beginning to be felt. In the year of his diamond jubilee the Emperor had experienced a certain pleasure in acquiring a new province, which would compensate a little for the territories lost during his reign, for which he felt himself responsible. But the wild mountain valleys of Bosnia had been acquired at a heavy price, rousing the animosity of Russia and the distrust of the western powers, particularly of England, who till now had relied on Austria to help her in maintaining the integrity of the Ottoman Empire. The Balkan cauldron was once more at boiling point and the only one to profit by the situation was Ferdinand of Bulgaria, who chose this moment to proclaim himself Tsar of an independent Bulgaria, an action which infuriated Tsar Nicholas of Russia, who denounced it as the insolent act of an upstart. But historically a prince of Bulgaria had a better right to the title of Tsar than any of the Romanoffs. In the Middle Ages, in the reign of Tsar Simeon, Bulgaria had been a great and powerful empire, at a time when in Russia there were no more than Grand Dukes of Kiev.

The first to congratulate the new Tsar was Katharina Schratt, for these were the kind of politics she understood. By now Ferdinand had found himself another wife, capable, intelligent and an excellent stepmother, with no illusions about her husband, with whom her relations were confined to strictly representational duties. Ferdinand was a constant visitor to Vienna, where one of his first visits was always to his 'dearest Frau Kathi'. With an ear finely attuned to the latest diplomatic rumours, he must have warned his friend of the obtuseness of Austria's policy, the old Emperor's obsession with the Balkans and his blindness to the larger issues at stake, the danger of the Anglo-French entente, the strengthening of the ties between France and Russia, and Germany's growing isolation.

King Edward VII had made two journeys to Ischl in the hope of winning Franz Josef to his side, if not as an ally, at least so as to ensure his neutrality in the event of a European war. The Emperor had received him with his habitual courtesy and had even gone to the lengths of accompanying him on a drive in his new automobile, a modern form of transport he detested. But he had remained deaf to all Edward's blandishments. He had never liked him as Prince of Wales and he liked him still less as King, not that he liked his nephew any better, for he regarded both Kaiser Wilhelm and his uncle as vulgarians. But he remained irrevocably loyal to the German alliance, a loyalty which was at once his strength and his undoing. He refused to listen to his chief of staff, Conrad von Hötzendorf, when he advocated preventive wars against both Italy and Serbia, the first of whom, though still a member of the Triple Alliance, was openly fomenting unrest in the south Tyrol and financing the *Irridentisti* in Trieste, while the latter was spreading revolutionary propaganda among the Slav populations of Croatia and Dalmatia. However untrustworthy she might be, Italy was still officially an ally and Serbia was still too insignificant to warrant the mobilizing of an army. Conrad von Hötzendorf was dismissed in December 1911, to be recalled twelve months later when all he had advocated had become inevitable and the little country 'too insignificant to fight against' was astounding Europe in the *Blitzkrieg* of the Balkan War.

In the summer of 1910 the eighty-year-old Franz Josef announced his intention of attending the military manoeuvres in Bosnia. The Archduchess Valerie and Frau Schratt united in begging him not to go. The exhaustion and discomfort of a journey made in the heat of summer, the risk of exposing himself to assassination in the remotest part of his Empire, would have made it a dangerous expedition for the youngest and healthiest of men. Four years later the Emperor was blamed for allowing Franz Ferdinand and his wife to risk their lives in going to Sarajevo, but he himself merely considered it a part of his duties to inspect his troops in his newly acquired province. The possibility of assassination was dismissed as '*un des risques du métier*'. All he worried about was the heat, and he wrote to Katharina Schratt,

> I hope it will not be too hot in Bosnia and that I shall withstand the whole thing well. From the schedule I am sending you at your request you will see that the rush could be worse and that my decrepitude will be taken into consideration. I am touched that you should wish to pray for me and I commend myself to your prayers during the whole of the Bosnia expedition.

The Emperor had need of Katharina's prayers, for members of a terrorist organization recruited and financed from Belgrade had already been sent to Sarajevo. One of them was waiting to assassinate him as he drove in an open carriage down the Appel Quay, a perfect target in his white uniform and green-feathered shako. The young man standing near the place from where, four years later, Gavrilo Princip was to fire his fatal shot had his revolver ready but never pulled the trigger. Later he confessed, 'I couldn't do it. There was so much dignity in his face' – dignity combined with a sublime indifference to death. The Emperor may have noted a scuffle in the crowd, but he never made a comment. He was pleased at his reception, the enthusiastic welcome given him by his Moslem subjects, for Sarajevo was predominantly a Moslem town, and he wrote to Katharina Schratt that 'It all went off far better than I had expected, and the troops were in splendid form.'

This was one of the last occasions on which the Emperor attended a military manoeuvre. From now on he gradually retired from public life. He no longer paid state visits to foreign capitals and in 1911 he attended a court ball for the last time. One of his only public appearances was at the country wedding of his great-nephew, the Archduke Karl to Zita of Bourbon-Parma. He was fond of Otto's son and at heart always looked upon him as the rightful heir to the throne. He was not making a brilliant marriage for a future emperor, but the bride was intelligent and handsome and came of good stock, for her eldest sister had succeeded in giving four healthy children to the effeminate Bulgarian Prince.

Apart from the two summer months at Ischl, Franz Josef now spent the whole of the year at Schönbrunn. His hours of work remained unchanged. At four-thirty in the morning he was already at his desk, though a growing debility now forced him to delegate certain duties to his heir apparent. These duties were grudgingly assigned, for Franz Josef could never conquer his aversion for Franz Ferdinand and his wife. He particularly resented the intimate friendship between the Archduke and the German Kaiser, who had known how to win the heart of the touchy, irascible Franz Ferdinand by treating his wife as royalty, behaviour which was in no way appreciated by the Austrian court.

The Emperor's life had become ever more lonely and Frau Schratt was often away on holiday. Now that she was approaching sixty she was feeling the strain of coping with the needs of an old man of whom she was the only friend, but to whom he was sometimes too tired to write. In a letter dated May 1912 we read, 'I am completely exhausted and the weakness of old age is growing very much worse. My spirits are sad and low.' But he still had the love and veneration of his people. In those last, uneasy years when Europe and in particular Austria-Hungary were moving inevitably towards war, there was still a feeling in Vienna that all would be well so long as the old Emperor was on the throne.

In the summer of 1912 the Tsar of Bulgaria paid his first state visit to Vienna since his coronation, and in spite of the great heat Franz Josef was waiting at the station to receive him with royal honours. '*Le Petit Ferdinand*' had travelled far since the day he set out for Orsova in a second-class carriage, a prince whose rights the powers had refused to recognize. Now the Ballhausplatz was out to woo Bulgaria, the traditional enemy of Serbia, and the proud Emperor of Austria had finally consented to reward him with the Order of the Golden Fleece.

But four months later came the shock of the Balkan League, Russia's revenge for the annexation of Bosnia-Herzegovina, when those four unnatural allies, Bulgaria, Serbia, Greece and Montenegro, financed by Russian loans and supplied with foreign arms, joined together in a so-called holy war to drive the Turks out of Europe. For over thirty years the great powers had been calling on the Turks to carry out reforms in Macedonia and the wily old Sultan Abdul Hamid had always prevaricated, playing one power against the other. When the Sultan was deposed it was hoped that the Turks would introduce a more liberal regime, but the present rulers in Constantinople were proving to be harsher, crueller and more bent on Ottomanizing their Christian subjects than any of their predecessors. The desperate resistance put up by the Macedonians, most of them of Bulgarian origin, resulted in appalling massacres. Refugees poured into Bulgaria, and of all the allies Ferdinand was the only one who went to war because he was forced to by public opinion, rather than in the hope of gain. The most unwarlike of men became involuntarily a hero, and the Bulgarian troops advancing into Thrace bore the worst brunt of the fighting. While the Serbs over-ran the whole of Macedonia, where the Turks put up little resistance, and the Greeks drove across the Thessalian plain in the race for Salonica, the Bulgarians captured Adrianople and advanced to within twenty miles of Constantinople.

At this moment one can hardly blame the romantic-minded Ferdinand if he was dazzled with a vision of Byzantium, and already saw himself attending mass in a reconsecrated Hagia Sofia. Those romantic aspirations, which in the past had led so many Russian tsars into costly and disastrous wars, were in the end to prove his undoing. With the coming of winter his soldiers remained bogged down in the mud of the Chataldja defences, while cholera and typhus took their toll. The geat powers, above all Russia who was alarmed by the course of events and had no intention of seeing the Bulgarian Tsar assume the throne of Byzantium, now called for an armistice. In London, at the conference tables of St James's Palace, Bulgaria found that for all her heroism it was Serbia who secured the lion's share of the spoils, and Greece, whose troops had arrived in Salonica twenty-four hours before the Bulgarians, who now claimed the city as her birthright.

The Balkan War, creating a 'greater Serbia', was disastrous for Austria, whose only success at the conference was in preventing Serbia from gaining access to the Adriatic by sponsoring an independent state of Albania, which only intensified the already bitter hatred of the Serbs. The western politicians, who had been full of praise for the 'gallant little Balkans', were now finding that dealing with them was impossible, since Serbia refused to hand over to Bulgaria her rightful share of Macedonia. When the ill-fated

London Conference finally came to an end, the Bulgarians were more determined to revenge themselves on their perfidious allies than on the Turks. Ferdinand returned to his capital to be given a hero's welcome, but among the cheering were shouts of 'Death to the Serbs'. Diplomats made an attempt to call on Russia to arbitrate. Russia delayed her reply, and in a fatal moment, under the influence of an angry and victorious army, Ferdinand gave the order to attack the Serbs and thereby branded Bulgaria as the aggressor.

On 9 July 1913 Franz Josef wrote to Katharina Schratt from Ischl, giving her as the latest news, 'Serbia has declared war on Bulgaria after the mobilization of Bulgaria.' No one knew better than Franz Josef that a second Balkan War would be even more disastrous for Austria than the first. Like jackals Bulgaria's former allies, Serbia, Greece and Montenegro, now joined by Romania, who came in for a share of the gains, fell on the impoverished and exhausted Bulgars, and it was only a question of weeks before the King was forced to seek an armistice. At the Treaty of Bucharest, a treaty Ferdinand never forgave, Bulgaria was forced to give up almost the whole of Macedonia to the Serbs and surrender southern Dobrudja, the lower reaches of the Danube, to the Romanians. The general opinion in Europe was that he would now have to abdicate. But the Bulgarians remained loyal to their 'Tsar', who in fighting had carried out the wishes of his people. His indomitable spirit rose above defeat. Within a few months he was back in Europe, presenting a brave face and an icy cynicism in front of those who had done nothing to help his country.

In his journal Hugo Thimig, the newly appointed Director of the Burgtheater, gives a vivid picture of King Ferdinand, whom he met dining with Frau Schratt at Hietzing:

20 November 1913. Last night at eight o'clock, a dinner with *die Schratt*. King Ferdinand of Bulgaria, Privy Counsellor Paul Schulz, the hostess, Fräulein Gössinger from the Burg and myself. On arrival I enquired of my hostess and Paul Schulz whether His Majesty was very crushed and depressed over the recent events which had had such tragic results for his country. But they both laughed and assured me he was as happy as a sandboy and enjoying himself hugely in Vienna. Thereupon His Majesty arrived blooming, affable, elegant as always

with a monocle, a lilac-coloured waistcoat and a beautifully cut frock coat; the Golden Fleece worn on a black cord under a snowy white cravat, the Bulgarian military cross in his buttonhole, charming, fascinating, and apparently in the best of spirits with an excellent appetite, ready to do justice to the food which is always superb in this house. The atmosphere was informal, the conversation animated and gay, to which the hostess contributed with her cosy, restful manner occasionally illuminated by some electrifying outburst. Paul Schulz told me in confidence that the King had taken a great enthusiasm for *die Marburg* [an actress] and was always giving her presents, but that I was on no account to tell our hostess.

It appears that at the age of sixty Katharina Schratt still refused to accept a rival.

King Ferdinand's visit to Vienna was not always as pleasant as this evening at the Gloriettegasse. In these very days the Serbians had released the text of a secret agreement made between him and King Peter before the outbreak of the first Balkan War, in which he pledged himself to come to his ally's help in the event of her being attacked by Austria-Hungary. Now he had to face an audience with the old Emperor at Schönbrunn, knowing everyone at court to be aware of his deceit. 'I consented to see him because we need Bulgaria,' wrote Franz Josef to Katharina Schratt, 'but I did not mince my words and I told him exactly what I thought of him.'

It was a sad situation for the great Habsburg Empire to be in need of Bulgaria, but at the end of the second Balkan War Austria found herself faced with a strong and aggressive Serbia who, from its former position as an insignificant little country, had almost overnight emerged into a dominating power in south-east Europe.

24

The End of an Epoch

'Do as you please,' the Emperor replied when Franz Ferdinand expressed his doubts regarding his forthcoming visit to Sarajevo. Four years had passed since Franz Josef had attended the summer manoeuvres in Bosnia, and had gone without the slightest hesitation. Admittedly times had changed. Serbian *agents-provocateurs* had doubled their activities, fomenting unrest among the Slav minorities. Franz Ferdinand was a brave man, but he had forebodings, apart from which he was not strong and, still suffering from the after-effects of tuberculosis, dreaded the apalling summer heat of that arid, treeless country. But the Military Governor's invitation had included the Duchess of Hohenberg, who in an Austrian province was to be treated for the first time with royal honours. Sophie's eagerness to go may well have influenced Franz Ferdinand's decision, and there were those who asserted that his enemies at court had exploited the Duchess's ambition in order to send the Archduke to an almost certain death. This was far from being the truth, but the Emperor saw no reason why the Archduke should not go to Bosnia, which was due for another royal visit.

On 26 June 1914 Franz Ferdinand set out for Sarajevo and the Emperor left for his summer holiday in Ischl, where he could look forward to the arrival of Frau Schratt who had interrupted her journey to Ischl to visit the shrine of Mariazell. In this uneasy summer of rumours and counter-rumours, certain responsible and moderate politicians who had served in former governments came to consult with Katharina Schratt, begging her to warn the Emperor that the war with Serbia, so earnestly advocated by Conrad von Hötzendorf and his followers, would inevitably drag in Russia and start a world war. Of all the roles she had ever had to play, Katharina was finding that of a political Egeria the most difficult. Franz Josef refused to believe that Russia would ever go to war over Serbia. And for the first time she realized that her beloved friend had grown too old to rule. In her simple childish piety she took refuge in prayer; at the shrine of Mariazell, where she had often found comfort in the past, she now prayed with a desperate fervour for her Emperor and her country.

It was a lovely summer's evening on 28 June, and Katharina Schratt was coming home from church when she saw a small crowd gathered round the post office. For a moment her heart stood still, for it was in Mariazell, at this very post office, that she first saw the black-bordered placard announcing the assassination of the Empress Elisabeth. This time it was a telegram exposed in the window, which read: 'Crown Prince, Archduke Franz Ferdinand and his wife the Duchess of Hohenberg assassinated at Sarajevo'. Her first thought was of the Emperor. How would he stand up to this terrible blow? No one, least of all Katharina Schratt, was under any illusion that Franz Josef would feel a deep personal loss. He had always disliked and distrusted the Archduke and his politics, and had never forgiven him for his marriage, but it was the first time that a Habsburg, the heir to the throne, had been assassinated on what was now Austrian soil.

The Archduchess Valerie wrote in her diary of her father's reaction: 'I found Papa amazingly fresh. Certainly he was shocked, and in speaking of the poor children he had tears in his eyes. But as I had imagined in advance he was not personally stricken. When I said that Karl would assuredly do well he said very solemnly and emphatically, "For me it is a relief from a great worry." ' He must have said the same to Katharina Schratt when they met on the morning after her return. Though appalled by the event, he was already talking of the Archduke Karl as if a divine providence had intervened to provide him with an heir worthy of being a Habsburg.

No one in Vienna had any doubt but that the nineteen-year-old Bosnian student who had fired the shot had acted on orders from Belgrade. The fact that the Serbian Minister in Vienna had attempted to warn the Ballhausplatz of a terrorist plot to assassinate the Archduke during his visit to Sarajevo appears for some reason to have been ignored. Exhausted by the Balkan Wars, the Serbs were not ready to fight, but they were unable to control the activities of their own extremists. The Prime Minister, Nicola Pásic, who in 1903 had been involved in the brutal murder of King Alexander and his wife, was hardly in a position to indict men with whom he had plotted in the past. All he did was to send a warning which would absolve his country from any participation in the plot, and for some unaccountable reason the warning was never handed on to the authorities in Sarajevo.

But though everyone in Vienna was ready to accuse Belgrade, no one in those first few days appears to have looked upon Franz Ferdinand's assassination as a cause for war. At court there was more concern over the complications arising from the Archduke's funeral; even in death Franz Ferdinand's *mésalliance* was not forgotten. The vindictiveness and pettiness, which dictated the actions of a Montenuovo and which the old Emperor made no attempt to contravene, even shocked those who had been opposed to Franz Ferdinand in his lifetime. The Duchess, who had died for her country, was granted no other insignia on her coffin than the gloves and fan of a lady-in-waiting. The lying-in-state in the Capuchin Church where, through his marriage, the Archduke had forfeited the right of burial, lasted no more than two hours. Then the gates were shut and the waiting crowds were turned away. After a requiem mass in the Augustiner Church the coffins were taken to the station, to be transported by train and ferry to the church of Artstetten on the Danube, where the Archduke had already prepared a vault for himself and his wife.

The entire ceremony was carried out in such a fashion as to arouse public indignation throughout the country. The Lord Chamberlain had decreed that the funeral cortège should pass through the streets without being given full military honours. But protests, not only from the public but also from Franz Ferdinand's nephew, the new heir apparent, forced him to change his plans. Both the army and the aristocracy turned up in strength to escort the coffins to the station. Thousands of mourners lined the streets, and despite the lateness of the hour, for it had been specially arranged for the funeral train to leave only at ten in the evening, the Westbahnhof was full to overflowing with people come to pay their last respects. This terrible day had a macabre end when a violent thunderstorm broke out at midnight and the ferry transporting the coffins over the Danube nearly capsized. Many found it hard to absolve the Emperor of his responsibility in having sanctioned the arrangements. There was criticism even in his family, from the chivalrous young Archduke Karl to Franz Ferdinand's loving stepmother, the Archduchess Marie Therese, who absented herself from court for many months thereafter.

Katharina Schratt was probably one of the few to understand a resentment which followed Franz Ferdinand to his grave. Time after time she had seen Franz Josef deny himself the chance of happiness by adhering to the rigid line of conduct expected of an Emperor and a Habsburg. How could he be expected to forgive Franz Ferdinand for having flouted these ideals and for the sake of his own selfish passions threaten to destroy the very mystique of royalty?

Meanwhile Europe was waiting on the Austrian reaction to the murder at Sarajevo. For the first few days the Ballhausplatz appeared too stunned to move. Aehrenthal was dead and his successor, the amiable, ineffectual Count Berchtold seemed utterly unable to grasp the gravity of the situation. No directive came from Schönbrunn, where the old Emperor sat at his desk painstakingly reading the reports from Sarajevo, where a provincial judge was carrying out investigations, trying to pin responsibility for the crime directly on Belgrade. Over a week was allowed to pass before the Ballhausplatz sent out one of their officials to corroborate the evidence, and still Europe watched in amazement the great sprawling Austro-Hungarian giant who for years had been talking of annihilating Serbia, and now that the perfect opportunity had come seemed incapable of waking from its lethargy.

At last came the first intonations of war. On 5 July the Austrian Ambassador to Berlin informed the German Kaiser that the assassination plot had been definitely planned by Belgrade, and that his government were making certain demands to Serbia which, should they be refused, would immediately lead to war. Kaiser Wilhelm appears to have assured the ambassador of Germany's support before he had even read the text of the Austrian terms. Two days later he committed himself still further in addressing a personal letter to Franz Josef, telling him that whatever complications might arise in Europe, Austria would always have Germany at her side.

Gradually war fever was mounting in Europe, with patriotic demonstrations in Paris in front of the veiled statue of Strasbourg, pan-Slav demonstrations in St Petersburg, and anti-German speeches in the British House of Commons. War fever had even penetrated to the lovely peaceful valleys of the Salzkammergut and in Ischl, at the Kurhaus and at Zauner's pastry shop, they talked of nothing else. At the Villa Felicitas Katharina Schratt listened to solid liberal politicians who a year ago had been inveighing against the warmongers in the government, now talking of the impossibility of a 'peaceful coexistence between a half German Empire and the uncivilized Balkans'.

The ultimatum to Serbia was sent out on 23 July and after all the weeks of prevarication a reply was demanded in two days. Diplomats accredited to the western powers, who saw copies of the note, regarded the terms as unacceptable by a proud, independent people like the Serbs. Particularly humiliating was the clause in which Austria claimed the right to send her own officials to participate in the suppression of Irridentist activity, and to carry out a thorough investigation of all those who might have been implicated in the crime. But in spite of the harshness of the terms, the Serbian Prime Minister Nicola Pásic appears to have been ready to accept them. His reply was already drafted when he suddenly changed his mind, whether on the promise of Russian support or on the strength of anti-Austrian feeling in the country is not known. On the morning of 25 July the Ballhausplatz was informed that a reply was on its way which would have made it impossible for Austria to go to war, but during the day the draft was suddenly changed and at seven o'clock in the evening the Emperor, who had been waiting in suspense all day, was told that Serbia had declared the terms to be unacceptable and that his ambassador had broken off relations and driven across the frontier.

Franz Josef's reaction was strangely apathetic. For a long time he did not speak, sitting in a heavy, brooding silence. Then he suddenly got up, saying, 'Well that's that,' as if after those hours of agonizing waiting the news had come almost as a relief. His War Minister, who was present, assured him that the Serbian resistance would be negligible and that the whole country could be over-run in less than two weeks. But he was too old for illusions. Quietly he sat down at his desk to sign the mobilization orders. On that same evening he visited Katharina Schratt. The hour was later than usual and she was sitting out on the verandah when she saw him cross the little bridge leading to her house, and knew by his stooping, halting walk that the worst must have happened. He looked so infinitely weary, so infinitely old, and in a low, hoarse voice he said, 'I have done my best but now it is the end.'

On 28 July, Austria-Hungary officially declared war on Serbia and Montenegro and on the same day Russia began to mobilize. On 30 July Germany declared war on Russia, and by midnight of 4 August Europe was at war. The Emperor Franz Josef, who had kept the peace for forty-eight years, had ignited the fuse of a world conflagration. In a proclamation addressed to his people he declared, 'After many long years of peace the machinations of a hostile power force me to take up my sword to preserve the honour of the monarchy, to defend its integrity and its power and to safeguard its possessions.'

Many years before Prince Bismarck had foretold that whatever might be the state of Austria, the Emperor Franz Josef would only have to gird his sword and mount his horse for all the various races of his Empire to rally to his cause. And now the miracle came true – Germans and Hungarians, Slavs and Jews came forward to volunteer for an army which for over three years defended frontiers which stretched from the Adriatic to the plains of Poland, and which later, after Italy had come into the war against the central powers, was extended to the bitter mountain fighting in the high Dolomites. Franz Josef, who was spared so little in his life, was at least spared the tragedy of the final break-up of an army of which he had been so proud and on whose loyalty he could always count. With his failing health he was now hardly more than a figurehead, but he was still the figurehead who kept the whole disintegrating fabric of the Empire together, and who to the end retained his integrity and his prestige.

When in January 1915 Italy adopted the policy of *sacro egoismo* and turned on her former ally, demanding as the price of her neutrality the whole of the Trentino and South Tyrol, the eighty-four-year-old Emperor's proud reply was to refuse even to consider the terms. Germany, on the contrary, was anxious to negotiate. At this critical moment in the war, her generals viewed with dismay the opening of another front. Nor was it Germany who was being asked to sacrifice provinces which for hundreds of years had been part of the Habsburg Empire. Unable to persuade or to coerce his ally into reconsidering its decision, the Kaiser resorted to other means. He remembered his former correspondence with Prince Eulenburg and the value his ambassador had placed on his friendship with Frau Schratt and the influence she had over the Emperor. But Eulenburg had now fallen into disgrace, hounded out of public life by his enemies and publicly put on trial for some half-forgotten homosexual scandal of his youth. At the time Kaiser Wilhelm had done nothing to save his friend from the vindictiveness of Baron Holstein, and the unfortunate Prince was now living as a self-imposed prisoner on his country estates. Failing Eulenburg, the Kaiser sent another ambassador, Prince Wedel, on a highly delicate mission to Vienna to contact a woman with whom he could only claim the barest acquaintance.

For the past four months Katharina Schratt had been running a hospital for officers at Hietzing, and for the first time in her life had come into contact with the full horrors of war. She had seen young men, many of them the sons of old friends, arrive blind and mutilated from the Russian front, and heard tell of the terrible hardships suffered during the winter fighting in the high Carpathians. She knew what the opening of another mountain front would mean, but when Prince Wedel, a polished and accomplished diplomat, tried to persuade her into using her influence over the Emperor in getting him to reconsider his decision and to give way to the Italian blackmail, all that was courageous and independent in her nature asserted itself, and she refused to be the bearer of advice for which she had nothing but contempt. Another attempt, this time by the Duke of Avarna, the Italian Ambassador to Vienna, to seek the mediation of Frau Schratt was equally unsuccessful. The *gnädige Frau* regretted that her duties at the hospital prevented her from seeing His Excellency, and in private she was heard to say that no treacherous Italian would ever cross her threshold.

Four months later, in May 1915, Italy declared war on the central powers. But by now Franz Josef had grown completely fatalistic, for he no longer had any illusion that his Empire could survive. The superb health he had enjoyed throughout his life had gone. The attacks of bronchitis were becoming more frequent, each one leaving him a little weaker. His last letter to Katharina Schratt was dated Easter 1915: 'Sincerest thanks dearest friend for the beautiful flowers and the good wishes which I return with all my heart. God save and protect you in these difficult times and keep your friendship for me till we meet again at one o'clock tomorrow.'

In these days she barely left the hospital, where she personally supervised the delicious meals which, as Vienna became increasingly short of food, were ever more difficult to provide. It upset her to see food left on a plate, and she would go up to some poor young officer who had lost his appetite and coax him into eating, laying a still lovely hand upon his shoulder and saying, 'Try to eat a little just to please me.' But in spite of her duties at the hospital she still went every day to Schönbrunn, where on fine days she would go out walking with the Emperor, or otherwise sit with him in his study, helping him to decipher documents he now found hard to read.

The year 1915, which saw Italy's defection brought Bulgaria into the war on the side of the central powers. Ferdinand had waited a year before committing himself, and with a flash of his former irony Franz Josef remarked, 'If the Bulgarian comes in on our side it must be because he thinks we are winning.' In February 1916 the King arrived in Vienna on an official visit and was presented by the Emperor with a baton of an Austrian field-marshal. 'This is the proudest moment of my life,' wrote Ferdinand to Katharina Schratt. But it was to be the last of the royal visits. The Emperor's personal physician, Dr Kerzl, declared that his patient could no longer stand the strain, and even the *gnädige Frau* was asked to curtail her visits.

At the beginning of November Franz Josef fell ill with bronchitis. The respiratory organs were affected and the attacks of coughing became so painful that he would sit up all night in an armchair rather than lie in bed. The doctors realized it was the end, and the young Archduke Karl was recalled from the Front. Katharina Schratt saw the Emperor for the last time on Sunday 19 November. It was St Elisabeth's Day, a day Franz Josef always dedicated to his wife, when he and Katharina would sit together and evoke the memory of that strange relationship which had bound the three of them together, harking back to their first meeting in von Angeli's studio, the picnics on the Jainzen and the walks in the Lainzer Tiergarten. This afternoon it was Katharina who did most of the talking as the Emperor was too weak to speak. When she left him the doctor asked her not to come the following day as His Majesty had need of rest. And when the telephone rang shortly after nine o'clock on the evening of Tuesday 21 November it was the Lord High Chamberlain Prince Montenuovo to tell her that the Emperor was dead. Half an hour later came the Emperor's faithful old valet, to tell her in a voice half choked in tears that His Majesty had bidden the *gnädige Frau* to come to the palace. Stupified with grief, it took her a moment to realize that 'His Majesty' now meant the young Archduke Karl.

Before leaving she went into the greenhouse to pick the last roses in bloom and, lacking the strength to walk, ordered the carriage to drive her to Schönbrunn. Here she found the halls and ante-rooms crowded with mourners, ministers and generals, many of them in tears, others silently praying. The officers on duty had orders to let her pass into the private apartments where only members of the imperial family were allowed to enter. The young Emperor came forward to meet her and, taking her by the arm, presented her to the Empress whom she had never met before. But the most surprising of all was the Archduchess Valerie, who in floods of tears came forward to embrace her, thanking her for the years of faithful friendship she had given to her father.

In his simple and austere bedroom Franz Joseph still lay on the plain iron bed on which he died. Tomorrow would come the high officers of state to clothe him with all the panoply and circumstance of Spanish etiquette, and prepare him for what was to be the last of the great Habsburg funerals. But now he was only a worn-out soldier who had died serving his country, and the friend of thirty years bent over him, uttering a silent prayer and placing two white roses in his gnarled old hands. Katharina Schratt was playing her last role in history, and as always she played it with dignity and grace. There was neither weeping nor hysterics, for hers was a grief too deep for tears. While the allied sovereigns and princes of the Empire converged on Vienna for the great state funeral, she remained quietly at Hietzing with the young officers whose sorrow in most cases was as genuine as her own.

Katharina Schratt only died in 1940, outliving Franz Josef by nearly twenty-four years. She witnessed the break-up of his army, the disintegration of his Empire, the abdication of the young Emperor Karl and foreign armies marching as victors through the town. She saw the Habsburg eagles trampled in the mud and the red flag flying over the Hofburg. Peace came, bringing with it the terrible aftermath of defeat: poverty and hunger, crashes on the stock exchange, the failure of banks and money become worthless almost overnight. Many of her friends were ruined, but Katharina Schratt was still rich in her possessions, and her generosity was never so evident as now. Every month some exquisite painted fan, some jewelled snuff box found its way to the auction rooms in the Dorotheergasse. But whether at Hietzing or on the Kärntner Ring she still kept open house, and many a pensioned actor was grateful for the substantial teas provided by the *gnädige Frau*, the trays of cakes and sandwiches sent round from Demel, the confectioner on the Kohlmarkt. A godson recalls the Sunday luncheons at Hietzing, the crowded table in the pretty rococo dining-room, the guests, mostly old colleagues from the Burg, many of them famous in their day, and the garden full of stray dogs for Katharina, as a lover of animals, had given a home to many a poor dog abandoned by those who could no longer afford to keep them.

She survived the misery and poverty of those post-war years, and with her passionate love of life adapted herself to the bourgeois standards of republican Austria, shorn of its grandeur. In her seventies she was still to be seen at the Salzburg Festival, taking a cure at Karlsbad, and in 1929, at seventy-six, she was still sufficiently adventurous to travel by aeroplane from Zurich to Vienna. Old friends from the past, Ferdinand of Bulgaria, now living in luxurious exile at Coburg, one of the few dethroned monarchs to keep his fortune, still came to Vienna bringing her exotic gifts of Lalique and Fabergé. But he was one of the few who remained out of all the admirers who once crowded her drawing-room. Toni, now married and retired from the diplomatic service, came to live with his mother on the Kärntnerring. Life was not always easy for the childless couple, for the gay, carefree young woman who had enchanted an Emperor had grown querulous and domineering with age, obsessed by money and miserable when it came to selling some of her jewels. In the 1930s Katharina asked her godson, who was attached to the Austrian Legation in London, to negotiate the sale of some valuable snuff boxes in the hope that Queen Mary might be interested. But the Queen and her advisers appear to have considered the price too high, and Katharina Schratt's collections were dispersed all over the world.

But whatever sacrifices she had to make, she never gave an interview to any of the journalists who pursued her throughout the 1930s, offering her large sums in foreign currencies. American publishers bidding for her memoirs were politely but firmly refused: 'I am an actress not a writer and I have nothing to say, for I was never a Pompadour, still less a Maintenon.' Sensational articles appeared from time to time on the 'Emperor's sweetheart' or the '*gnädige Frau* of Schönbrunn', but Katharina Schratt did not even trouble to read them.

She was still living in the spring of 1938 when the Nazis invaded Austria, and her last political gesture at the age of eighty-four was to pull down the blinds of her windows on the Kärntnerring when Hitler drove in triumph through the town. Of all the malicious gossip she had had to contend with over the years, nothing angered her so much as the story fabricated by the Nazis of her having accepted a pension from Herr Hitler.

From now on she rarely ventured out of the house, until she died quite peacefully on an April day in 1940, guarding to the end the secrets of an undefined romance which keeps us guessing after over sixty years.

Select Bibliography

Acton, Lord, *Cambridge Modern History 1870–1898* (Cambridge, 1934)

Baernreither (Joseph), ed. J. Redlich, *Fragments of a Political Diary* (London, 1930)

Barea, Isla, *Vienna: Legend and Reality* (New York, 1966)

Battenberg, Prince Alexander von, *Kampf unter drei Zaren* (Vienna, 1920)

Bourgoing, Jean de, *Briefe Kaiser Franz Josef an Frau Katharina Schratt* (Vienna, 1949)

Bülow, Prince Bernhard von, *Memoirs* vol I (London, 1931)

Christomanos, Constantine, *Tagebuchblätter* (Vienna, 1899)

Constant, Stephen, *Foxy Ferdinand, Csar of Bulgaria* (London, 1979)

Corti, E. C., *Der Alte Kaiser Franz Joseph I vom Berliner Kongress bis zu seinem Tode* (Graz, 1956)

  Mensch und Herrscher (Graz, 1956)

Crankshaw, Edward, *The Fall of the House of Habsburg* (London, 1963)

Dingelstedt, Franz von, *Aus der Briefmappe eines Burgtheater-Direktors* (Vienna, 1925)

Dedijer, Vladimir, *The Road to Sarajevo* (London, 1967)

Eulenburg, Prince Philip, *Aus Fünfzig Jahren* (Berlin, 1923)

Fugger, Princess Nora, *The Glory of the Habsburgs* (London, 1932)

Gainham, Sarah, *The Habsburg Twilight* (London, 1979)

Hamann, Brigitte, *Rudolf, Kronprinz und Rebell* (Vienna, 1978)

Haslip, Joan, *The Lonely Empress* (London, 1965)

Heere, Franz, *Franz Josef* (Cologne, 1978)

Henning, Fred, *Ringstrassensymphonie* 4 vols (Vienna, 1964)

Ketterl, Eugene, *The Emperor Franz Josef, an intimate study by his valet* (London, 1929)

Kielmansegg, Count, *Kaiserhaus, Staatsmänner und Politiker* (Vienna, 1966)

Kürenburg, Joachim von, *Woman of Vienna: A Romantic Biography of Katharina Schratt* (London, 1955)

Larisch, Countess Marie Louise, *My Past* (London, 1914)

Laube, Heinrich, *Das Wiener Stadttheater* (Leipzig, 1875)

  Errinnerungen 1841–1881 (Vienna, 1882)

Macdonald, John, *Czar Ferdinand and his People* (London, 1913)

Mailer, Hermann, *Katharina Schratt, Ein Lebensbild* (Vienna, 1947)

Margutti, General von, *The Emperor Francis Joseph and his Times* (London, 1921)

Mitis, O., *Das Leben des Kronprinzen Rudolf* (Leipzig, 1928)

Namier, Sir Louis, *Vanished Supremacies* (London, 1958)

Nostitz, George (ed.), *Kaiser Franz Josef's und Kaiserin Elisabeth's Briefe 1859, 1898* 2 vols (Munich, 1966)

Paget, Lady Walpurga, *Embassies of Other Days* (London, 1913)

Radziwill, Princess Catherine, *The Austrian Court from Within* (London, 1916)

Schiel, Irmgard *Stephanie* (Stuttgart, 1979)

Schnitzler, Arthur, *My Youth in Vienna* (London, 1970)

Schorske, Carl, *Fin de Siècle Vienna, Politics and Culture (London, 1979)*

Sztaray, Countess Irma, *Aus den letzten Jahren der Kaiserin Elisabeth* (Vienna, 1909)

Taylor, A. P., *The Habsburg Monarchy* (London, 1941)

Thimig, Hugo, *Aus dem Alten und Neuen Burgtheater* (Zurich, 1920)

  Hugo Thimig erzählt aus seinem Lenen (Graz/Cologne, 1962)

Vetséra, Baronin Helene von, *Denkschrift der Baronin von Vetsera* (privately printed, 1889)

Wagner-Jauregg, Dr, *Errinnerungen an die Affaire Girardi* (Vienna, 1900)

Previously unpublished material

The Schratt-Kiss papers: letters from the Emperor Franz Josef to Frau Katharina Schratt 1886–1915 (Dial Press, New York)

Extracts and rough copies of letters from Katharina Schratt to Emperor Franz Josef 1886–1912 (Dial Press, New York)

Correspondence between Ferdinand of Bulgaria and Katharina Schratt (Dial Press, New York)

Letter from Baron Franz von Hawerda to Katharina Schratt, February 1889 (Dial Press, New York)

Copy of legacy drawn up by Emperor Franz Josef in favour of Katharina Schratt, February 1889 (Dial Press, New York)

Letter from Katharina Schratt to Frau Katharina Rosen, Monte Carlo, 1904 (by kind permission of Madame Johanna Nebehay)

Correspondence between Katharina Schratt and Dr Paul Schlenther at the time of her resignation from the Burgtheater, 1900, 1901 (Haus-, Hof- und Staats-Archiv, General Intendanz des Burgtheaters, Karton 188)

Index